SEATTLE
TRAVEL GUIDE
2016

SHOPS, RESTAURANTS, ARTS, ENTERTAINMENT & NIGHTLIFE

The Most Positively Reviewed And Recommended Places In The City

SEATTLE
TRAVEL GUIDE
2016

SHOPS, RESTAURANTS, ARTS, ENTERTAINMENT & NIGHTLIFE

SEATTLE TRAVEL GUIDE 2016
Shops, Restaurants, Arts, Entertainment & Nightlife

© James F. Hayward, 2016
© E.G.P. Editorial, 2016

Printed in USA.

ISBN-13: 978-1517623807
ISBN-10: 1517623804

Copyright © 2016
All rights reserved.

INDEX

SHOPS
Top 500 Shops - 9

RESTAURANTS
Top 500 Restaurants - 47

ARTS & ENTERTAINMENT
Top 500 Arts & Entertainment - 85

NIGHTLIFE SPOTS
Top 500 Nightlife Spots - 123

SEATTLE TRAVEL GUIDE 2016
Shops, Restaurants, Arts, Entertainment & Nightlife

*This directory is dedicated to Seattle Business Owners and Managers
who provide the experience that the locals and tourists enjoy.
Thanks you very much for all that you do and thank for being the "People Choice".*

*Thanks to everyone that posts their reviews online and
the amazing reviews sites that make our life easier.*

*The places listed in this book are the most positively reviewed
and recommended by locals and travelers from around the world.*

*Thank you for your time and enjoy the directory that is
designed with locals and tourist in mind!*

TOP 500 SHOPS
The Most Recommended by Locals & Trevelers
(From #1 to #500)

#1
Pike Place Market
Category: Fruits, Veggies, Farmers Market, Shopping Center
Average Price: Modest
Area: Downtown
Address: 85 Pike St
Seattle, WA 98101
Phone: (206) 682-7453

#2
University Village
Category: Shopping Center
Average Price: Expensive
Area: University District
Address: 2623 NE University Village St
Seattle, WA 98105
Phone: (206) 523-0622

#3
Pacific Place
Category: Shopping Center
Average Price: Expensive
Area: Downtown
Address: 600 Pine St
Seattle, WA 98101
Phone: (206) 405-2655

#4
Frock Shop
Category: Women's Clothing
Average Price: Modest
Area: Phinney Ridge
Address: 6500 Phinney Ave N
Seattle, WA 98103
Phone: (206) 297-1638

#5
Nordstrom
Category: Accessories, Men's Clothing, Women's Clothing
Average Price: Expensive
Area: Downtown
Address: 500 Pine St
Seattle, WA 98101
Phone: (206) 628-2111

#6
Meadow
Category: Women's Clothing, Home Decor
Average Price: Modest
Area: Queen Anne
Address: 1959 6th Ave W
Seattle, WA 98119
Phone: (206) 659-4963

#7
Momo
Category: Women's Clothing, Men's Clothing, Home Decor
Average Price: Expensive
Area: International District
Address: 600 S Jackson St
Seattle, WA 98104
Phone: (206) 329-4736

#8
Babeland
Category: Adult
Average Price: Modest
Area: First Hill, Capitol Hill
Address: 707 E Pike St
Seattle, WA 98122
Phone: (206) 328-2914

#9
LUCCA Great Finds
Category: Home Decor
Average Price: Modest
Area: Ballard
Address: 5332 Ballard Ave NW
Seattle, WA 98107
Phone: (206) 782-7337

#10
The Dress Theory
Category: Bridal, Formal Wear
Average Price: Modest
Area: Phinney Ridge
Address: 7222 Linden Ave
Seattle, WA 98103
Phone: (206) 550-7948

#11
Ten Thousand Villages
Category: Home Decor, Jewelry
Average Price: Modest
Area: Roosevelt
Address: 6417 Roosevelt Way NE
Seattle, WA 98115
Phone: (206) 524-9223

#12
Andaluz
Category: Fashion, Jewelry, Flowers, Gifts
Average Price: Modest
Area: Columbia City
Address: 4908 Rainier Ave S
Seattle, WA 98118
Phone: (206) 760-1900

#13
Ye Olde Curiosity Shop
Category: Toy Store, Flowers, Gifts
Average Price: Modest
Area: Waterfront
Address: 1001 Alaskan Way
Seattle, WA 98104
Phone: (206) 682-5844

#14
Westwood Village
Category: Shopping Center
Average Price: Modest
Area: Roxhill
Address: 2600 SW Barton St
Seattle, WA 98126
Phone: (206) 508-1671

#15
Gold Dogs Vintage
Category: Vintage, Leather Goods, Women's Clothing
Average Price: Modest
Area: Fremont
Address: 3519 B Fremont Pl N
Seattle, WA 98103
Phone: (206) 499-1811

#16
Horseshoe
Category: Women's Clothing
Average Price: Expensive
Area: Ballard
Address: 5344 Ballard Ave NW
Seattle, WA 98107
Phone: (206) 547-9639

#17
Laura Bee Designs
Category: Jewelry, Accessories
Average Price: Modest
Area: Ballard
Address: 6418 20th Ave NW
Seattle, WA 98107
Phone: (206) 789-4044

#18
Fred Meyer
Category: Grocery, Drugstore
Average Price: Modest
Area: Ballard
Address: 915 NW 45th St
Seattle, WA 98107
Phone: (206) 297-4300

#19
Diva Dollz
Category: Women's Clothing, Jewelry, Shoe Store
Average Price: Expensive
Area: Downtown, Pioneer Square
Address: 624 1st Ave
Seattle, WA 98104
Phone: (206) 652-2299

#20
Sell Your Sole Consignment Boutique
Category: Women's Clothing, Vintage
Average Price: Modest
Area: Belltown
Address: 2121 1st Ave Seattle, WA 98121
Phone: (206) 443-2616

#21
Jax Joon
Category: Accessories, Women's Clothing, Home Decor
Average Price: Modest
Area: Ballard
Address: 5338 Ballard Ave NW St
Seattle, WA 98107
Phone: (206) 789-8777

#22
Queen Anne Dispatch
Category: Women's Clothing, Accessories, Shipping Center
Average Price: Modest
Area: Queen Anne
Address: 2212 Queen Anne Ave N
Seattle, WA 98109
Phone: (206) 286-1024

#23
Velouria
Category: Women's Clothing, Jewelry
Average Price: Expensive
Area: Ballard
Address: 2205 NW Market St
Seattle, WA 98107
Phone: (206) 788-0330

#24
Portage Bay Goods
Category: Gift Shop, Baby Gear, Furniture
Average Price: Modest
Area: Fremont
Address: 621 N 35th St
Seattle, WA 98103
Phone: (206) 547-5221

#25
Pretty Parlor
Category: Vintage
Average Price: Modest
Area: Capitol Hill
Address: 119 Summit Ave E
Seattle, WA 98102
Phone: (206) 405-2883

#26
Butter Home
Category: Home Decor, Cards, Stationery
Average Price: Modest
Area: Capitol Hill
Address: 1531 Melrose Ave
Seattle, WA 98122
Phone: (206) 623-2626

#27
Three Birds
Category: Home & Garden, Flowers, Gifts
Average Price: Expensive
Area: Queen Anne
Address: 2107 Queen Anne Ave N
Seattle, WA 98119
Phone: (206) 686-7664

#28
Throwbacks Northwest
Category: Sports Wear, Hats
Average Price: Modest
Area: Capitol Hill
Address: 1205 E Pike St
Seattle, WA 98122
Phone: (206) 402-4855

Seattle Travel Guide 2016 / Shops, Restaurants, Arts, Entertainment & Nightlife

#29
City Target
Category: Department Store, Drugstore, Grocery
Average Price: Modest
Area: Downtown
Address: 1401 2nd Ave
Seattle, WA 98101
Phone: (206) 494-3250

#30
Westlake Center
Category: Shopping Center
Average Price: Modest
Area: Downtown
Address: 400 Pine Street
Seattle, WA 98101
Phone: (206) 467-1600

#31
Lifelong Thrift Store
Category: Vintage, Thrift Store
Average Price: Inexpensive
Area: First Hill
Address: 1017 E Union St
Seattle, WA 98102
Phone: (206) 957-1655

#32
Essenza
Category: Cosmetics, Beauty Supply, Skin Care, Jewelry
Average Price: Expensive
Area: Fremont
Address: 615 N 35th St
Seattle, WA 98103
Phone: (206) 547-4895

#33
Totokaelo
Category: Women's Clothing, Shoe Store
Average Price: Expensive
Area: Capitol Hill
Address: 1523 10th Ave
Seattle, WA 98122
Phone: (206) 623-3582

#34
Evo
Category: Men's Clothing, Women's Clothing, Outdoor Gear
Average Price: Expensive
Area: Fremont
Address: 3500 Stone Way N
Seattle, WA 98103
Phone: (206) 973-4470

#35
Damsalfly
Category: Women's Clothing
Average Price: Modest
Area: Ballard
Address: 5338 Ballard Ave NW
Seattle, WA 98107
Phone: (206) 297-8146

#36
REI
Category: Outdoor Gear, Sports Wear, Bikes
Average Price: Expensive
Area: South Lake Union
Address: 222 Yale Ave N
Seattle, WA 98109
Phone: (206) 223-1944

#37
Omzappy
Category: Women's Clothing, Jewelry
Average Price: Modest
Area: University District
Address: 1409 NE 45th St
Seattle, WA 98105
Phone: (800) 661-1762

#38
Fini
Category: Accessories
Average Price: Modest
Area: Downtown
Address: 86 Pine St
Seattle, WA 98101
Phone: (206) 443-0563

#39
Moksha Clothing & Accessories
Category: Women's Clothing, Jewelry, Men's Clothing
Average Price: Modest
Area: University District
Address: 4542 University Way NE
Seattle, WA 98105
Phone: (206) 632-2622

#40
Macy's
Category: Department Store, Men's Clothing, Women's Clothing
Average Price: Modest
Area: Downtown
Address: 1601 Third Avenue
Seattle, WA 98181
Phone: (206) 506-6000

#41
The Polka Dot Jersey
Category: Bike Repair, Maintenance, Bikes
Average Price: Modest
Area: Leschi
Address: 121 Lakeside Ave
Seattle, WA 98122
Phone: (206) 328-5400

#42
Gather
Category: Vintage
Average Price: Modest
Area: Columbia City
Address: 4863 Rainier Ave S
Seattle, WA 98118
Phone: (206) 760-0674

#43
Costco
Category: Tires, Wholesale Store, Gas & Service Station
Average Price: Modest
Area: Industrial District
Address: 4401 4th Ave S
Seattle, WA 98134
Phone: (206) 674-1220

#44
Endless Knot
Category: Women's Clothing, Accessories
Average Price: Modest
Area: Belltown
Address: 2300 1st Ave
Seattle, WA 98121
Phone: (206) 448-0355

#45
Kobo At Higo
Category: Home Decor, Furniture Store, Art Gallery
Average Price: Modest
Area: International District
Address: 602-608 S Jackson St
Seattle, WA 98104
Phone: (206) 381-3000

#46
Target
Category: Department Store, Drugstore, Grocery
Average Price: Modest
Area: Northgate
Address: 302 NE Northgate Way
Seattle, WA 98125
Phone: (206) 494-0897

#47
Show Pony
Category: Accessories, Women's Clothing, Jewelry
Average Price: Modest
Area: Fremont
Address: 702 N 35th St
Seattle, WA 98103
Phone: (206) 706-4188

#48
Retail Therapy
Category: Jewelry, Women's Clothing, Lingerie
Average Price: Modest
Area: First Hill, Capitol Hill
Address: 905 E Pike St
Seattle, WA 98122
Phone: (206) 324-4092

#49
Fremont Vintage Mall
Category: Antiques, Vinyl Records
Average Price: Modest
Area: Fremont
Address: 3419 Fremont Pl N
Seattle, WA 98103
Phone: (206) 548-9140

#50
Second Ascent
Category: Outdoor Gear
Average Price: Modest
Area: Ballard
Address: 5209 Ballard Ave NW
Seattle, WA 98107
Phone: (206) 545-8810

#51
Les Amis
Category: Women's Clothing, Accessories
Average Price: Expensive
Area: Fremont
Address: 3420 Evanston Avenue N.
Seattle, WA 98103
Phone: (206) 632-2877

#52
Trove Vintage Boutique
Category: Women's Clothing, Vintage, Bridal
Average Price: Modest
Area: Ballard
Address: 2204 NW Market St
Seattle, WA 98107
Phone: (206) 297-6068

#53
Archie Mcphee
Category: Toy Store
Average Price: Inexpensive
Area: Wallingford
Address: 1300 N 45th St
Seattle, WA 98103
Phone: (206) 297-0240

#54
The Dreaming
Category: Comic Books, Hobby Shop
Average Price: Modest
Area: University District
Address: 5226 University Way NE
Seattle, WA 98105
Phone: (206) 525-9394

#55
District Fabric
Category: Fabric Store
Average Price: Modest
Area: Fremont
Address: 513 N 36th St A
Seattle, WA 98103
Phone: (206) 629-8795

#56
Two Big Blondes
Category: Women's Clothing, Vintage, Plus Size Fashion
Average Price: Inexpensive
Area: Atlantic
Address: 2501 S Jackson St
Seattle, WA 98144
Phone: (206) 762-8620

Seattle Travel Guide 2016 / Shops, Restaurants, Arts, Entertainment & Nightlife

#57
The Finerie
Category: Accessories, Men's Clothing, Women's Clothing
Average Price: Expensive
Area: Downtown
Address: 1215 1st Ave
Seattle, WA 98101
Phone: (206) 652-4664

#58
The Sneakery
Category: Shoe Store
Average Price: Modest
Area: Ballard, Phinney Ridge
Address: 612 NW 65th Ave
Seattle, WA 98127
Phone: (206) 297-1786

#59
Goodwill Outlet
Category: Vintage, Thrift Store,
Average Price: Inexpensive
Area: Industrial District
Address: 1765 6th Ave S
Seattle, WA 98134
Phone: (206) 957-5516

#60
Bootyland
Category: Children's Clothing
Average Price: Modest
Area: Capitol Hill
Address: 1317 E Pine St
Seattle, WA 98122
Phone: (206) 328-0636

#61
The Sock Monster
Category: Fashion
Average Price: Modest
Area: Wallingford
Address: 1909 N 45th St
Seattle, WA 98103
Phone: (206) 724-0123

#62
Daiso
Category: Department Store, Discount Store
Average Price: Inexpensive
Area: International District
Address: 710 6th Ave S
Seattle, WA 98104
Phone: (206) 355-4084

#63
Kick It Boots & Stompwear
Category: Women's Clothing, Accessories
Average Price: Modest
Area: Ballard
Address: 2607 NW Market St
Seattle, WA 98107
Phone: (206) 784-3399

#64
Metropolis
Category: Cards, Stationery
Average Price: Modest
Area: Phinney Ridge
Address: 7319 Greenwood Ave N
Seattle, WA 98103
Phone: (206) 782-7002

#65
Goodwill
Category: Vintage, Thrift Store
Average Price: Inexpensive
Area: International District
Address: 1400 S Lane St
Seattle, WA 98144
Phone: (206) 860-5711

#66
Seven Hills Running Shop
Category: Sports Wear
Average Price: Modest
Area: Magnolia
Address: 3139 W Government Way
Seattle, WA 98199
Phone: (206) 941-5866

#67
DSW Designer Shoe Warehouse
Category: Shoe Store
Average Price: Modest
Area: Northgate
Address: 401 Northeast Northgate Way
Seattle, WA 98125
Phone: (206) 367-1289

#68
Smallclothes
Category: Vintage, Children's Clothing
Average Price: Modest
Area: Admiral
Address: 3215 California Ave SW
Seattle, WA 98116
Phone: (206) 923-2222

#69
Coastal Surf Boutique
Category: Women's Clothing, Sports Wear, Men's Clothing
Average Price: Modest
Area: Alki
Address: 2532 Alki Ave SW
Seattle, WA 98116
Phone: (206) 933-5605

#70
Indian Summer
Category: Vintage
Average Price: Modest
Area: Capitol Hill
Address: 534 Summit Ave E
Seattle, WA 98102
Phone: (206) 588-0717

#71
Monster Art And Clothing
Category: Art Gallery, Women's Clothing
Average Price: Modest
Area: Ballard
Address: 5000 20th Ave NW
Seattle, WA 98107
Phone: (206) 789-0037

#72
Ketch
Category: Women's Clothing
Average Price: Expensive
Area: Ballard
Address: 5317 Ballard Ave
Seattle, WA 98107
Phone: (206) 402-4589

#73
Hands Of The World
Category: Jewelry, Accessories, Arts, Crafts
Average Price: Modest
Area: Downtown
Address: 1501 Pike Pl
Seattle, WA 98101
Phone: (206) 622-1696

#74
Stuhlberg's
Category: Cards, Stationery, Home Decor, Toy Store
Average Price: Expensive
Area: Queen Anne
Address: 1801 Queen Anne Ave N
Seattle, WA 98109
Phone: (206) 352-2351

#75
Schmancy
Category: Toy Store
Average Price: Modest
Area: Downtown, Belltown
Address: 1930 2nd Ave
Seattle, WA 98101
Phone: (206) 728-8008

#76
Goodwill
Category: Thrift Store, Vintage
Average Price: Inexpensive
Area: University District
Address: 4552 University Way NE
Seattle, WA 98105
Phone: (206) 547-1487

#77
Northgate Mall
Category: Shopping Center
Average Price: Modest
Area: Northgate
Address: 401 NE Northgate Way
Seattle, WA 98125
Phone: (206) 362-4778

#78
Louis Vuitton
Category: Luggage, Leather Goods, Accessories
Average Price: Exclusive
Area: Downtown
Address: 416 University St
Seattle, WA 98101
Phone: (206) 749-0711

#79
Trichome
Category: Home Decor
Average Price: Modest
Area: International District
Address: 618 S Jackson St
Seattle, WA 98104
Phone: (206) 905-9884

#80
Daiso
Category: Department Store, Discount Store
Average Price: Inexpensive
Area: Downtown
Address: 400 Pine St, Ste 1005
Seattle, WA 98101
Phone: (206) 447-6211

#81
Kuhlman
Category: Men's Clothing, Women's Clothing, Bespoke Clothing
Average Price: Expensive
Area: Belltown
Address: 2419 1st Ave
Seattle, WA 98121
Phone: (206) 441-1999

#82
Crossroads Trading Co.
Category: Vintage, Men's Clothing, Women's Clothing
Average Price: Inexpensive
Area: University District
Address: 4300 University Way NE
Seattle, WA 98105
Phone: (206) 632-3111

#83
Kobo
Category: Art Gallery, Home Decor
Average Price: Modest
Area: Capitol Hill
Address: 814 E Roy
Seattle, WA 98102
Phone: (206) 726-0704

#84
Retrofit Home
Category: Furniture Store, Home Decor
Average Price: Modest
Area: Capitol Hill
Address: 1103 East Pike
Seattle, WA 98122
Phone: (206) 568-4663

#85
H&M
Category: Men's Clothing, Women's Clothing
Average Price: Inexpensive
Area: Downtown
Address: 520 Pike St
Seattle, WA 98101
Phone: (206) 623-0592

#86
Labels
Category: Vintage,
Women's Clothing, Children's Clothing
Average Price: Inexpensive
Area: Phinney Ridge
Address: 7212 Greenwood Ave N
Seattle, WA 98103
Phone: (206) 781-1194

#87
Wild At Heart
Category: Adult
Average Price: Modest
Area: Ballard
Address: 1111 NW Leary Way
Seattle, WA 98107
Phone: (206) 782-5538

#88
Nena
Category: Art Gallery, Gift Shop
Average Price: Modest
Area: Madrona
Address: 1105 34th Ave
Seattle, WA 98122
Phone: (206) 860-4282

#89
Seattle Seahawks Pro Shop
Category: Sports Wear
Average Price: Expensive
Area: Sodo
Address: 800 Occidental Ave S
Seattle, WA 98134
Phone: (206) 682-2900

#90
Nordstrom Rack
Category: Department Store
Average Price: Modest
Area: Downtown
Address: 400 Pine St
Seattle, WA 98101
Phone: (206) 448-8522

#91
University Book Store
Category: Bookstore, Art Supplies, Computers
Average Price: Modest
Area: University District
Address: 4326 University Way NE
Seattle, WA 98105
Phone: (800) 335-7323

#92
QFC
Category: Grocery, Drugstore
Average Price: Modest
Area: Lower Queen Anne
Address: 500 Mercer St
Seattle, WA 98109
Phone: (206) 352-4020

#93
Fred Meyer
Category: Grocery, Drugstore,
Department Store
Average Price: Modest
Area: Greenwood
Address: 100 NW 85th St
Seattle, WA 98117
Phone: (206) 784-9600

#94
Urban Outfitters
Category: Men's Clothing,
Women's Clothing, Home Decor
Average Price: Expensive
Area: Downtown
Address: 1507 5th Ave
Seattle, WA 98101
Phone: (206) 381-3777

#95
Ugly Baby And La Ru
Category: Cards, Stationery,
Gift Shop, Embroidery, Crochet
Average Price: Modest
Area: Downtown
Address: 1525 1st Ave
Seattle, WA 98101
Phone: (206) 696-0089

#96
Wish
Category: Women's Clothing
Average Price: Modest
Area: Wallingford
Address: 4419 Wallingford Ave N
Seattle, WA 98103
Phone: (206) 522-9474

#97
Four Winds Artful Living
Category: Home Decor
Average Price: Modest
Area: Queen Anne
Address: 1521 Queen Anne Ave N
Seattle, WA 98109
Phone: (206) 282-0472

#98
The Elliott Bay Book Company
Category: Bookstore
Average Price: Modest
Area: Capitol Hill
Address: 1521 10th Ave
Seattle, WA 98122
Phone: (206) 624-6600

#99
The Belfry
Category: Antiques
Average Price: Modest
Area: Pioneer Square
Address: 309A 3rd Ave S
Seattle, WA 98104
Phone: (206) 682-2951

#100
Pema Kharpo
Category: Gift Shop
Average Price: Modest
Area: Greenwood
Address: 8554 Greenwood Ave N
Seattle, WA 98103
Phone: (206) 297-2054

#101
The Metro Clothing Co
Category: Women's Clothing, Accessories, Men's Clothing
Average Price: Expensive
Area: Capitol Hill
Address: 231 Broadway E
Seattle, WA 98102
Phone: (206) 726-7978

#102
Le OBJECTS
& Timothy De Clue Design
Category: Home Decor, Antiques, Furniture Store
Average Price: Modest
Area: Georgetown
Address: 1226 S Bailey
Seattle, WA 98108
Phone: (206) 604-4958

#103
QFC
Category: Grocery, Drugstore
Average Price: Modest
Area: University District
Address: 2746 NE 45th St
Seattle, WA 98105
Phone: (206) 523-5160

#104
Value Village
Category: Vintage, Thrift Store
Average Price: Inexpensive
Area: Crown Hill
Address: 8532 15th Ave NW
Seattle, WA 98117
Phone: (206) 783-4648

#105
Driftwood Consignment
Category: Vintage, Women's Clothing
Average Price: Modest
Area: Madrona
Address: 1135 34th Ave
Seattle, WA 98122
Phone: (206) 941-6828

#106
Fireworks Gallery
Category: Jewelry, Accessories, Home Decor
Average Price: Modest
Area: Downtown
Address: 400 Pine St
Seattle, WA 98101
Phone: (206) 682-8707

#107
West Seattle Fabric Company
Category: Fabric Store
Average Price: Modest
Area: Admiral
Address: 2210 California Ave SW
Seattle, WA 98116
Phone: (206) 257-1083

#108
Fremont Sunday Street Market
Category: Flea Market
Average Price: Inexpensive
Area: Fremont
Address: 400 N 34th St
Seattle, WA 98103
Phone: (206) 781-6776

#109
Zovo Lingerie
Category: Women's Clothing, Lingerie
Average Price: Expensive
Area: University District
Address: 4612 26th Ave NE
Seattle, WA 98105
Phone: (206) 525-9686

#110
Laguna Vintage Pottery
Category: Home Decor
Average Price: Expensive
Area: Pioneer Square
Address: 116 S Washington St
Seattle, WA 98104
Phone: (206) 682-6162

#111
Red Light Vintage & Costume
Category: Vintage, Costumes
Average Price: Modest
Area: Capitol Hill
Address: 312 Broadway E
Seattle, WA 98102
Phone: (206) 329-2200

#112
Restaurant Depot
Category: Wholesale Store
Average Price: Modest
Area: Industrial District
Address: 3670 E Marginal Way S
Seattle, WA 98134
Phone: (206) 381-1555

Seattle Travel Guide 2016 / Shops, Restaurants, Arts, Entertainment & Nightlife

#113
Magic Mouse Toys
Category: Toy Store
Average Price: Modest
Area: Pioneer Square
Address: 603 1st Ave
Seattle, WA 98104
Phone: (206) 682-8097

#114
T.J. Maxx
Category: Department Store
Average Price: Inexpensive
Area: Mapleleaf, Northgate
Address: 11029 Roosevelt Way NE
Seattle, WA 98125
Phone: (206) 363-9511

#115
Valley Of Roses
Category: Men's Clothing,
Women's Clothing, Vintage
Average Price: Inexpensive
Area: University District
Address: 4748 University Way NE
Seattle, WA 98105
Phone: (206) 522-6887

#116
Atlas Clothing
Category: Vintage
Average Price: Modest
Area: Fremont
Address: 3509 Fremont Place N
Seattle, WA 98103
Phone: (206) 323-0960

#117
Magus Books
Category: Bookstore
Average Price: Inexpensive
Area: University District
Address: 1408 NE 42nd St
Seattle, WA 98105
Phone: (206) 633-1800

#118
Revival Shop Seattle
Category: Vintage,
Women's Clothing, Antiques
Average Price: Modest
Area: Capitol Hill
Address: 229 Broadway E
Seattle, WA 98102
Phone: (206) 395-6414

#119
Old Seattle Paperworks
Category: Antiques, Home Decor, Art Gallery
Average Price: Modest
Area: Downtown
Address: 1514 Pike Place
Seattle, WA 98101
Phone: (206) 623-2870

#120
Wide World Books & Maps
Category: Bookstore, Luggage
Average Price: Modest
Area: Wallingford
Address: 4411 Wallingford Ave N
Seattle, WA 98103
Phone: (206) 634-3453

#121
Metsker Maps
Category: Hobby Shop
Average Price: Modest
Area: Downtown
Address: 1511 1st Ave
Seattle, WA 98101
Phone: (206) 623-8747

#122
Harvard Market
Category: Shopping Center
Average Price: Inexpensive
Area: First Hill
Address: 1401 Broadway
Seattle, WA 98122
Phone: (206) 324-0187

#123
Alexandra's Exclusively Designer Consignment
Category: Vintage
Average Price: Modest
Area: Downtown, Belltown
Address: 412 Olive Way
Seattle, WA 98101
Phone: (206) 623-1214

#124
Crossroads Trading Co.
Category: Vintage,
Men's Clothing, Women's Clothing
Average Price: Modest
Area: Capitol Hill
Address: 325 Broadway E
Seattle, WA 98102
Phone: (206) 328-5867

#125
Cicada
Category: Women's Clothing,
Bridal, Accessories
Average Price: Modest
Area: Downtown
Address: 1121 1st Avenue
Seattle, WA 98101
Phone: (206) 652-2434

#126
Card Kingdom
Category: Hobby Shop
Average Price: Modest
Area: Ballard
Address: 5105 Leary Ave NW
Seattle, WA 98107
Phone: (206) 523-2273

#127
Burnt Sugar & Frankie
Category: Shoe Store, Jewelry, Accessories
Average Price: Expensive
Area: Fremont
Address: 601 N 35th St
Seattle, WA 98103
Phone: (888) 545-0699

#128
Hub And Bespoke
Category: Women's Clothing, Men's Clothing
Average Price: Expensive
Area: Fremont
Address: 513 N 36th St
Seattle, WA 98103
Phone: (206) 547-5730

#129
Stussy
Category: Shopping
Average Price: Modest
Area: Capitol Hill
Address: 1108 Pike St
Seattle, WA 98101
Phone: (206) 467-5030

#130
Ballard Home Comforts
Category: Furniture Store, Home Decor
Average Price: Modest
Area: Ballard
Address: 5334 Ballard Ave NW
Seattle, WA 98107
Phone: (206) 781-1040

#131
Shiga's Imports
Category: Home Decor, Furniture Store, Kitchen & Bath
Average Price: Inexpensive
Area: University District
Address: 4306 University Way NE
Seattle, WA 98105
Phone: (206) 633-2400

#132
Hointer
Category: Men's Clothing, Women's Clothing
Average Price: Expensive
Area: Wallingford
Address: 400 NE 45th St
Seattle, WA 98105
Phone: (650) 241-9105

#133
E Smith Mercantile
Category: Cocktail Bar, Gift Shop, American
Average Price: Modest
Area: Pioneer Square
Address: 208 1st Ave S
Seattle, WA 98104
Phone: (206) 641-7250

#134
Once Upon A Time
Category: Children's Clothing, Toy Store, Baby Gear, Furniture
Average Price: Modest
Area: Queen Anne
Address: 1622 Queen Anne Ave N
Seattle, WA 98109
Phone: (206) 284-7260

#135
City Of Hope Second Hand Rose Thrift Shop
Category: Thrift Store
Average Price: Inexpensive
Area: Greenwood, Phinney Ridge
Address: 203 N 85th St
Seattle, WA 98103
Phone: (206) 784-0298

#136
Fireworks Gallery
Category: Jewelry, Accessories
Average Price: Modest
Area: University District
Address: 2617 NE Village St
Seattle, WA 98105
Phone: (206) 527-2858

#137
Buffalo Exchange
Category: Vintage, Men's Clothing, Women's Clothing
Average Price: Modest
Area: University District
Address: 4530 University Way NE
Seattle, WA 98105
Phone: (206) 545-0175

#138
Goodwill
Category: Vintage, Thrift Store,
Average Price: Inexpensive
Area: Ballard
Address: 6400 8th Ave NW
Seattle, WA 98107
Phone: (206) 957-5544

#139
Lambs Ear Shoes
Category: Shoe Store
Average Price: Expensive
Area: Fremont
Address: 617 N 35th St
Seattle, WA 98103
Phone: (206) 632-2626

#140
Top Ten Toys
Category: Toy Store, Art Supplies
Average Price: Modest
Area: Greenwood
Address: 120 N 85th St
Seattle, WA 98103
Phone: (206) 782-0098

#141
Veridis
Category: Men's Clothing, Women's Clothing
Average Price: Expensive
Area: Capitol Hill
Address: 1205 E Pike St
Seattle, WA 98122
Phone: (206) 402-3789

#142
Watson Kennedy Fine Home
Category: Home Decor
Average Price: Expensive
Area: Downtown
Address: 1022 1st Ave
Seattle, WA 98104
Phone: (206) 652-8350

#143
Anthropologie
Category: Women's Clothing, Accessories
Average Price: Expensive
Area: University District
Address: 2520 NE University Village St
Seattle, WA 98105
Phone: (206) 985-2101

#144
TWIST
Category: Jewelry
Average Price: Expensive
Area: Downtown
Address: 600 Pine St
Seattle, WA 98101
Phone: (206) 315-8080

#145
Clover Toys
Category: Toy Store, Children's Clothing
Average Price: Expensive
Area: Ballard
Address: 5333 Ballard Ave NW
Seattle, WA 98107
Phone: (206) 782-0715

#146
J.Crew
Category: Women's Clothing, Men's Clothing, Accessories
Average Price: Expensive
Area: Downtown
Address: 600 Pine Street
Seattle, WA 98101
Phone: (206) 652-9788

#147
Banana Republic
Category: Women's Clothing, Accessories
Average Price: Expensive
Area: Downtown
Address: 500 Pike St
Seattle, WA 98101
Phone: (206) 622-2303

#148
Ada's Technical Books & Cafe
Category: Bookstore, Coffee, Tea, Café
Average Price: Modest
Area: Capitol Hill
Address: 425 15th Ave E
Seattle, WA 98112
Phone: (206) 322-1058

#149
Kinokuniya Bookstore
Category: Bookstore, Comic Books, Music, Dvds
Average Price: Modest
Area: International District
Address: 525 S Weller St
Seattle, WA 98104
Phone: (206) 587-2477

#150
The Curious Nest
Category: Antiques, Jewelry, Art Gallery
Average Price: Expensive
Area: Ravenna
Address: 2916 NE 55th St
Seattle, WA 98105
Phone: (206) 729-6378

#151
Trendy Wendy
Category: Women's Clothing
Average Price: Modest
Area: Capitol Hill
Address: 211 Broadway E
Seattle, WA 98102
Phone: (206) 322-6642

#152
Mishu Boutique
Category: Women's Clothing, Men's Clothing, Leather Goods
Average Price: Modest
Area: Capitol Hill
Address: 321 Broadway E
Seattle, WA 98102
Phone: (206) 802-8022

#153
Dream
Category: Women's Clothing
Average Price: Modest
Area: Fremont
Address: 3427 Fremont Pl N
Seattle, WA 98103
Phone: (206) 547-1211

#154
Urban Earth
Category: Nursery, Gardening, Home Decor
Average Price: Modest
Area: Fremont
Address: 1051 N 35th St
Seattle, WA 98103
Phone: (206) 632-1760

#155
Cost Plus World Market
Category: Furniture Store, Beer, Wine, Spirits, Home Decor
Average Price: Modest
Area: Belltown
Address: 2103 Western Ave
Seattle, WA 98121
Phone: (206) 443-1055

#156
QFC
Category: Grocery, Drugstore
Average Price: Modest
Area: Northgate
Address: 11100 Roosevelt Way NE
Seattle, WA 98125
Phone: (206) 361-4849

#157
Pacific Galleries Antique Mall & Auction House.
Category: Antiques, Shopping Center, Art Gallery
Average Price: Expensive
Area: Industrial District
Address: 241 S Lander St
Seattle, WA 98134
Phone: (206) 292-3999

#158
Alive And Well
Category: Men's Clothing
Average Price: Modest
Area: First Hill, Capitol Hill
Address: 705A E Pike St
Seattle, WA 98122
Phone: (206) 453-4705

#159
Safeway
Category: Grocery, Drugstore
Average Price: Modest
Area: Roosevelt
Address: 7300 Roosevelt Way NE
Seattle, WA 98115
Phone: (206) 525-6348

#160
Classic Consignment
Category: Vintage
Average Price: Modest
Area: Ballard
Address: 5514 24th Ave NW
Seattle, WA 98107
Phone: (206) 781-7061

#161
No Parking On Pike
Category: Vintage
Average Price: Modest
Area: Capitol Hill
Address: 1102 E Pike
Seattle, WA 98122
Phone: (206) 322-7453

#162
Kirk Albert Vintage Furnishings
Category: Home Decor, Furniture Store
Average Price: Expensive
Area: Georgetown
Address: 5517 Airport Way S
Seattle, WA 98108
Phone: (206) 931-6208

#163
35th North
Category: Sporting Goods, Shoe Store
Average Price: Modest
Area: Capitol Hill
Address: 1100 E Pike St
Seattle, WA 98122
Phone: (206) 320-1252

#164
Sassafras
Category: Women's Clothing, Jewelry, Accessories
Average Price: Modest
Area: Belltown
Address: 2307 1st Ave
Seattle, WA 98121
Phone: (206) 420-7057

#165
Underu4men
Category: Men's Clothing, Swimwear
Average Price: Expensive
Area: Capitol Hill
Address: 709 Broadway E
Seattle, WA 98102
Phone: (206) 324-6446

#166
Castle Megastore
Category: Adult
Average Price: Modest
Area: Capitol Hill
Address: 206 Broadway East
Seattle, WA 98102
Phone: (206) 204-0126

#167
Red Light Vintage Clothing
Category: Vintage, Costumes
Average Price: Modest
Area: University District
Address: 4560 University Way NE
Seattle, WA 98105
Phone: (206) 545-4044

#168
Pink Gorilla
Category: Toy Store, Electronics
Average Price: Modest
Area: International District
Address: 601 S King St
Seattle, WA 98104
Phone: (206) 264-2434

#169
Lemon Drop
Category: Vintage
Average Price: Modest
Area: Ballard
Address: 5818 24th Ave NW
Seattle, WA 98107
Phone: (206) 547-1840

#170
Lucky Vintage
Category: Vintage
Average Price: Modest
Area: University District
Address: 4742 University Way NE
Seattle, WA 98105
Phone: (206) 523-6621

#171
Luly Yang Couture
Category: Bridal, Women's Clothing
Average Price: Exclusive
Area: Downtown
Address: 1218 4th Ave
Seattle, WA 98101
Phone: (206) 623-8200

#172
Tina's On Madison
Category: Fabric Store
Average Price: Expensive
Area: Madison Park
Address: 4232 E Madison St
Seattle, WA 98112
Phone: (206) 328-0803

#173
Used Furniture
Category: Furniture Store
Average Price: Inexpensive
Area: Capitol Hill
Address: 117 Summit Ave E
Seattle, WA 98102
Phone: (206) 261-7999

#174
Stop N Shop Thrift Store
Category: Thrift Store
Average Price: Inexpensive
Area: Junction
Address: 4504 California Ave SW
Seattle, WA 98116
Phone: (206) 932-4044

#175
Edge Of The Circle Books
Category: Bookstore
Average Price: Modest
Area: First Hill, Capitol Hill
Address: 701 E Pike St
Seattle, WA 98122
Phone: (206) 726-1999

#176
Anthropologie
Category: Women's Clothing, Accessories
Average Price: Expensive
Area: Downtown
Address: 1509 5th Ave
Seattle, WA 98101
Phone: (206) 381-5900

#177
Woolly Mammoth
Category: Shoe Store
Average Price: Modest
Area: University District
Address: 4303 University Way NE
Seattle, WA 98105
Phone: (206) 632-3254

#178
Presence Art Of Living
Category: Women's Clothing, Men's Clothing, Jewelry
Average Price: Modest
Area: Capitol Hill
Address: 713 Broadway E
Seattle, WA 98102
Phone: (206) 325-5530

#179
Artist & Craftsman Supply
Category: Art Supplies
Average Price: Modest
Area: University District
Address: 4350 8th Ave NE
Seattle, WA 98105
Phone: (206) 545-0091

#180
Forever 21
Category: Women's Clothing, Men's Clothing
Average Price: Inexpensive
Area: Downtown
Address: 601 Pine St
Seattle, WA 98101
Phone: (206) 623-2154

#181
Seattle Mystery Bookshop
Category: Bookstore
Average Price: Modest
Area: Downtown, Pioneer Square
Address: 117 Cherry St
Seattle, WA 98104
Phone: (206) 587-5737

#182
Swansons Nursery
Category: Nursery, Gardening
Average Price: Expensive
Area: Olympic Manor
Address: 9701 15th Ave NW
Seattle, WA 98117
Phone: (206) 782-2543

#183
Platinum Records
Category: Electronics, Music, Dvds, Vinyl Records
Average Price: Modest
Area: First Hill, Capitol Hill
Address: 915 E Pike St
Seattle, WA 98122
Phone: (206) 324-8032

#184
Stitches
Category: Fabric Store, Knitting Supplies
Average Price: Modest
Area: First Hill, Capitol Hill
Address: 711 E Pike St
Seattle, WA 98122
Phone: (206) 709-0707

#185
Mario's
Category: Women's Clothing, Accessories, Men's Clothing
Average Price: Exclusive
Area: Downtown
Address: 1513 6th Ave
Seattle, WA 98101
Phone: (206) 223-1461

#186
Party At Display & Costume
Category: Party Supplies, Costumes
Average Price: Modest
Area: Northgate
Address: 11201 Roosevelt Way NE
Seattle, WA 98125
Phone: (206) 362-4810

#187
American Eagle Outfitters
Category: Women's Clothing, Men's Clothing
Average Price: Modest
Area: Downtown
Address: 1420 5th Ave
Seattle, WA 98101
Phone: (206) 264-4994

#188
Aprie
Category: Women's Clothing
Average Price: Modest
Area: Capitol Hill
Address: 310 Broadway E
Seattle, WA 98102
Phone: (206) 324-1255

#189
Nordstrom
Category: Department Store
Average Price: Expensive
Area: Northgate
Address: 401 NE Northgate Way
Seattle, WA 98125
Phone: (206) 364-8800

#190
Glassybaby
Category: Flowers, Gifts, Home & Garden
Average Price: Expensive
Area: Madrona
Address: 3406 E Union St
Seattle, WA 98122
Phone: (206) 518-9071

#191
QFC
Category: Grocery, Drugstore
Average Price: Modest
Area: Capitol Hill
Address: 417 Broadway E
Seattle, WA 98102
Phone: (206) 328-6920

#192
Mercer Street Books
Category: Bookstore
Average Price: Inexpensive
Area: Lower Queen Anne
Address: 7 Mercer St
Seattle, WA 98109
Phone: (206) 282-7687

#193
Express
Category: Accessories, Men's Clothing, Women's Clothing
Average Price: Modest
Area: Downtown
Address: 600 Pine St
Seattle, WA 98101
Phone: (206) 652-8481

#194
Outdoor Emporium
Category: Sporting Goods
Average Price: Modest
Area: Industrial District
Address: 1701 4th Ave S
Seattle, WA 98134
Phone: (206) 624-6550

#195
The Paper Feather
Category: Cards, Stationery
Average Price: Modest
Area: Downtown
Address: 1520 Western Ave
Seattle, WA 98101
Phone: (206) 395-8720

#196
Zanadu Comics
Category: Toy Store, Comic Books
Average Price: Modest
Area: Belltown
Address: 1923 3rd Ave
Seattle, WA 98101
Phone: (206) 443-1316

#197
Nube Green
Category: Home Decor, Women's Clothing, Children's Clothing
Average Price: Expensive
Area: Capitol Hill
Address: 921 E Pine St
Seattle, WA 98122
Phone: (206) 402-4515

#198
Cookin
Category: Kitchen & Bath
Average Price: Modest
Area: Madison Park
Address: 4224 E Madison St
Seattle, WA 98112
Phone: (206) 328-2665

#199
Easy Street Records And Café
Category: Music, Dvds, Coffee, Tea, Breakfast & Brunch
Average Price: Inexpensive
Area: Junction
Address: 4559 California Ave SW
Seattle, WA 98116
Phone: (206) 938-3279

#200
Peter Miller Architecture And Design Books
Category: Bookstore
Average Price: Modest
Area: Belltown
Address: 2326 2nd Ave
Seattle, WA 98121
Phone: (206) 441-4114

#201
Glasswing
Category: Men's Clothing, Women's Clothing, Furniture Store
Average Price: Expensive
Area: Capitol Hill
Address: 1525 Melrose Ave
Seattle, WA 98122
Phone: (206) 641-7646

#202
Alexandria Rossoff Jewels & Rare Finds
Category: Jewelry
Average Price: Expensive
Address: 411 University St
Seattle, WA 98101
Phone: (206) 381-3949

#203
Fluidride
Category: Bikes
Average Price: Expensive
Area: University District
Address: 723 NE Northlake Way
Seattle, WA 98105
Phone: (206) 499-3469

#204
Click! Design That Fits
Category: Jewelry, Home Decor
Average Price: Modest
Area: Junction
Address: 4540 California Ave SW
Seattle, WA 98116
Phone: (206) 328-9252

#205
Twice Sold Tales
Category: Bookstore
Average Price: Inexpensive
Area: Capitol Hill
Address: 1833 Harvard Ave
Seattle, WA 98102
Phone: (206) 324-2421

#206
Dolce Bleu
Category: Bridal, Formal Wear
Average Price: Modest
Area: Industrial District
Address: 3220 1st Ave S
Seattle, WA 98134
Phone: (206) 420-7320

#207
Gamma Ray Games
Category: Hobby Shop
Average Price: Modest
Area: Capitol Hill
Address: 411 E Pine St
Seattle, WA 98122
Phone: (206) 838-9445

#208
Space Oddity Vintage Furniture
Category: Home Decor, Furniture Store
Average Price: Modest
Area: Ballard
Address: 5318 22nd Ave NW
Seattle, WA 98107
Phone: (206) 322-6704

#209
Cherry Consignment
Category: Vintage
Average Price: Modest
Area: Junction
Address: 4142 California Ave SW
Seattle, WA 98116
Phone: (206) 933-7479

#210
Carmilia's
Category: Women's Clothing
Average Price: Expensive
Area: Junction
Address: 4528 California Ave SW
Seattle, WA 98116
Phone: (206) 935-1929

#211
Casita International
Category: Home Decor, Fashion, Jewelry
Average Price: Modest
Area: Capitol Hill
Address: 423 15th Ave E
Seattle, WA 98112
Phone: (206) 322-7800

#212
Zebraclub
Category: Women's Clothing, Accessories, Men's Clothing
Average Price: Modest
Area: Downtown
Address: 1901 1st Ave
Seattle, WA 98101
Phone: (206) 448-7452

#213
Bellefleur Lingerie Boutique
Category: Lingerie
Average Price: Expensive
Area: Fremont
Address: 3504 Fremont Pl N
Seattle, WA 98103
Phone: (206) 545-0222

#214
Singles Going Steady
Category: Music, Dvds, Vinyl Records
Average Price: Modest
Area: Belltown
Address: 2219 2nd Ave
Seattle, WA 98121
Phone: (206) 441-7396

#215
Bliss
Category: Women's Clothing, Accessories
Average Price: Expensive
Area: Fremont
Address: 3501 Fremont Ave N
Seattle, WA 98103
Phone: (206) 632-6695

#216
Target
Category: Department Store, Grocery, Drugstore
Average Price: Modest
Area: Roxhill
Address: 2800 SW Barton St
Seattle, WA 98126
Phone: (206) 932-1153

#217
HAMMER + AWL
Category: Men's Clothing, Accessories
Average Price: Modest
Area: Madrona
Address: 3315 E Pike St
Seattle, WA 98122
Phone: (206) 992-7444

#218
Safeway
Category: Grocery, Drugstore
Average Price: Modest
Area: Lower Queen Anne
Address: 516 1st Ave W
Seattle, WA 98119
Phone: (206) 494-1685

#219
Made In Washington
Category: Specialty Food, Home Decor, Gift Shop
Average Price: Modest
Area: Downtown
Address: 400 Pine St
Seattle, WA 98101
Phone: (206) 623-9753

#220
Sports Authority
Category: Sporting Goods
Average Price: Modest
Area: Northgate
Address: 328 NE Northgate Way
Seattle, WA 98125
Phone: (206) 838-7783

#221
Barneys New York
Category: Department Store
Average Price: Exclusive
Area: Downtown
Address: 600 Pine St
Seattle, WA 98101
Phone: (206) 622-6300

#222
Peridot Boutique
Category: Women's Clothing, Accessories
Average Price: Modest
Area: Lower Queen Anne
Address: 532 Queen Anne Ave N
Seattle, WA 98109
Phone: (206) 687-7130

#223
Cash & Carry
Category: Grocery, Wholesale Store
Average Price: Inexpensive
Area: Industrial District
Address: 1760 4th Ave S
Seattle, WA 98134
Phone: (206) 343-7156

#224
Crackerjack Contemporary Crafts
Category: Jewelry, Arts, Crafts, Art Gallery
Average Price: Modest
Area: Wallingford
Address: 1815 N 45th St
Seattle, WA 98103
Phone: (206) 547-4983

Seattle Travel Guide 2016 / Shops, Restaurants, Arts, Entertainment & Nightlife

#225
John Fluevog
Category: Shoe Store
Average Price: Expensive
Area: Downtown
Address: 205 Pine St
Seattle, WA 98101
Phone: (206) 441-1065

#226
Ancient Grounds
Category: Coffee, Tea, Art Gallery
Average Price: Inexpensive
Area: Downtown
Address: 1220 1st Ave
Seattle, WA 98101
Phone: (206) 749-0747

#227
Lion Heart Book Store
Category: Bookstore
Average Price: Inexpensive
Area: Downtown
Address: 1501 Pike Pl
Seattle, WA 98101
Phone: (206) 903-6511

#228
Re-Soul
Category: Shoe Store, Accessories
Average Price: Expensive
Area: Ballard
Address: 5319 Ballard Ave NW
Seattle, WA 98107
Phone: (206) 789-7312

#229
Filson
Category: Shoe Store, Sports Wear, Luggage
Average Price: Expensive
Area: Industrial District
Address: 1555 4th Ave S
Seattle, WA 98134
Phone: (206) 622-3147

#230
Old Navy
Category: Men's Clothing, Women's Clothing, Children's Clothing
Average Price: Inexpensive
Area: Downtown
Address: 511 Pine St
Seattle, WA 98101
Phone: (206) 623-1800

#231
Secret Garden Bookshop
Category: Bookstore
Average Price: Modest
Area: Ballard
Address: 2214 NW Market St
Seattle, WA 98107
Phone: (206) 789-5006

#232
Fireworks Gallery
Category: Jewelry, Accessories
Average Price: Expensive
Area: Pioneer Square
Address: 210 1st Ave S
Seattle, WA 98104
Phone: (206) 682-8707

#233
Shoprite
Category: Department Store
Average Price: Inexpensive
Area: Capitol Hill
Address: 432 15th Ave E
Seattle, WA 98112
Phone: (206) 328-5138

#234
Vixen Day Spa & Boutique
Category: Day Spa, Women's Clothing
Average Price: Modest
Area: Magnolia
Address: 3209 W Mcgraw St
Seattle, WA 98199
Phone: (206) 281-9399

#235
Unveiled Bridal Boutique
Category: Bridal, Accessories
Average Price: Modest
Area: Magnolia
Address: 2425 33rd Ave W
Seattle, WA 98199
Phone: (206) 402-6880

#236
Ballard Consignment Store
Category: Antiques, Furniture Store, Vintage
Average Price: Modest
Area: Ballard
Address: 5459 Leary Ave NW
Seattle, WA 98107
Phone: (206) 859-9956

#237
Local Color
Category: Coffee, Tea, Art Gallery
Average Price: Inexpensive
Area: Downtown
Address: 1600 Pike Pl
Seattle, WA 98101
Phone: (206) 728-1717

#238
Mr. Johnson's Antiques
Category: Antiques
Average Price: Modest
Area: Montlake
Address: 2315 24th Ave E
Seattle, WA 98112
Phone: (206) 322-6033

#239
Tea Cozy Yarn Shop
Category: Knitting Supplies, Coffee, Tea, Framing
Average Price: Modest
Area: Ballard
Address: 5816 24th Ave NW
Seattle, WA 98107
Phone: (206) 783-3322

#240
Childish Things
Category: Vintage, Children's Clothing, Maternity Wear
Average Price: Inexpensive
Area: Greenwood
Address: 10002 Holman Rd NW
Seattle, WA 98177
Phone: (206) 789-1498

#241
Federal Army & Navy Surplus
Category: Outdoor Gear
Average Price: Modest
Area: Belltown
Address: 2112 1st Ave
Seattle, WA 98121
Phone: (206) 443-1818

#242
The Walking Company
Category: Shoe Store
Average Price: Expensive
Area: Downtown
Address: 1428 4th Ave
Seattle, WA 98101
Phone: (206) 624-9215

#243
Clementine
Category: Women's Clothing, Shoe Store
Average Price: Expensive
Area: Junction
Address: 4447 California Ave SW
Seattle, WA 98127
Phone: (206) 935-9400

#244
Sylvia's Swimwear
Category: Swimwear
Average Price: Modest
Area: Mapleleaf
Address: 9596 1st Ave NE
Seattle, WA 98115
Phone: (206) 985-7946

#245
International Model Toys
Category: Toy Store, Hobby Shop
Average Price: Expensive
Area: International District
Address: 524 S King St
Seattle, WA 98104
Phone: (206) 682-8534

#246
Urban Outfitters
Category: Women's Clothing, Men's Clothing, Accessories
Average Price: Expensive
Area: Capitol Hill
Address: 401 Broadway E
Seattle, WA 98102
Phone: (206) 322-1800

#247
Hardwick's
Category: Hardware Store
Average Price: Modest
Area: University District
Address: 4214 Roosevelt Way NE
Seattle, WA 98105
Phone: (206) 632-1203

#248
Recycled Cycles
Category: Bikes, Bike Rentals
Average Price: Modest
Area: University District
Address: 1007 NE Boat St
Seattle, WA 98105
Phone: (206) 547-4491

#249
Spin Cycle
Category: Music, Dvds, Vinyl Records, Videos, Video Game
Average Price: Modest
Area: Capitol Hill
Address: 321 Broadway Ave E
Seattle, WA 98102
Phone: (206) 971-0267

#250
Kasala Outlet
Category: Furniture Store, Outlet Store, Home Decor
Average Price: Modest
Area: Industrial District
Address: 1946 Occidental Ave S
Seattle, WA 98134
Phone: (206) 340-4112

#251
City People's Mercantile
Category: Hardware Store, Home Decor, Furniture Store
Average Price: Modest
Area: Laurelhurst
Address: 5440 Sand Point Way NE
Seattle, WA 98105
Phone: (206) 524-1200

#252
Greenwood Space Travel Supply
Category: Hobby Shop
Average Price: Modest
Area: Greenwood, Phinney Ridge
Address: 8414 Greenwood Ave N
Seattle, WA 98103
Phone: (206) 725-2625

#253
Dollar Tree
Category: Discount Store, Department Store
Average Price: Inexpensive
Area: University District
Address: 4535 University Way NE
Seattle, WA 98105
Phone: (206) 547-5680

#254
Byrnie Utz Hats
Category: Accessories,
Men's Clothing, Women's Clothing
Average Price: Expensive
Area: Downtown
Address: 310 Union St
Seattle, WA 98101
Phone: (206) 623-0233

#255
Yazdi
Category: Women's Clothing, Accessories
Average Price: Expensive
Area: Wallingford
Address: 1815 N 45th St
Seattle, WA 98103
Phone: (206) 547-6008

#256
SPUN Sustainable Collective
Category: Women's Clothing,
Accessories, Home Decor
Average Price: Expensive
Area: Capitol Hill
Address: 1515 14th Ave
Seattle, WA 98122
Phone: (206) 328-2102

#257
Urban Outfitters
Category: Women's Clothing,
Men's Clothing, Jewelry
Average Price: Expensive
Area: University District
Address: 4518 University Way NE
Seattle, WA 98105
Phone: (206) 632-0409

#258
Liave
Category: Home Decor, Furniture Store
Average Price: Modest
Area: Downtown
Address: 1205 Western Ave
Seattle, WA 98101
Phone: (206) 364-0748

#259
Super Jock 'N Jill
Category: Sports Wear
Average Price: Modest
Area: Greenlake
Address: 7210 E Green Lake Dr N
Seattle, WA 98115
Phone: (206) 522-7711

#260
Kitchen N Things
Category: Kitchen & Bath
Average Price: Expensive
Area: Ballard
Address: 2322 NW Market St
Seattle, WA 98107
Phone: (206) 784-8717

#261
Ophelia's Books
Category: Bookstore
Average Price: Inexpensive
Area: Fremont
Address: 3504 Fremont Ave N
Seattle, WA 98103
Phone: (206) 632-3759

#262
The Soap Box
Category: Kitchen & Bath
Average Price: Modest
Area: Downtown
Address: 1916 Pike Pl
Seattle, WA 98101
Phone: (206) 441-5680

#263
Shop Task
Category: Sporting Goods
Average Price: Modest
Area: University District
Address: 1100 NE 47th St
Seattle, WA 98105
Phone: (206) 402-4966

#264
Chihuly Garden And Glass
Category: Art Gallery, Museum
Average Price: Modest
Area: Lower Queen Anne
Address: 305 Harrison St
Seattle, WA 98109
Phone: (206) 753-4940

#265
The Red Balloon Company
Category: Cards, Stationery,
Toy Store, Party Supplies
Average Price: Modest
Area: Capitol Hill
Address: 417 15th Ave E
Seattle, WA 98112
Phone: (206) 467-0318

#266
Modele's Consignment Home Furnishings
Category: Furniture Store
Average Price: Modest
Area: South Lake Union
Address: 964 Denny Way
Seattle, WA 98109
Phone: (206) 287-9942

#267
Gargoyles Statuary
Category: Home Decor, Art Gallery
Average Price: Modest
Area: University District
Address: 4550 University Way NE
Seattle, WA 98105
Phone: (206) 632-4940

#268
Winner's Circle
Category: Shoe Store, Men's Clothing
Average Price: Modest
Area: Capitol Hill
Address: 1353 E Olive Way
Seattle, WA 98122
Phone: (206) 860-6879

#269
Optical-Nerve
Category: Eyewear, Opticians
Average Price: Inexpensive
Area: South Lake Union, Westlake
Address: 904 Dexter Ave N
Seattle, WA 98109
Phone: (206) 282-2120

#270
Goorin Bros.
Category: Accessories, Hats
Average Price: Modest
Area: Downtown
Address: 1610 1st Ave
Seattle, WA 98101
Phone: (206) 443-8082

#271
Take 2
Category: Women's Clothing, Vintage
Average Price: Modest
Area: Capitol Hill
Address: 430 15th Ave E
Seattle, WA 98112
Phone: (206) 324-2569

#272
West Elm
Category: Furniture Store, Home Decor, Kitchen & Bath
Average Price: Modest
Area: South Lake Union, Denny Triangle
Address: 2201 Westlake Ave
Seattle, WA 98121
Phone: (206) 467-5798

#273
Capers Home
Category: Furniture Store, Home Decor
Average Price: Modest
Area: Junction
Address: 4525 California Ave SW
Seattle, WA 98116
Phone: (206) 932-0371

#274
Brooks Brothers
Category: Men's Clothing, Women's Clothing
Average Price: Expensive
Area: Downtown
Address: 1330 5th Ave
Seattle, WA 98101
Phone: (206) 624-4400

#275
Chloe And Dillon
Category: Women's Clothing, Men's Clothing
Average Price: Expensive
Area: Eastlake
Address: 2345 Eastlake Ave E
Seattle, WA 98102
Phone: (206) 457-5086

#276
Distant Lands
Category: Furniture Store, Antiques, Home Decor
Average Price: Expensive
Area: Pioneer Square
Address: 109 1st Ave S
Seattle, WA 98104
Phone: (206) 340-2868

#277
Sprocketts Recycled Bicycles
Category: Bikes
Average Price: Inexpensive
Area: Magnolia
Address: 2823 Thorndyke Ave W
Seattle, WA 98199
Phone: (360) 929-5313

#278
Market Street Shoes
Category: Shoe Store
Average Price: Expensive
Area: Ballard
Address: 2232 NW Market St
Seattle, WA 98107
Phone: (206) 783-1670

#279
The Spanish Table
Category: Grocery, Beer, Wine, Spirits, Kitchen & Bath
Average Price: Modest
Area: Downtown
Address: 1426 Western Ave
Seattle, WA 98101
Phone: (206) 682-2827

#280
The Boston Street Baby Store
Category: Children's Clothing, Accessories
Average Price: Modest
Area: Downtown
Address: 1902 Post Alley
Seattle, WA 98127
Phone: (206) 634-0580

Seattle Travel Guide 2016 / Shops, Restaurants, Arts, Entertainment & Nightlife

#281
Dutch Bike Co.
Category: Bikes, Bike Rentals
Average Price: Inexpensive
Area: Ballard
Address: 4905 Leary Ave NW
Seattle, WA 98107
Phone: (206) 789-1678

#282
Fleurt
Category: Florist
Average Price: Modest
Area: Junction
Address: 4536 California Ave SW
Seattle, WA 98116
Phone: (206) 937-1103

#283
Fancy
Category: Jewelry, Bridal
Average Price: Modest
Area: Belltown
Address: 1914 2nd Ave
Seattle, WA 98101
Phone: (206) 956-2945

#284
Parfumerie Nasreen
Category: Cosmetics, Beauty Supply
Average Price: Exclusive
Area: Downtown
Address: 1005 1st Ave
Seattle, WA 98104
Phone: (206) 682-3459

#285
Sela's Small Couture
Category: Baby Gear, Furniture, Children's Clothing
Average Price: Modest
Area: Queen Anne
Address: 610 W Mcgraw St
Seattle, WA 98119
Phone: (206) 216-4423

#286
Cotton Caboodle
Category: Children's Clothing, Women's Clothing
Average Price: Inexpensive
Area: Interbay, Belltown
Address: 3136 Elliott Ave
Seattle, WA 98121
Phone: (206) 352-3763

#287
Mia Bella
Category: Women's Clothing, Vintage
Average Price: Expensive
Area: Roosevelt
Address: 6507 Roosevelt Way NE
Seattle, WA 98115
Phone: (206) 523-1083

#288
De Medici Ming Fine Paper
Category: Cards, Stationery
Average Price: Modest
Area: Downtown
Address: 1222 1st Ave
Seattle, WA 98101
Phone: (206) 624-1983

#289
Safeway
Category: Grocery, Drugstore, Beer, Wine, Spirits
Average Price: Modest
Area: Central District
Address: 2201 E Madison St
Seattle, WA 98122
Phone: (206) 494-1518

#290
Ross Dress For Less
Category: Department Store
Average Price: Inexpensive
Area: Downtown
Address: 301 Pike St
Seattle, WA 98101
Phone: (206) 623-6781

#291
White House Black Market
Category: Women's Clothing
Average Price: Expensive
Area: Downtown
Address: 600 Pine St, Ste 301
Seattle, WA 98101
Phone: (206) 382-6242

#292
Book Larder
Category: Bookstore, Cooking School
Average Price: Modest
Area: Fremont
Address: 4252 Fremont Ave N
Seattle, WA 98103
Phone: (206) 397-4271

#293
Title Nine
Category: Sports Wear, Women's Clothing
Average Price: Expensive
Area: Greenlake
Address: 7000 Woodlawn Ave NE
Seattle, WA 98115
Phone: (206) 522-1425

#294
Buffalo Exchange
Category: Vintage, Men's Clothing, Women's Clothing
Average Price: Modest
Area: Ballard
Address: 2232 NW Market St
Seattle, WA 98107
Phone: (206) 297-5920

#295
Baraka Gemstones & Jewelry
Category: Jewelry, Watches, Gold Buyer, Bridal
Average Price: Modest
Area: Ballard
Address: 1521 NW 54th St
Seattle, WA 98107
Phone: (425) 422-9290

#296
The Crypt
Category: Adult, Leather Goods
Average Price: Modest
Area: Capitol Hill
Address: 1516 11th Ave
Seattle, WA 98122
Phone: (206) 325-3882

#297
Paper Delights
Category: Cards, Stationery
Average Price: Expensive
Area: Wallingford
Address: 2205 N 45th St
Seattle, WA 98103
Phone: (206) 547-1002

#298
Open Books
Category: Bookstore
Average Price: Modest
Area: Wallingford
Address: 2414 N 45th St
Seattle, WA 98103
Phone: (206) 633-0811

#299
Ross Dress For Less
Category: Department Store, Discount Store
Average Price: Inexpensive
Area: Northgate
Address: 300 NE Northgate Way
Seattle, WA 98125
Phone: (206) 364-2111

#300
Mort's Cabin
Category: Home Decor, Furniture Store
Average Price: Expensive
Area: Eastlake
Address: 2241 Eastlake Ave E
Seattle, WA 98102
Phone: (206) 323-6678

#301
Max And Quinn's Atomic Boys Shop-O-Rama
Category: Toy Store, Candy Store
Average Price: Modest
Area: Admiral
Address: 4311 SW Admiral Way
Seattle, WA 98116
Phone: (206) 938-3255

#302
A To Z
Category: Women's Clothing, Accessories
Average Price: Modest
Area: Ravenna
Address: 2920 NE Blakeley St
Seattle, WA 98105
Phone: (206) 729-3545

#303
20/20 Cycle
Category: Bikes
Average Price: Modest
Area: Central District
Address: 2020 E Union St
Seattle, WA 98122
Phone: (206) 568-3090

#304
Blue Owl Workshop
Category: Men's Clothing
Average Price: Expensive
Area: Fremont
Address: 707 N 35th St 2 Fl
Seattle, WA 98103
Phone: (206) 849-6500

#305
Blue Highway Games
Category: Hobby Shop, Toy Store
Average Price: Modest
Area: Queen Anne
Address: 2203 Queen Anne Ave N
Seattle, WA 98109
Phone: (206) 282-0540

#306
Sandylew
Category: Women's Clothing, Accessories
Average Price: Expensive
Area: Downtown
Address: 1408 1st Ave
Seattle, WA 98101
Phone: (206) 903-0303

#307
Northwest Art & Frame
Category: Art Supplies, Framing, Cards, Stationery
Average Price: Modest
Area: Fairmount Park, Junction
Address: 4733 California Ave SW
Seattle, WA 98116
Phone: (206) 937-5507

#308
Venue Work Studio + Boutique
Category: Jewelry, Home Decor, Art Gallery
Average Price: Expensive
Area: Ballard
Address: 5408 22nd Ave NW
Seattle, WA 98107
Phone: (206) 789-3335

#309
Ross Dress For Less
Category: Department Store
Average Price: Inexpensive
Area: Mount Baker
Address: 3820 Rainier Ave S
Seattle, WA 98118
Phone: (206) 722-3016

#310
Again And A Gain
Category: Vintage, Children's Clothing,
Baby Gear, Furniture
Average Price: Modest
Area: Fairmount Park
Address: 4832 California Ave SW
Seattle, WA 98116
Phone: (206) 933-2060

#311
Hitchcock
Category: Jewelry
Average Price: Expensive
Area: Madrona
Address: 1406 34th Ave
Seattle, WA 98122
Phone: (206) 838-7173

#312
Zenith Supplies
Category: Hobby Shop, Kitchen & Bath
Average Price: Modest
Area: Roosevelt
Address: 6300 Roosevelt Way NE
Seattle, WA 98115
Phone: (206) 525-7997

#313
QFC Quality Food Center
Category: Grocery, Drugstore
Average Price: Modest
Area: Pinehurst
Address: 1531 NE 145th St
Seattle, WA 98155
Phone: (206) 363-5717

#314
Victoria's Secret
Category: Lingerie
Average Price: Modest
Area: Downtown
Address: 600 Pine St
Seattle, WA 98101
Phone: (206) 467-1834

#315
Far4
Category: Home Decor,
Art Gallery, Interior Design
Average Price: Expensive
Area: Downtown
Address: 1020 1st Ave
Seattle, WA 98104
Phone: (206) 621-8831

#316
Insurrection
Category: Men's Clothing, Leather Goods,
Motorcycle Gear
Average Price: Expensive
Area: Greenwood, Phinney Ridge
Address: 8403 1/2 Greenwood Ave
Seattle, WA 98103
Phone: (206) 782-5752

#317
Trouvaille
Category: Vintage, Women's Clothing
Average Price: Exclusive
Area: Ballard
Address: 5335 Ballard Ave NW
Seattle, WA 98107
Phone: (206) 829-8539

#318
The Erotic Bakery
Category: Bakery, Cards, Stationery
Average Price: Modest
Area: Wallingford
Address: 2323 N 45th St
Seattle, WA 98103
Phone: (206) 545-6969

#319
Lululemon Athletica
Category: Sports Wear,
Women's Clothing, Yoga
Average Price: Expensive
Area: Downtown
Address: 600 Pine St
Seattle, WA 98101
Phone: (206) 682-1286

#320
Jive Time Records
Category: Vinyl Records
Average Price: Inexpensive
Area: Fremont
Address: 3506 Fremont Ave N
Seattle, WA 98103
Phone: (206) 632-5483

#321
QFC
Category: Grocery, Drugstore
Average Price: Modest
Area: Junction
Address: 4550 42nd Ave SW
Seattle, WA 98116
Phone: (206) 923-6390

#322
Vintage & Moore
Category: Antiques, Jewelry, Thrift Store
Average Price: Modest
Area: Pioneer Square
Address: 157 S Jackson St
Seattle, WA 98104
Phone: (206) 623-1408

#323
Bartell Drugs
Category: Drugstore, Photography Store, Services, Grocery
Average Price: Modest
Area: Magnolia
Address: 2222 32nd Ave W
Seattle, WA 98199
Phone: (206) 282-2880

#324
Megan Mary Olander
Category: Florist
Average Price: Modest
Area: Capitol Hill
Address: 1911 E Aloha St
Seattle, WA 98112
Phone: (206) 623-6660

#325
Gap
Category: Men's Clothing, Women's Clothing, Children's Clothing
Average Price: Modest
Area: Downtown
Address: 1530 5th Ave
Seattle, WA 98101
Phone: (206) 254-8000

#326
Sholdt
Category: Jewelry
Average Price: Expensive
Area: Industrial District
Address: 3130 Airport Way S
Seattle, WA 98134
Phone: (206) 623-2334

#327
Consign Design
Category: Furniture Store
Average Price: Modest
Area: Interbay, Queen Anne
Address: 1630 15th Ave W
Seattle, WA 98119
Phone: (206) 345-0009

#328
Urban Surf
Category: Sporting Goods
Average Price: Modest
Area: Wallingford
Address: 2100 N Northlake Way
Seattle, WA 98103
Phone: (206) 545-9463

#329
Eco-Elements
Category: Bookstore
Average Price: Modest
Area: Downtown
Address: 1530 1st Ave
Seattle, WA 98101
Phone: (206) 467-7745

#330
Crate & Barrel
Category: Furniture Store, Home Decor, Kitchen & Bath
Average Price: Expensive
Area: University District
Address: 2680 NE 49th St
Seattle, WA 98105
Phone: (206) 937-9939

#331
Speedy Reedy
Category: Bikes, Sports Wear
Average Price: Modest
Area: Wallingford
Address: 1300-C N Northlake Way
Seattle, WA 98103
Phone: (206) 632-9879

#332
Forever XXI
Category: Women's Clothing
Average Price: Inexpensive
Area: Northgate
Address: 401 NE Northgate Way
Seattle, WA 98125
Phone: (206) 365-5056

#333
Sole Food
Category: Shoe Store, Accessories
Average Price: Expensive
Area: University District
Address: 2619 NE Village Ln
Seattle, WA 98105
Phone: (206) 526-7184

#334
Solstice Sunglasses
Category: Eyewear, Opticians, Accessories
Average Price: Expensive
Area: Downtown
Address: 600 Pine Street, Suite 345
Seattle, WA 98101
Phone: (206) 381-8866

#335
Aprie
Category: Women's Clothing
Average Price: Expensive
Area: University District
Address: 4546 University Way NE
Seattle, WA 98105
Phone: (206) 547-6800

#336
Anderson's Comfort Footwear
Category: Shoe Store
Average Price: Expensive
Area: First Hill
Address: 1012 Madison St
Seattle, WA 98104
Phone: (206) 682-1737

#337
Kasala Furniture
Category: Furniture Store,
Carpeting, Home Decor
Average Price: Expensive
Area: Downtown
Address: 1505 Western Ave
Seattle, WA 98101
Phone: (206) 623-7795

#338
Rene Ropas
Category: Women's Clothing, Vintage
Average Price: Modest
Area: Belltown
Address: 2604 Western Ave
Seattle, WA 98121
Phone: (206) 552-1275

#339
Play It Again Sports
Category: Sports Wear, Bikes, Outdoor Gear
Average Price: Modest
Area: South Lake Union
Address: 1304 Stewart St
Seattle, WA 98109
Phone: (206) 264-9255

#340
Zara
Category: Department Store,
Women's Clothing, Men's Clothing
Average Price: Modest
Area: Downtown
Address: 400 Pine St
Seattle, WA 98101
Phone: (206) 204-6440

#341
Rite Aid
Category: Drugstore, Convenience Store
Average Price: Inexpensive
Area: Lower Queen Anne
Address: 802 Third Avenue
Seattle, WA 98104
Phone: (206) 623-0577

#342
H&M
Category: Men's Clothing, Women's Clothing
Average Price: Modest
Area: University District
Address: 2604 NE University Village
Seattle, WA 98105
Phone: (206) 729-4942

#343
Microsoft Store
Category: Electronics, Computers,
Mobile Phones
Average Price: Expensive
Area: University District
Address: 2624 NE University Village Street
Seattle, WA 98105
Phone: (206) 834-0680

#344
Future Vapor
Category: Vape Shop
Average Price: Modest
Area: Capitol Hill
Address: 1828 B 12th Ave
Seattle, WA 98122
Phone: (206) 323-9654

#345
Gucci
Category: Leather Goods,
Men's Clothing, Women's Clothing
Average Price: Exclusive
Area: Downtown
Address: 1302 Fifth Avenue
Seattle, WA 98101
Phone: (206) 682-1730

#346
Sonic Boom Records
Category: Music, Dvds, Vinyl Records
Average Price: Modest
Area: Ballard
Address: 2209 NW Market St
Seattle, WA 98107
Phone: (206) 297-2666

#347
Safeway
Category: Grocery, Drugstore,
Gas & Service Station
Average Price: Modest
Area: Ballard
Address: 1423 NW Market St
Seattle, WA 98107
Phone: (206) 784-6480

#348
Lucky Dry Goods
Category: Vintage, Men's Clothing,
Women's Clothing
Average Price: Expensive
Area: Ballard
Address: 5424 Ballard Ave NW
Seattle, WA 98107
Phone: (206) 789-8191

#349
Canopy Blue
Category: Women's Clothing
Average Price: Expensive
Area: Washington Park
Address: 3121 E Madison St
Seattle, WA 98112
Phone: (206) 323-1115

#350
Card Exchange
Category: Hobby Shop
Average Price: Modest
Area: Bitter Lake
Address: 14020 Aurora Ave N
Seattle, WA 98133
Phone: (206) 440-5467

#351
Safeway
Category: Grocery, Drugstore
Average Price: Modest
Area: Greenwood
Address: 8704 Greenwood Ave N
Seattle, WA 98103
Phone: (206) 494-0433

#352
Fantasy Unlimited
Category: Adult, Lingerie, Women's Clothing
Average Price: Expensive
Area: Denny Triangle
Address: 2027 Westlake Ave
Seattle, WA 98121
Phone: (206) 682-0167

#353
Destee-Nation Shirt Co
Category: Men's Clothing, Women's Clothing
Average Price: Modest
Area: Fremont
Address: 3412 Evanston Ave N
Seattle, WA 98103
Phone: (206) 547-5993

#354
Sephora
Category: Cosmetics, Beauty Supply
Average Price: Modest
Area: Downtown
Address: 415 Pine St
Seattle, WA 98101
Phone: (206) 624-7003

#355
Savvy Mattress Outlet Northgate
Category: Outlet Store, Mattresses, Discount Store
Average Price: Modest
Area: Northgate
Address: 543 NE Northgate Way
Seattle, WA 98125
Phone: (206) 257-0763

#356
Fury Womens Consignment
Category: Vintage, Thrift Store
Average Price: Modest
Area: Capitol Hill
Address: 2810 E Madison St
Seattle, WA 98112
Phone: (206) 329-6829

#357
So Much Yarn
Category: Arts, Crafts, Knitting Supplies
Average Price: Modest
Area: Downtown
Address: 1525 First Ave
Seattle, WA 98121
Phone: (206) 443-0727

#358
Sugarlump
Category: Children's Clothing, Maternity Wear
Average Price: Inexpensive
Area: Madison Valley
Address: 2709 E Madison St
Seattle, WA 98112
Phone: (206) 860-5083

#359
La Tienda Folk Art Gallery
Category: Jewelry, Art Gallery, Cards, Stationery
Average Price: Modest
Area: Ballard
Address: 2050 NW Market St
Seattle, WA 98107
Phone: (206) 297-3605

#360
Fast Girl Skates
Category: Sporting Goods
Average Price: Expensive
Area: Wallingford
Address: 252 NE 45th St
Seattle, WA 98105
Phone: (206) 274-8250

#361
Mountain To Sound Outfitters
Category: Outdoor Gear, Rafting, Kayaking, Paddleboarding
Average Price: Modest
Area: Fairmount Park
Address: 3602 SW Alaska St
Seattle, WA 98126
Phone: (206) 935-7669

#362
Bad Woman Yarn
Category: Arts, Crafts
Average Price: Modest
Area: Wallingford
Address: 1815 N 45th St
Seattle, WA 98103
Phone: (206) 547-5384

#363
Cash & Carry
Category: Grocery, Wholesale Store
Average Price: Inexpensive
Area: Haller Lake
Address: 13102 Stone Ave N
Seattle, WA 98133
Phone: (206) 364-1733

#364
Sur La Table
Category: Kitchen & Bath
Average Price: Modest
Area: Downtown
Address: 84 Pine St
Seattle, WA 98101
Phone: (206) 448-2244

Seattle Travel Guide 2016 / Shops, Restaurants, Arts, Entertainment & Nightlife

#365
Rosebud Bicycle Builds
Category: Bikes
Average Price: Expensive
Area: Ballard
Address: 700 NW 42nd St
Seattle, WA 98107
Phone: (206) 595-2874

#366
Pier 55 Shirt Co
Category: Fashion
Average Price: Modest
Area: Waterfront
Address: 1101 Alaskan Way
Seattle, WA 98101
Phone: (206) 624-4040

#367
Ecigexpress
Category: Tobacco Shop, Vape Shop
Average Price: Modest
Area: Pioneer Square
Address: 118 1st Ave S
Seattle, WA 98104
Phone: (206) 397-3993

#368
Susan Wheeler Home
Category: Antiques, Home Decor, Furniture Store
Average Price: Expensive
Area: Georgetown
Address: 5515 Airport Way S.
Seattle, WA 98108
Phone: (360) 402-5080

#369
Seattle Shirt Company
Category: Fashion
Average Price: Modest
Area: Downtown
Address: 103 Pike St
Seattle, WA 98101
Phone: (206) 621-7330

#370
Galway Traders
Category: Shopping
Average Price: Modest
Area: Phinney Ridge
Address: 7518 15th Ave NW
Seattle, WA 98117
Phone: (206) 784-9343

#371
Frida: Fineries & Frocks
Category: Art Gallery, Fashion
Average Price: Modest
Area: Georgetown
Address: 5905 Airport Way S
Seattle, WA 98108
Phone: (206) 767-0331

#372
Phoenix Comics And Games
Category: Bookstore, Hobby Shop, Comic Books
Average Price: Modest
Area: Capitol Hill
Address: 113 Broadway E
Seattle, WA 98102
Phone: (206) 328-4554

#373
Value Village
Category: Thrift Store
Average Price: Inexpensive
Area: Capitol Hill
Address: 1525 11th Ave
Seattle, WA 98122
Phone: (206) 322-7789

#374
Shoe Advantage
Category: Shoe Store
Average Price: Modest
Area: Roosevelt
Address: 1008 NE 65th St
Seattle, WA 98115
Phone: (206) 524-7722

#375
Surf Ballard
Category: Outdoor Gear, Surfing, Surf Shop
Average Price: Modest
Area: Sunset Hill
Address: 6300 Seaview Ave NW
Seattle, WA 98107
Phone: (206) 726-7878

#376
Queen Anne Book Company
Category: Bookstore
Average Price: Modest
Area: Queen Anne
Address: 1811 Queen Anne Ave N
Seattle, WA 98109
Phone: (206) 284-2427

#377
Surplus Too Army Navy
Category: Shopping
Average Price: Inexpensive
Area: Industrial District
Address: 85 S Lander St
Seattle, WA 98134
Phone: (206) 447-0117

#378
Men's Wearhouse
Category: Men's Clothing, Formal Wear
Average Price: Modest
Area: Northgate
Address: 500 Ne Northgate Way
Seattle, WA 98125
Phone: (206) 366-8344

#379
Dandelion Botanical Company
Category: Cosmetics, Beauty Supply, Drugstore, Health Market
Average Price: Modest
Area: Ballard
Address: 5424 Ballard Ave NW
Seattle, WA 98107
Phone: (206) 545-8892

#380
American Apparel
Category: Men's Clothing, Women's Clothing, Accessories
Average Price: Expensive
Area: Capitol Hill
Address: 200 Broadway E
Seattle, WA 98102
Phone: (206) 709-8100

#381
Rhinestone Rosie
Category: Antiques, Accessories, Jewelry
Average Price: Expensive
Area: Queen Anne
Address: 606 W Crockett St
Seattle, WA 98119
Phone: (206) 283-4605

#382
L'Occitane
Category: Cosmetics, Beauty Supply
Average Price: Exclusive
Area: Downtown
Address: 600 Pine St
Seattle, WA 98101
Phone: (206) 903-6693

#383
Motion Boardshop
Category: Outdoor Gear
Average Price: Modest
Area: Greenlake
Address: 8306 Aurora Ave N
Seattle, WA 98103
Phone: (206) 372-5268

#384
Greenwood Truevalue Hardware
Category: Hardware Store, Plumbing
Average Price: Modest
Area: Phinney Ridge
Address: 7201 Greenwood Ave N
Seattle, WA 98103
Phone: (206) 783-2900

#385
Hawaii General Store & Gallery
Category: Party Supplies, Florist, Specialty Food
Average Price: Modest
Area: Wallingford
Address: 258 NE 45th St
Seattle, WA 98105
Phone: (206) 633-5233

#386
Junction True Value Hardware
Category: Hardware Store
Average Price: Modest
Area: Junction
Address: 4747 44th Ave SW
Seattle, WA 98116
Phone: (206) 932-0450

#387
Camelion Design
Category: Furniture Store, Home Decor
Average Price: Expensive
Area: Ballard
Address: 5330 Ballard Ave NW
Seattle, WA 98107
Phone: (206) 783-7125

#388
Panache
Category: Men's Clothing, Women's Clothing
Average Price: Inexpensive
Area: Capitol Hill
Address: 225 Broadway E
Seattle, WA 98102
Phone: (206) 726-3300

#389
Outdoor Research Retail Store
Category: Outdoor Gear, Sports Wear
Average Price: Expensive
Area: Industrial District
Address: 2203 1st Ave S
Seattle, WA 98134
Phone: (206) 971-1496

#390
Cash & Carry
Category: Grocery, Wholesale Store
Average Price: Modest
Area: Ballard
Address: 1155 NW Ballard Way
Seattle, WA 98107
Phone: (206) 789-7242

#391
Planet Happy Toys
Category: Toy Store
Average Price: Modest
Area: Ravenna
Address: 2914 NE 55th St
Seattle, WA 98105
Phone: (206) 729-0154

#392
Kassie Keith Curiosities & Home Decor
Category: Antiques, Home Decor
Average Price: Exclusive
Area: Georgetown
Address: 5951 Airport Way S
Seattle, WA 98108
Phone: (206) 420-3158

Seattle Travel Guide 2016 / Shops, Restaurants, Arts, Entertainment & Nightlife

#393
Best Buy
Category: Computer Repair, Computers, Electronics
Average Price: Modest
Area: Northgate
Address: 330 NE Northgate Way
Seattle, WA 98125
Phone: (206) 306-7663

#394
Lucky Brand
Category: Men's Clothing, Women's Clothing
Average Price: Expensive
Area: University District
Address: 2614 NE University Village
Seattle, WA 98105
Phone: (206) 529-8104

#395
Dreamstrands Comics & Such
Category: Comic Books
Average Price: Inexpensive
Area: Greenwood, Phinney Ridge
Address: 115 N 85th St
Seattle, WA 98103
Phone: (206) 297-3737

#396
Chartreuse International
Category: Antiques, Furniture Store
Average Price: Expensive
Area: Belltown
Address: 2609 1st Ave
Seattle, WA 98121
Phone: (206) 328-4844

#397
Beats & Bohos
Category: Women's Clothing, Vintage, Vinyl Records
Average Price: Modest
Area: Phinney Ridge
Address: 7200 Greenwood Ave N
Seattle, WA 98103
Phone: (206) 395-4468

#398
Area 51
Category: Furniture Store
Average Price: Expensive
Area: Capitol Hill
Address: 401 E Pine St
Seattle, WA 98122
Phone: (206) 568-4782

#399
Quiksilver
Category: Sports Wear, Surfing, Swimwear
Average Price: Modest
Area: Downtown
Address: 2030 First Ave .
Seattle, WA 98121
Phone: (206) 441-4879

#400
Isadora's Antique Jewelry
Category: Jewelry, Watches
Average Price: Expensive
Area: Downtown
Address: 1601 1st Ave
Seattle, WA 98101
Phone: (206) 441-7711

#401
Counterbalance Bicycles
Category: Bikes, Bike Rentals
Average Price: Modest
Area: University District
Address: 2943 NE Blakeley St
Seattle, WA 98105
Phone: (206) 922-3555

#402
Carhartt
Category: Men's Clothing, Women's Clothing, Children's Clothing
Average Price: Modest
Area: Downtown
Address: 409 Pike St.
Seattle, WA 98101
Phone: (206) 470-2503

#403
Macy's
Category: Department Store, Men's Clothing, Women's Clothing
Average Price: Modest
Area: Northgate
Address: 401 NE Northgate Way # 602
Seattle, WA 98125
Phone: (206) 440-6000

#404
University Village Shopping Center
Category: Shopping Center
Average Price: Expensive
Area: University District
Address: 2673 NE University Vlg Ste 7
Seattle, WA 98105
Phone: (206) 523-0622

#405
TAP Plastics
Category: Arts, Crafts, Hardware Store, Hobby Shop
Average Price: Modest
Area: South Lake Union, Westlake
Address: 710 9th Avenue North
Seattle, WA 98109
Phone: (206) 389-5900

#406
Lola Pop
Category: Shoe Store, Accessories, Women's Clothing
Average Price: Expensive
Area: Fremont
Address: 711 N 35th St
Seattle, WA 98103
Phone: (206) 547-2071

#407
Digs
Category: Furniture Store, Baby Gear, Furniture, Home Decor
Average Price: Expensive
Area: Ballard
Address: 2002 NW Market St
Seattle, WA 98107
Phone: (206) 457-5709

#408
Ravenna Third Place Books
Category: Bookstore
Average Price: Modest
Area: Ravenna
Address: 6504 20th Ave NE
Seattle, WA 98115
Phone: (206) 525-2347

#409
Fuego
Category: Women's Clothing
Average Price: Modest
Area: Northgate
Address: 401 NE Northgate Way
Seattle, WA 98125
Phone: (206) 364-0306

#410
Maxines Floral And Gift
Category: Flowers, Gifts
Average Price: Expensive
Area: Mapleleaf
Address: 8811 Roosevelt Way NE
Seattle, WA 98115
Phone: (206) 523-4200

#411
Merryweather Books
Category: Bookstore
Average Price: Inexpensive
Area: Junction
Address: 4537 California Avenue SW
Seattle, WA 98116
Phone: (206) 935-7325

#412
Amita The Art Of Gifts
Category: Women's Clothing, Jewelry, Accessories
Average Price: Expensive
Area: Wallingford
Address: 1815 N 45th St
Seattle, WA 98103
Phone: (206) 632-7998

#413
Safeway
Category: Grocery, Drugstore, Gas & Service Station
Average Price: Modest
Area: White Center
Address: 9620 28th Ave SW
Seattle, WA 98127
Phone: (206) 935-3996

#414
Road Runner Sports
Category: Shoe Store, Sports Wear
Average Price: Expensive
Area: Greenlake
Address: 7020 Woodlawn Ave NE
Seattle, WA 98115
Phone: (206) 517-5100

#415
Kavu World
Category: Sports Wear
Average Price: Expensive
Area: Ballard
Address: 5419 Ballard Ave NW
Seattle, WA 98107
Phone: (206) 783-0060

#416
Our Fabric Stash
Category: Fabric Store
Average Price: Inexpensive
Area: International District
Address: 666 S Jackson St
Seattle, WA 98104
Phone: (206) 981-0152

#417
Couth Buzzard Books Espresso Buono
Category: Bookstore, Coffee, Tea
Average Price: Inexpensive
Area: Greenwood, Phinney Ridge
Address: 8310 Greenwood Ave
Seattle, WA 98103
Phone: (206) 436-2960

#418
Many Moons Trading Co
Category: Vintage
Average Price: Inexpensive
Area: Junction
Address: 4461 California Ave SW
Seattle, WA 98116
Phone: (206) 937-3481

#419
Cintli Fine Mexican Jewelry
Category: Jewelry, Accessories
Average Price: Modest
Area: Downtown
Address: 1501 Pike Pl
Seattle, WA 98101
Phone: (206) 262-0794

#420
The Smoke House
Category: Tobacco Shop
Average Price: Modest
Area: Brighton
Address: 6301 Rainier Ave S
Seattle, WA 98118
Phone: (206) 414-5566

Seattle Travel Guide 2016 / Shops, Restaurants, Arts, Entertainment & Nightlife

#421
Rejuvenation
Category: Home Decor, Hardware Store
Average Price: Expensive
Area: Industrial District
Address: 2910 1st Ave S
Seattle, WA 98117
Phone: (206) 382-1901

#422
Sleepers In Seattle
Category: Furniture Store
Average Price: Modest
Area: Fairmount Park, Junction
Address: 4741 California Ave SW
Seattle, WA 98116
Phone: (206) 932-8500

#423
Furnishments
Category: Home Decor, Home Staging
Average Price: Modest
Area: Phinney Ridge
Address: 7218 Greenwood Ave N
Seattle, WA 98103
Phone: (206) 841-9030

#424
Zion's Gate Records
Category: Music, Dvds, Vinyl Records
Average Price: Expensive
Area: Capitol Hill
Address: 1100 E Pike St
Seattle, WA 98122
Phone: (206) 568-5446

#425
The Fiber Gallery
Category: Arts, Crafts
Average Price: Modest
Area: Greenwood, Phinney Ridge
Address: 8212 Greenwood Ave N
Seattle, WA 98103
Phone: (206) 706-4197

#426
Madewell
Category: Women's Clothing, Accessories
Average Price: Expensive
Area: University District
Address: 2666 NE University Village St
Seattle, WA 98105
Phone: (206) 525-0151

#427
Branford Bike
Category: Bikes
Average Price: Exclusive
Area: Capitol Hill
Address: 2404 10th Ave E
Seattle, WA 98102
Phone: (206) 323-1218

#428
Modern Design Sofas
Category: Furniture Store
Average Price: Modest
Area: Downtown
Address: 915 Western Ave
Seattle, WA 98104
Phone: (206) 652-8374

#429
Goodwill
Category: Thrift Store, Vintage
Average Price: Modest
Area: South Lake Union
Address: 411 Westlake Ave N
Seattle, WA 98109
Phone: (206) 812-6625

#430
Curious Kidstuff
Category: Toy Store
Average Price: Modest
Area: Fairmount Park, Junction
Address: 4740 California Ave SW
Seattle, WA 98116
Phone: (206) 937-8788

#431
Bedrooms & More
Category: Furniture Store, Mattresses
Average Price: Modest
Area: Wallingford
Address: 300 NE 45th St
Seattle, WA 98105
Phone: (206) 633-4494

#432
Math 'N' Stuff
Category: Toy Store, Art Supplies, Bookstore
Average Price: Modest
Area: Mapleleaf
Address: 8926 Roosevelt Way NE
Seattle, WA 98115
Phone: (206) 522-8891

#433
The Audio Connection
Category: Electronics
Average Price: Modest
Area: University District
Address: 5621 University Way NE
Seattle, WA 98105
Phone: (206) 524-7251

#434
Watson Kennedy Fine Living
Category: Home Decor, Flowers, Gifts
Average Price: Expensive
Area: Downtown
Address: 86 Pine St
Seattle, WA 98101
Phone: (206) 443-6281

#435
Antique Liquidators
Category: Antiques
Average Price: Expensive
Area: South Lake Union
Address: 503 Westlake Ave N
Seattle, WA 98109
Phone: (206) 623-2740

#436
Blue Sky Bridal
Category: Bridal
Average Price: Modest
Area: Greenwood, Phinney Ridge
Address: 311 N 77th St
Seattle, WA 98103
Phone: (206) 783-8700

#437
Red Ticking
Category: Home Decor
Average Price: Expensive
Area: Capitol Hill
Address: 2802 E Madison St
Seattle, WA 98112
Phone: (206) 322-9890

#438
Spacebase Gift Shop
Category: Gift Shop
Average Price: Modest
Area: Lower Queen Anne
Address: 400 Broad St
Seattle, WA 98109
Phone: (206) 905-2100

#439
Tatyana Boutique
Category: Accessories, Women's Clothing
Average Price: Expensive
Area: Capitol Hill
Address: 400 Broadway E
Seattle, WA 98102
Phone: (206) 329-5220

#440
Retroactive Kids
Category: Toy Store, Children's Clothing
Average Price: Modest
Area: Columbia City
Address: 4859 Rainier Ave S
Seattle, WA 98118
Phone: (206) 932-3154

#441
Home Office Supply Company
Category: Office Equipment
Average Price: Modest
Area: Belltown
Address: 2606 2nd Ave
Seattle, WA 98121
Phone: (206) 448-8677

#442
American Apparel
Category: Accessories, Men's Clothing, Women's Clothing, Children's Clothing
Average Price: Expensive
Area: University District
Address: 4345 University Way NE
Seattle, WA 98105
Phone: (206) 547-0399

#443
Ponytail Jewelry Studio
Category: Jewelry
Average Price: Modest
Area: Ballard
Address: 2603 NW Market St
Seattle, WA 98107
Phone: (206) 724-0585

#444
Silver Platters
Category: Music, Dvds, Vinyl Records, Bookstore
Average Price: Modest
Area: Industrial District
Address: 2930 1st Ave S
Seattle, WA 98134
Phone: (206) 283-3472

#445
Funky Jane's
Category: Vintage
Average Price: Modest
Area: Junction
Address: 4455 California Ave SW
Seattle, WA 98116
Phone: (206) 937-2637

#446
Papyrus
Category: Cards, Stationery, Bookstore
Average Price: Expensive
Area: University District
Address: 2660 NE University Vlg
Seattle, WA 98105
Phone: (206) 523-0055

#447
Michael Reed Black Antiques
Category: Antiques
Average Price: Modest
Area: Lower Queen Anne
Address: 125 W Mercer St
Seattle, WA 98119
Phone: (206) 284-9581

#448
Sound Sports
Category: Shoe Store, Sporting Goods
Average Price: Modest
Area: Downtown
Address: 80 Madison St
Seattle, WA 98104
Phone: (206) 624-6717

Seattle Travel Guide 2016 / Shops, Restaurants, Arts, Entertainment & Nightlife

#449
Baby & Co
Category: Women's Clothing, Accessories, Jewelry
Average Price: Exclusive
Area: Downtown
Address: 1936 1st Ave
Seattle, WA 98101
Phone: (206) 448-4077

#450
Pharmaca Integrative Pharmacy
Category: Drugstore
Average Price: Expensive
Area: Madison Park
Address: 4130 E Madison St
Seattle, WA 98112
Phone: (206) 324-0701

#451
Golden Age Collectables
Category: Comic Books, Toy Store
Average Price: Modest
Area: Downtown
Address: 1501 Pike Place Market
Seattle, WA 98101
Phone: (206) 622-9799

#452
Goodwill
Category: Thrift Store
Average Price: Modest
Area: Capitol Hill
Address: 115 Belmont Ave E
Seattle, WA 98102
Phone: (206) 812-7583

#453
Albertsons
Category: Grocery, Drugstore
Average Price: Modest
Area: Bitter Lake
Address: 13050 Aurora Ave N
Seattle, WA 98133
Phone: (206) 306-8780

#454
Free People
Category: Women's Clothing
Average Price: Modest
Area: University District
Address: 2623 NE University Village St
Seattle, WA 98105
Phone: (206) 523-0622

#455
Black Market Skates
Category: Sporting Goods, Men's Clothing, Vinyl Records
Average Price: Modest
Area: Denny Triangle
Address: 2404 7th Ave
Seattle, WA 98121
Phone: (206) 462-1343

#456
Nordstrom Rack
Category: Department Store
Average Price: Modest
Area: Northgate
Address: 401 NE Northgate Way
Seattle, WA 98125
Phone: (206) 641-3300

#457
Aveda Store
Category: Cosmetics, Beauty Supply
Average Price: Modest
Area: University District
Address: 2622 NE University Village, Ste 727 Seattle, WA 98105
Phone: (206) 526-2610

#458
Mattress Depot USA
Category: Mattresses
Average Price: Modest
Area: Northgate
Address: 823 NE Northgate Way
Seattle, WA 98125
Phone: (206) 361-4561

#459
Sally Beauty Supply
Category: Cosmetics, Beauty Supply
Average Price: Inexpensive
Area: Downtown
Address: 1527 3rd Ave
Seattle, WA 98101
Phone: (206) 262-1635

#460
Safeway
Category: Drugstore, Grocery
Average Price: Modest
Area: Mount Baker
Address: 3820 Rainier Ave S
Seattle, WA 98118
Phone: (206) 725-9575

#461
Indoor Sun Shoppe
Category: Home & Garden, Lighting Fixtures, Equipment
Average Price: Inexpensive
Area: Fremont
Address: 160 N Canal St
Seattle, WA 98103
Phone: (206) 634-3727

#462
Sephora
Category: Cosmetics, Beauty Supply
Average Price: Modest
Area: University District
Address: 2618 NE University Village St
Seattle, WA 98105
Phone: (206) 526-9110

Seattle Travel Guide 2016 / Shops, Restaurants, Arts, Entertainment & Nightlife

#463
Twilight Gallery & Boutique
Category: Art Gallery, Jewelry
Average Price: Modest
Area: Junction
Address: 4306 SW Alaska St
Seattle, WA 98116
Phone: (206) 933-2444

#464
Soaring Heart Natural Bed Company
Category: Mattresses
Average Price: Expensive
Area: Queen Anne
Address: 101 Nickerson St
Seattle, WA 98109
Phone: (206) 282-1717

#465
Nancy Meyer Fine Lingerie
Category: Lingerie
Average Price: Exclusive
Area: Downtown
Address: 1318 5th Ave
Seattle, WA 98101
Phone: (206) 625-9200

#466
The Vajra
Category: Flowers, Gifts
Average Price: Modest
Area: Capitol Hill
Address: 518 Broadway E
Seattle, WA 98102
Phone: (206) 323-7846

#467
Leroy Men's Wear
Category: Men's Clothing
Average Price: Modest
Area: Downtown
Address: 201 Pike St
Seattle, WA 98101
Phone: (206) 682-1033

#468
Art Primo
Category: Art Supplies
Average Price: Modest
Area: Georgetown
Address: 6601 E Marginal Way S
Seattle, WA 98108
Phone: (206) 365-4083

#469
Tricoter
Category: Arts, Crafts, Knitting Supplies
Average Price: Exclusive
Area: Washington Park
Address: 3121 E Madison St
Seattle, WA 98112
Phone: (206) 328-6505

#470
Armadillo Consignment
Category: Home Decor, Vintage, Furniture Store
Average Price: Modest
Area: Broadview
Address: 12421 Greenwood Ave N
Seattle, WA 98133
Phone: (206) 363-6700

#471
Paris Miki
Category: Eyewear, Opticians
Average Price: Modest
Area: Sodo, International District
Address: 600 5th Ave S
Seattle, WA 98104
Phone: (206) 652-8436

#472
Red Wagon Toys
Category: Toy Store
Average Price: Modest
Area: Madison Park
Address: 4218B E Madison St
Seattle, WA 98112
Phone: (206) 453-5306

#473
QFC
Category: Grocery, Department Store
Average Price: Modest
Area: Roxhill
Address: 2500 SW Barton St
Seattle, WA 98126
Phone: (206) 935-0585

#474
Pistil Design
Category: Florist
Average Price: Modest
Area: Queen Anne
Address: 1422 Queen Anne Ave N
Seattle, WA 98109
Phone: (206) 612-0973

#475
Everrest Mattress
Category: Furniture Store, Mattresses
Average Price: Modest
Area: Interbay, Queen Anne
Address: 1408 Elliott Ave W
Seattle, WA 98119
Phone: (206) 284-9531

#476
Barnes & Noble
Category: Bookstore, Newspapers & Magazines, Music, Dvds
Average Price: Modest
Area: Downtown
Address: 600 Pine St
Seattle, WA 98101
Phone: (206) 264-0156

Seattle Travel Guide 2016 / Shops, Restaurants, Arts, Entertainment & Nightlife

#477
Free People
Category: Women's Clothing, Accessories
Average Price: Expensive
Area: Downtown
Address: 101 Stewart St
Seattle, WA 98101
Phone: (206) 441-3659

#478
Metrix Create:Space
Category: Electronics
Average Price: Inexpensive
Area: Capitol Hill
Address: 623A Broadway E
Seattle, WA 98102
Phone: (206) 357-9406

#479
Frye Art Museum
Category: Museum, Art Gallery
Average Price: Inexpensive
Area: First Hill
Address: 704 Terry Ave
Seattle, WA 98104
Phone: (206) 622-9250

#480
Coach
Category: Leather Goods, Accessories
Average Price: Expensive
Area: Downtown
Address: 600 Pine St
Seattle, WA 98101
Phone: (206) 264-0372

#481
Seattle Antiques Market
Category: Antiques
Average Price: Modest
Area: Downtown
Address: 1400 Alaskan Way
Seattle, WA 98101
Phone: (206) 623-6115

#482
Recess
Category: Men's Clothing, Shoe Store
Average Price: Expensive
Area: University District
Address: 5235 University Way NE
Seattle, WA 98105
Phone: (206) 729-5099

#483
Kym's Kiddy Corner
Category: Children's Clothing, Baby Gear, Furniture
Average Price: Modest
Area: Pinehurst
Address: 11721 15th Ave NE
Seattle, WA 98125
Phone: (206) 361-5974

#484
Katterman's Sand Point Pharmacy
Category: Drugstore
Average Price: Modest
Area: Laurelhurst
Address: 5400 Sand Point Way NE
Seattle, WA 98105
Phone: (206) 524-2211

#485
Bartell Drugs
Category: Drugstore, Photography Store, Services, Grocery
Average Price: Modest
Area: First Hill
Address: 1101 Madison St
Seattle, WA 98104
Phone: (206) 340-1066

#486
Tiffany & Co.
Category: Jewelry
Average Price: Exclusive
Area: Ravenna, University District
Address: 4618 26th Ave NE
Seattle, WA 98105
Phone: (206) 522-1000

#487
Dis N That
Category: Flowers, Gifts
Average Price: Expensive
Area: Mount Baker
Address: 2802 S Mcclellan St
Seattle, WA 98144
Phone: (206) 327-9351

#488
Walgreens
Category: Drugstore, Cosmetics, Beauty Supply, Convenience Store
Average Price: Inexpensive
Area: South Lake Union
Address: 566 Denny Way
Seattle, WA 98109
Phone: (206) 204-1982

#489
Found It
Category: Antiques
Average Price: Modest
Area: Roosevelt
Address: 6820 Roosevelt Way NE
Seattle, WA 98115
Phone: (206) 517-5047

#490
Ecig N' Vape
Category: Vape Shop
Average Price: Modest
Area: Greenlake
Address: 8012 Aurora Ave N
Seattle, WA 98103
Phone: (206) 397-4421

#491
Kiki Corona Fashion & More
Category: Women's Clothing
Average Price: Inexpensive
Area: Westwood
Address: 9448 Delridge Way SW
Seattle, WA 98127
Phone: (206) 762-5141

#492
Cuttysark Nautical Antiques
Category: Antiques
Average Price: Modest
Area: Pioneer Square
Address: 320 1st Ave S
Seattle, WA 98104
Phone: (206) 262-1265

#493
Mockingbird Books & Finch Café
Category: Coffee, Tea, Bookstore
Average Price: Modest
Area: Greenlake
Address: 7220 Woodlawn Ave NE
Seattle, WA 98115
Phone: (206) 518-5886

#494
Perfectly Outgrown
Category: Personal Shopping, Baby Gear, Furniture, Vintage
Average Price: Inexpensive
Area: Lower Queen Anne
Address: 305 Harrison St
Seattle, WA 98109
Phone: (206) 948-3223

#495
The Land Of Nod
Category: Toy Store, Furniture Store
Average Price: Expensive
Area: University District
Address: 2660 NE 49th St
Seattle, WA 98105
Phone: (206) 527-9900

#496
Beadworld
Category: Art Supplies, Jewelry
Average Price: Modest
Area: Mapleleaf
Address: 9520 Roosevelt Way NE
Seattle, WA 98115
Phone: (206) 523-0530

#497
Communique Cards & Gifts
Category: Cards, Stationery, Gift Shop
Average Price: Modest
Area: Queen Anne
Address: 2211 Queen Anne Ave N
Seattle, WA 98109
Phone: (206) 284-4111

#498
Kerf Design
Category: Furniture Store, Interior Design
Average Price: Expensive
Area: Interbay
Address: 3635-A Thorndyke Ave W
Seattle, WA 98119
Phone: (206) 954-8677

#499
J.Crew
Category: Men's Clothing, Women's Clothing, Accessories
Average Price: Expensive
Area: University District
Address: 2660 NE University Village Street
Seattle, WA 98105
Phone: (206) 523-6066

#500
Lush
Category: Cosmetics, Beauty Supply
Average Price: Expensive
Area: Downtown
Address: 400 Pine St, Ste 100
Seattle, WA 98101
Phone: (206) 624-5874

TOP 500 RESTAURANTS
The Most Recommended by Locals & Trevelers
(From #1 to #500)

Seattle Travel Guide 2016 / Shops, Restaurants, Arts, Entertainment & Nightlife

#1
Paseo
Cuisines: Caribbean, Sandwiches, Cuban
Average Price: Inexpensive
Area: Fremont
Address: 4225 Fremont Ave N
Seattle, WA 98103
Phone: (206) 545-7440

#2
The Butcher And The Baker
Cuisines: Butcher, Bakery, Sandwiches
Average Price: Modest
Area: Greenlake
Address: 6412 Latona Ave NE
Seattle, WA 98115
Phone: (206) 414-3100

#3
Radiator Whiskey
Cuisines: American, Cocktail Bar
Average Price: Modest
Area: Downtown
Address: 94 Pike St
Seattle, WA 98101
Phone: (206) 467-4268

#4
Pike Place Chowder
Cuisines: Seafood, American, Soup
Average Price: Inexpensive
Area: Downtown
Address: 1530 Post Aly
Seattle, WA 98101
Phone: (206) 267-2537

#5
Blind Pig Bistro
Cuisines: American
Average Price: Expensive
Area: Eastlake
Address: 2238 Eastlake Ave E
Seattle, WA 98102
Phone: (206) 329-2744

#6
Barnacle
Cuisines: Wine Bar, Seafood, Tapas
Average Price: Modest
Area: Ballard
Address: 4743 Ballard Ave NW
Seattle, WA 98107
Phone: (206) 706-3379

#7
Brimmer & Heeltap
Cuisines: Gastropub, American
Average Price: Modest
Area: Ballard
Address: 425 NW Market St
Seattle, WA 98107
Phone: (206) 420-2534

#8
Itadakimasu
Cuisines: Korean, Japanese, Hawaiian
Average Price: Modest
Area: University District
Address: 4743 Brooklyn Ave NE
Seattle, WA 98105
Phone: (206) 659-0722

#9
Some Random Bar
Cuisines: Pub, American
Average Price: Modest
Area: Belltown
Address: 2604 1st Ave
Seattle, WA 98121
Phone: (206) 745-2185

#10
Westward
Cuisines: American, Breakfast & Brunch
Average Price: Modest
Area: Wallingford
Address: 2501 N Northlake Way
Seattle, WA 98103
Phone: (206) 552-8215

#11
Ten On 9th
Cuisines: Cocktail Bar, American
Average Price: Modest
Area: South Lake Union
Address: 227 9th Ave N
Seattle, WA 98109
Phone: (206) 792-7221

#12
Toulouse Petit
Cuisines: Cajun, Creole, Breakfast & Brunch, Bar
Average Price: Modest
Area: Lower Queen Anne
Address: 601 Queen Anne Ave N
Seattle, WA 98109
Phone: (206) 432-9069

#13
Witness
Cuisines: Southern, Cocktail Bar
Average Price: Modest
Area: Capitol Hill
Address: 410 Broadway E
Seattle, WA 98102
Phone: (206) 329-0248

#14
List
Cuisines: Italian, Tapas
Average Price: Modest
Area: Belltown
Address: 2226 1st Ave
Seattle, WA 98121
Phone: (206) 441-1000

#15
The Pink Door
Cuisines: Italian
Average Price: Modest
Area: Downtown
Address: 1919 Post Alley
Seattle, WA 98101
Phone: (206) 443-3241

#16
Bottlehouse
Cuisines: Wine Bar, Tapas
Average Price: Modest
Area: Madrona
Address: 1416 34th Ave
Seattle, WA 98122
Phone: (206) 708-7164

#17
Resto
Cuisines: Seafood, Steakhouse
Average Price: Modest
Area: Capitol Hill
Address: 421 E Thomas St
Seattle, WA 98102
Phone: (206) 734-6104

#18
Paseo
Cuisines: Caribbean, Sandwiches, Cuban
Average Price: Inexpensive
Area: Sunset Hill
Address: 6226 Seaview Ave NW
Seattle, WA 98107
Phone: (206) 789-3100

#19
Geo's Cuban & Creole Cafe
Cuisines: Cajun, Creole, Cuban
Average Price: Inexpensive
Area: Sunset Hill
Address: 6301 Seaview Ave NW
Seattle, WA 98107
Phone: (206) 706-3117

#20
Cask & Trotter
Cuisines: Barbeque
Average Price: Modest
Area: South Lake Union, Westlake
Address: 711 Westlake Ave
Seattle, WA 98109
Phone: (206) 453-4756

#21
Tilikum Place Café
Cuisines: European, American
Average Price: Modest
Area: Belltown
Address: 407 Cedar St
Seattle, WA 98121
Phone: (206) 282-4830

#22
Tanglewood Supreme
Cuisines: Seafood, American
Average Price: Modest
Area: Magnolia
Address: 3216 W Wheeler St
Seattle, WA 98199
Phone: (206) 708-6235

#23
Phoenecia
Cuisines: Tapas Bar, Wine Bar, Pizza
Average Price: Modest
Area: Alki
Address: 2716 Alki Ave SW
Seattle, WA 98116
Phone: (206) 935-6550

#24
Art Of The Table
Cuisines: American, Greek
Average Price: Exclusive
Area: Fremont
Address: 1054 N 39th St
Seattle, WA 98103
Phone: (206) 282-0942

#25
The Sixgill
Cuisines: American, Tapas, Pub
Average Price: Modest
Area: Fremont
Address: 3417 Evanston Ave N
Seattle, WA 98103
Phone: (206) 466-2846

#26
Villa Escondida
Cuisines: Mexican, Breakfast & Brunch
Average Price: Inexpensive
Area: Capitol Hill
Address: 219 Broadway E
Seattle, WA 98102
Phone: (206) 324-0475

#27
Local 360
Cuisines: American, Breakfast & Brunch
Average Price: Modest
Area: Belltown
Address: 2234 1st Ave
Seattle, WA 98121
Phone: (206) 441-9360

#28
Restaurant Zoë
Cuisines: American, Bar
Average Price: Expensive
Area: Central District
Address: 1318 E Union St
Seattle, WA 98122
Phone: (206) 256-2060

#29
Martino's
Cuisines: American
Average Price: Modest
Area: Phinney Ridge
Address: 7410 Greenwood Ave
Seattle, WA 98103
Phone: (206) 397-4689

#30
Bongos
Cuisines: Cuban, Caribbean
Average Price: Inexpensive
Area: Phinney Ridge
Address: 6501 Aurora Ave N
Seattle, WA 98103
Phone: (206) 420-8548

#31
Queen Bee Cafe
Cuisines: Café
Average Price: Inexpensive
Area: Central District, Capitol Hill
Address: 2200 E Madison St
Seattle, WA 98112
Phone: (206) 757-6314

#32
The Walrus And The Carpenter
Cuisines: Seafood, Live/Raw Food, Tapas
Average Price: Expensive
Area: Ballard
Address: 4743 Ballard Ave NW
Seattle, WA 98107
Phone: (206) 395-9227

#33
Tacos Chukis
Cuisines: Mexican
Average Price: Inexpensive
Area: Capitol Hill
Address: 219 Broadway E
Seattle, WA 98102
Phone: (206) 328-4447

#34
Serious Pie
Cuisines: Pizza
Average Price: Modest
Area: Belltown
Address: 316 Virginia St
Seattle, WA 98121
Phone: (206) 838-7388

#35
Morsel
Cuisines: Coffee, Tea, Comfort Food, Breakfast & Brunch
Average Price: Inexpensive
Area: University District
Address: 4754 University Way NE
Seattle, WA 98105
Phone: (206) 268-0154

#36
Lola
Cuisines: Greek, Mediterranean, Breakfast & Brunch
Average Price: Modest
Area: Belltown
Address: 2000 4th Ave
Seattle, WA 98121
Phone: (206) 441-1430

#37
Il Corvo Pasta
Cuisines: Italian
Average Price: Modest
Area: Pioneer Square
Address: 217 James St
Seattle, WA 98104
Phone: (206) 538-0999

#38
Tat's Delicatessen
Cuisines: Deli, Cheesesteaks, Sandwiches
Average Price: Inexpensive
Area: Pioneer Square
Address: 159 Yesler Way
Seattle, WA 98104
Phone: (206) 264-8287

#39
Petra Mediterranean Bistro
Cuisines: Mediterranean, Middle Eastern, Greek
Average Price: Modest
Area: Belltown
Address: 2501 4th Ave
Seattle, WA 98121
Phone: (206) 728-5389

#40
The Whale Wins
Cuisines: American, Tapas
Average Price: Expensive
Area: Wallingford
Address: 3506 Stone Way N
Seattle, WA 98103
Phone: (206) 632-9425

#41
Betty
Cuisines: Specialty Food, Cocktail Bar
Average Price: Modest
Area: Queen Anne
Address: 1507 Queen Anne Ave N
Seattle, WA 98109
Phone: (206) 352-3773

#42
Piroshky Piroshky
Cuisines: Bakery, Russian
Average Price: Inexpensive
Area: Downtown
Address: 1908 Pike Pl
Seattle, WA 98101
Phone: (206) 441-6068

#43
Farestart
Cuisines: American
Average Price: Modest
Area: Denny Triangle
Address: 700 Virginia St
Seattle, WA 98101
Phone: (206) 267-7601

#44
Honeyhole
Cuisines: Bar, Sandwiches
Average Price: Inexpensive
Area: First Hill, Capitol Hill
Address: 703 E Pike St
Seattle, WA 98122
Phone: (206) 709-1399

#45
Pestle Rock
Cuisines: Thai
Average Price: Modest
Area: Ballard
Address: 2305 NW Market St
Seattle, WA 98107
Phone: (206) 466-6671

#46
Palace Kitchen
Cuisines: American, Bar, Desserts
Average Price: Modest
Area: Denny Triangle
Address: 2030 5th Ave
Seattle, WA 98121
Phone: (206) 448-2001

#47
St. Clouds
Cuisines: American
Average Price: Modest
Area: Madrona
Address: 1131 34th Ave
Seattle, WA 98122
Phone: (206) 726-1522

#48
Grub
Cuisines: American,
Breakfast & Brunch, Sandwiches
Average Price: Modest
Area: Queen Anne
Address: 7 Boston St
Seattle, WA 98109
Phone: (206) 216-3628

#49
Hue Ky Mi Gia
Cuisines: Vietnamese, Cantonese
Average Price: Inexpensive
Area: International District
Address: 1207 S Jackson St
Seattle, WA 98144
Phone: (206) 568-1268

#50
Salumi Artisan Cured Meats
Cuisines: Italian, Deli, Meat Shop
Average Price: Modest
Area: Pioneer Square
Address: 309 3rd Ave S
Seattle, WA 98104
Phone: (206) 621-8772

#51
Tippe And Drague Alehouse
Cuisines: American, Pub
Average Price: Modest
Area: Beacon Hill
Address: 3315 Beacon Ave S
Seattle, WA 98144
Phone: (206) 538-0094

#52
Quinn's
Cuisines: American, Pub
Average Price: Modest
Area: First Hill, Capitol Hill
Address: 1001 E Pike St
Seattle, WA 98122
Phone: (206) 325-7711

#53
Skillet Diner - Capitol Hill
Cuisines: Breakfast & Brunch, American
Average Price: Modest
Area: Central District
Address: 1400 E Union St
Seattle, WA 98122
Phone: (206) 512-2000

#54
The Zig Zag Café
Cuisines: American, Cocktail Bar
Average Price: Modest
Area: Downtown
Address: 1501 Western Ave
Seattle, WA 98101
Phone: (206) 625-1146

#55
Babirusa
Cuisines: Bar, American
Average Price: Modest
Area: Eastlake
Address: 2236 Eastlake Ave E
Seattle, WA 98102
Phone: (206) 329-2744

#56
Revel
Cuisines: Asian Fusion, Korean
Average Price: Modest
Area: Fremont
Address: 403 N 36th St
Seattle, WA 98103
Phone: (206) 547-2040

#57
Lovage
Cuisines: Do-It-Yourself Food, Salad
Average Price: Inexpensive
Area: Downtown
Address: 1526 1st Ave
Seattle, WA 98101
Phone: (206) 486-2160

#58
Lecōsho
Cuisines: American
Average Price: Modest
Area: Downtown
Address: 89 University St
Seattle, WA 98101
Phone: (206) 623-2101

#59
Ravish
Cuisines: American,
Breakfast & Brunch, Cocktail Bar
Average Price: Modest
Area: Eastlake
Address: 2956 Eastlake Ave E
Seattle, WA 98102
Phone: (206) 913-2497

#60
Gastropod
Cuisines: Gastropub, Brewerie
Average Price: Modest
Area: Industrial District
Address: 3201 1st Ave S
Seattle, WA 98134
Phone: (206) 403-1228

#61
Mashawi Mediterranean Cuisine
Cuisines: Mediterranean, Lebanese
Average Price: Modest
Area: Lower Queen Anne
Address: 366 Roy St
Seattle, WA 98109
Phone: (206) 282-0078

#62
The Barbeque Pit
Cuisines: Barbeque
Average Price: Inexpensive
Area: Central District
Address: 2509 E Cherry St
Seattle, WA 98122
Phone: (206) 724-0005

#63
Black Bottle
Cuisines: American, Gastropub, Tapas
Average Price: Modest
Area: Belltown
Address: 2600 1st Ave
Seattle, WA 98121
Phone: (206) 441-1500

#64
Palisade
Cuisines: Seafood, Steakhouse, Asian Fusion
Average Price: Expensive
Area: Magnolia
Address: 2601 W Marina Pl
Seattle, WA 98199
Phone: (206) 285-1000

#65
Rockcreek Seafood & Spirits
Cuisines: Seafood
Average Price: Expensive
Area: Fremont
Address: 4300 Fremont Ave N
Seattle, WA 98103
Phone: (206) 557-7532

#66
Pho Bac
Cuisines: Vietnamese, Sandwiches
Average Price: Inexpensive
Area: Denny Triangle
Address: 1809 Minor Ave
Seattle, WA 98101
Phone: (206) 621-8816

#67
Box And Bottle
Cuisines: American
Average Price: Modest
Area: Greenwood
Address: 8576 Greenwood Ave N
Seattle, WA 98103
Phone: (206) 258-4985

#68
BOKA Restaurant + Bar
Cuisines: American, Bar
Average Price: Modest
Area: Downtown
Address: 1010 1st Ave
Seattle, WA 98104
Phone: (206) 357-9000

#69
Japonessa
Cuisines: Japanese, Sushi Bar
Average Price: Modest
Area: Downtown
Address: 1400 1st Ave
Seattle, WA 98101
Phone: (206) 971-7979

#70
Restaurant Roux
Cuisines: Cajun, Creole, Southern
Average Price: Modest
Area: Fremont
Address: 4201 Fremont Ave N
Seattle, WA 98103
Phone: (206) 547-5420

Seattle Travel Guide 2016 / Shops, Restaurants, Arts, Entertainment & Nightlife

#71
Rain City Burgers
Cuisines: Burgers
Average Price: Inexpensive
Area: Roosevelt
Address: 6501 Roosevelt Way NE
Seattle, WA 98115
Phone: (206) 525-3542

#72
Cafe Turko
Cuisines: Turkish, Mediterranean, Halal
Average Price: Modest
Area: Fremont
Address: 754 N 34th St
Seattle, WA 98103
Phone: (206) 284-9954

#73
Altura
Cuisines: Italian
Average Price: Exclusive
Area: Capitol Hill
Address: 617 Broadway E
Seattle, WA 98102
Phone: (206) 402-6749

#74
Calozzi's Cheesesteaks
Cuisines: Cheesesteaks, Sandwiches
Average Price: Inexpensive
Area: Downtown
Address: 1306 4th Ave
Seattle, WA 98101
Phone: (206) 623-1330

#75
The Harvest Vine
Cuisines: Tapas Bar, Spanish, Basque
Average Price: Expensive
Area: Madison Valley
Address: 2701 E Madison St
Seattle, WA 98112
Phone: (206) 320-9771

#76
Elliott's Oyster House
Cuisines: Seafood, Live/Raw Food
Average Price: Expensive
Area: Waterfront
Address: 1201 Alaskan Way
Seattle, WA 98101
Phone: (206) 623-4340

#77
Calozzi's Cheesesteaks
Cuisines: Cheesesteaks, Sandwiches
Average Price: Inexpensive
Area: Georgetown
Address: 7016 E Marginal Way S
Seattle, WA 98108
Phone: (206) 762-1777

#78
Knee High Stocking Co.
Cuisines: American, Cocktail Bar
Average Price: Modest
Area: Capitol Hill
Address: 1356 E Olive Way
Seattle, WA 98122
Phone: (206) 979-7049

#79
Humble Pie
Cuisines: Pizza
Average Price: Modest
Area: International District
Address: 525 Rainier Ave S
Seattle, WA 98144
Phone: (206) 329-5133

#80
Burgundian
Cuisines: Bar, American
Average Price: Modest
Area: Wallingford
Address: 2253 N 56th St
Seattle, WA 98103
Phone: (206) 420-8943

#81
Italian Family Pizza
Cuisines: Pizza, Italian
Average Price: Inexpensive
Area: Downtown
Address: 1206 1st Ave
Seattle, WA 98101
Phone: (206) 538-0040

#82
Royal Grinders
Cuisines: Sandwiches, Ice Cream, Gelato
Average Price: Inexpensive
Area: Fremont
Address: 3526 Fremont Pl N
Seattle, WA 98103
Phone: (206) 545-7560

#83
Cicchetti
Cuisines: Mediterranean, Tapas
Average Price: Modest
Area: Eastlake
Address: 121 E Boston St
Seattle, WA 98102
Phone: (206) 859-4155

#84
Liam's
Cuisines: Wine Bar, American
Average Price: Modest
Area: University District
Address: 2685 NE 46th St
Seattle, WA 98105
Phone: (206) 527-6089

Seattle Travel Guide 2016 / Shops, Restaurants, Arts, Entertainment & Nightlife

#85
A La Bonne Franquette
Cuisines: French
Average Price: Modest
Area: Mount Baker
Address: 1421 31st Ave S
Seattle, WA 98144
Phone: (206) 568-7715

#86
Le Caviste
Cuisines: Wine Bar, French
Average Price: Modest
Area: Denny Triangle
Address: 1919 7th Ave
Seattle, WA 98101
Phone: (206) 728-2657

#87
Biscuit Bitch
Cuisines: Breakfast & Brunch, Coffee, Tea, Sandwiches
Average Price: Inexpensive
Area: Downtown
Address: 1909 1st Ave
Seattle, WA 98101
Phone: (206) 441-7999

#88
Tallulah's
Cuisines: Café, Breakfast & Brunch
Average Price: Modest
Area: Capitol Hill
Address: 550 19th Ave E
Seattle, WA 98112
Phone: (206) 860-0077

#89
Metropolitan Grill
Cuisines: American, Steakhouse
Average Price: Exclusive
Area: Downtown
Address: 820 2nd Ave
Seattle, WA 98104
Phone: (206) 624-3287

#90
The People's Burger
Cuisines: Food Truck, Burgers, American
Average Price: Inexpensive
Area: Sodo
Address: 922 Occidental Ave S
Seattle, WA 98134
Phone: (425) 471-5781

#91
Circa
Cuisines: American
Average Price: Modest
Area: Admiral
Address: 2605 California Ave SW
Seattle, WA 98116
Phone: (206) 923-1102

#92
Artisan Cafe
Cuisines: Coffee, Tea, Sandwiches, Ice Cream
Average Price: Inexpensive
Area: Belltown
Address: 2523 5th Ave
Seattle, WA 98121
Phone: (206) 441-8885

#93
Café Besalu
Cuisines: Bakery, Coffee, Tea, French
Average Price: Inexpensive
Area: Ballard
Address: 5909 24th Ave NW
Seattle, WA 98107
Phone: (206) 789-1463

#94
Sunrice
Cuisines: Korean
Average Price: Inexpensive
Area: Laurelhurst
Address: 3513 NE 45th St
Seattle, WA 98105
Phone: (206) 841-2454

#95
Mr. Gyros
Cuisines: Greek, Middle Eastern, Mediterranean
Average Price: Inexpensive
Area: Greenwood, Phinney Ridge
Address: 8411 Greenwood Ave N
Seattle, WA 98103
Phone: (206) 706-7472

#96
Din Tai Fung
Cuisines: Taiwanese, Shanghainese, Dim Sum
Average Price: Modest
Area: University District
Address: 2621 NE 46th St
Seattle, WA 98105
Phone: (206) 525-0958

#97
Mediterranean Kitchen Kabob House
Cuisines: Mediterranean, Lebanese
Average Price: Inexpensive
Area: First Hill
Address: 1009 Boren Ave
Seattle, WA 98104
Phone: (206) 467-5046

#98
Serious Biscuit
Cuisines: Breakfast & Brunch, Sandwiches, Bakery
Average Price: Modest
Area: South Lake Union
Address: 401 Westlake Ave N
Seattle, WA 98109
Phone: (206) 436-0050

#99
Matt's In The Market
Cuisines: American
Average Price: Expensive
Area: Downtown
Address: 94 Pike St
Seattle, WA 98101
Phone: (206) 467-7909

#100
Taylor Shellfish Farms
Cuisines: Seafood Market, Seafood, Live/Raw Food
Average Price: Modest
Area: Capitol Hill
Address: 1521 Melrose Ave
Seattle, WA 98122
Phone: (206) 501-4321

#101
Bar Cantinetta
Cuisines: Bar, Tapas, Italian
Average Price: Modest
Area: Madison Valley
Address: 2811 E Madison St
Seattle, WA 98112
Phone: (206) 329-1501

#102
Cafe Pettirosso
Cuisines: Coffee, Tea, Beer, Wine, Spirits, American
Average Price: Modest
Area: Capitol Hill
Address: 1101 E Pike St
Seattle, WA 98122
Phone: (206) 324-2233

#103
The Kingfish Cafe
Cuisines: Southern, Breakfast & Brunch, Soul Food
Average Price: Modest
Area: Capitol Hill
Address: 602 19th Ave E
Seattle, WA 98112
Phone: (206) 320-8757

#104
St. Dames
Cuisines: Gastropub, Vegetarian, Breakfast & Brunch
Average Price: Modest
Area: Columbia City
Address: 4525 Martin Luther King Way S
Seattle, WA 98108
Phone: (206) 725-8879

#105
The Hi Spot Cafe
Cuisines: American
Average Price: Modest
Area: Madrona
Address: 1410 34th Ave
Seattle, WA 98122
Phone: (206) 325-7905

#106
The Masonry
Cuisines: Bar, Pizza, Italian
Average Price: Modest
Area: Lower Queen Anne
Address: 20 Roy St
Seattle, WA 98109
Phone: (206) 453-4375

#107
5 Spot
Cuisines: American, Breakfast & Brunch
Average Price: Modest
Area: Queen Anne
Address: 1502 Queen Anne Ave N
Seattle, WA 98109
Phone: (206) 285-7768

#108
How To Cook A Wolf
Cuisines: Italian, Tapas
Average Price: Expensive
Area: Queen Anne
Address: 2208 Queen Anne Ave N
Seattle, WA 98109
Phone: (206) 838-8090

#109
Hello Robin
Cuisines: Bakery, Café
Average Price: Inexpensive
Area: Capitol Hill
Address: 522 19th Ave E
Seattle, WA 98112
Phone: (206) 735-7970

#110
Cascina Spinasse
Cuisines: Italian
Average Price: Expensive
Area: Capitol Hill
Address: 1531 14th Ave
Seattle, WA 98122
Phone: (206) 251-7673

#111
Mike's Noodle House
Cuisines: Cantonese
Average Price: Inexpensive
Area: International District
Address: 418 Maynard Ave S
Seattle, WA 98104
Phone: (206) 389-7099

#112
Araya's Place
Cuisines: Thai, Vegan, Vegetarian
Average Price: Modest
Area: Capitol Hill
Address: 2808 E Madison St
Seattle, WA 98112
Phone: (206) 402-6634

Seattle Travel Guide 2016 / Shops, Restaurants, Arts, Entertainment & Nightlife

#113
San Fernando Roasted Chicken
Cuisines: Peruvian
Average Price: Modest
Area: Central District
Address: 900 Rainier Ave S
Seattle, WA 98144
Phone: (206) 331-3763

#114
Mojito
Cuisines: Cuban, Colombian, Venezuelan
Average Price: Modest
Area: Mapleleaf
Address: 7545 Lake City Way NE
Seattle, WA 98115
Phone: (206) 525-3162

#115
Ha!
Cuisines: Comfort Food, Bar
Average Price: Modest
Area: Fremont
Address: 4256 Fremont Ave N
Seattle, WA 98103
Phone: (206) 588-1169

#116
Tsukushinbo
Cuisines: Japanese, Sushi Bar
Average Price: Modest
Area: International District
Address: 515 S Main St
Seattle, WA 98104
Phone: (206) 467-4004

#117
Sand Point Grill
Cuisines: American
Average Price: Modest
Area: Laurelhurst
Address: 5412 Sand Point Way NE
Seattle, WA 98105
Phone: (206) 729-1303

#118
Pica Border Grill
Cuisines: Mexican
Average Price: Inexpensive
Area: Junction
Address: 4151 California Ave SW
Seattle, WA 98116
Phone: (206) 935-5555

#119
Tsue Chong Co
Cuisines: Ethnic Food, Chinese
Average Price: Inexpensive
Area: International District
Address: 800 S Weller St
Seattle, WA 90104
Phone: (206) 623-0801

#120
Market Grill
Cuisines: Seafood
Average Price: Modest
Area: Downtown
Address: 1509 Pike Pl
Seattle, WA 98101
Phone: (206) 682-2654

#121
Shawn O'Donnell's American Grill & Irish Pub
Cuisines: Irish, Burgers, Fish & Chips
Average Price: Modest
Area: Pioneer Square
Address: 508 2nd Ave
Seattle, WA 98104
Phone: (206) 602-6380

#122
Madison Kitchen
Cuisines: Café, Sandwiches
Average Price: Modest
Area: Madison Park
Address: 4122 E Madison St
Seattle, WA 98112
Phone: (206) 557-4639

#123
Pam's Kitchen
Cuisines: Trinidadian
Average Price: Modest
Area: University District
Address: 5000 University Way NE
Seattle, WA 98105
Phone: (206) 696-7010

#124
Ugly Mug Café
Cuisines: Café, Sandwiches
Average Price: Inexpensive
Area: University District
Address: 1309 NE 43rd St
Seattle, WA 98105
Phone: (206) 547-3219

#125
Now Make Me A Sandwich
Cuisines: Food Truck, Sandwiches, American
Average Price: Inexpensive
Area: Crown Hill
Address: 9057 8th Ave NW
Seattle, WA 98117
Phone: (206) 714-5090

#126
Rain Shadow Meats Squared
Cuisines: Sandwiches, Meat Shop, Butcher
Average Price: Modest
Area: Pioneer Square
Address: 404 Occidental Ave S
Seattle, WA 98104
Phone: (206) 467-4854

#127
Re:Public
Cuisines: American, Bar
Average Price: Modest
Area: South Lake Union
Address: 429 Westlake Ave N
Seattle, WA 98109
Phone: (206) 467-5300

#128
Taste Of The Caribbean
Cuisines: Caribbean
Average Price: Modest
Area: Central District
Address: 1212 E Jefferson St
Seattle, WA 98122
Phone: (425) 270-8743

#129
Tacos El Asadero
Cuisines: Mexican, Food Truck, Sandwiches
Average Price: Inexpensive
Area: Mount Baker
Address: 3517 Rainier Ave S
Seattle, WA 98118
Phone: (206) 722-9977

#130
Arosa Café
Cuisines: Coffee, Tea, Sandwiches, Belgian
Average Price: Inexpensive
Area: First Hill
Address: 1310 Madison St
Seattle, WA 98104
Phone: (206) 329-5881

#131
Saigon Deli
Cuisines: Vietnamese, Deli, Sandwiches
Average Price: Inexpensive
Area: International District
Address: 1237 S Jackson St
Seattle, WA 98144
Phone: (206) 322-3700

#132
8oz Burger & Co
Cuisines: Burgers, Bar
Average Price: Modest
Area: First Hill
Address: 1401 Broadway
Seattle, WA 98122
Phone: (206) 466-5989

#133
Taylor Shellfish Oyster Bar
Cuisines: Seafood, Live/Raw Food
Average Price: Modest
Area: Lower Queen Anne
Address: 124 Republican St
Seattle, WA 98109
Phone: (206) 501-4442

#134
The Leary Traveler
Cuisines: Pub, American
Average Price: Modest
Area: Fremont
Address: 4356 Leary Way NW
Seattle, WA 98107
Phone: (206) 783-4805

#135
Kimchi House
Cuisines: Korean, Deli, Sandwiches
Average Price: Inexpensive
Area: Ballard
Address: 5809 24th Ave NW
Seattle, WA 98107
Phone: (206) 784-5322

#136
Sweet Iron
Cuisines: Belgian, Breakfast & Brunch
Average Price: Inexpensive
Area: Downtown
Address: 1200 3rd Ave
Seattle, WA 98101
Phone: (206) 682-3336

#137
Marination Station
Cuisines: Korean, Asian Fusion, Hawaiian
Average Price: Inexpensive
Area: First Hill, Capitol Hill
Address: 1412 Harvard Ave
Seattle, WA 98122
Phone: (206) 325-8226

#138
Ping's Dumpling House
Cuisines: Chinese
Average Price: Inexpensive
Area: International District
Address: 508 S King St
Seattle, WA 98104
Phone: (206) 623-6764

#139
Michou
Cuisines: Deli, Sandwiches
Average Price: Inexpensive
Area: Downtown
Address: 1904 Pike Pl
Seattle, WA 98101
Phone: (206) 448-4758

#140
Caffè Senso Unico
Cuisines: Coffee, Tea, Café, Sandwiches
Average Price: Inexpensive
Area: Denny Triangle
Address: 622 Olive Way
Seattle, WA 98101
Phone: (206) 264-7611

Seattle Travel Guide 2016 / Shops, Restaurants, Arts, Entertainment & Nightlife

#141
Pomerol
Cuisines: French
Average Price: Expensive
Area: Fremont
Address: 127 N 36th St
Seattle, WA 98103
Phone: (206) 632-0135

#142
Cheeky Cafe
Cuisines: Asian Fusion, Comfort Food, Breakfast & Brunch
Average Price: Modest
Area: Central District
Address: 1700 S Jackson St
Seattle, WA 98144
Phone: (206) 322-9895

#143
George's Sausage & Delicatessen
Cuisines: Deli, Polish, Grocery
Average Price: Inexpensive
Area: First Hill
Address: 907 Madison St
Seattle, WA 98104
Phone: (206) 622-1491

#144
Volunteer Park Cafe & Marketplace
Cuisines: Coffee, Tea, American, Bakery
Average Price: Modest
Area: Capitol Hill
Address: 1501 17th Ave E
Seattle, WA 98112
Phone: (206) 328-3155

#145
The Noble Fir
Cuisines: Bar, Tapas
Average Price: Modest
Area: Ballard
Address: 5316 Ballard Ave NW
Seattle, WA 98107
Phone: (206) 420-7425

#146
Le Pichet
Cuisines: French, Tapas
Average Price: Modest
Area: Downtown
Address: 1933 1st Ave
Seattle, WA 98101
Phone: (206) 256-1499

#147
Americana
Cuisines: American, Breakfast & Brunch
Average Price: Modest
Area: Capitol Hill
Address: 219 Broadway E
Seattle, WA 98102
Phone: (206) 328-4604

#148
Maneki
Cuisines: Japanese, Sushi Bar
Average Price: Modest
Area: International District
Address: 304 6th Ave S
Seattle, WA 98104
Phone: (206) 622-2631

#149
Shawarma King
Cuisines: Mediterranean, Egyptian
Average Price: Inexpensive
Area: University District
Address: 5004 University Way NE
Seattle, WA 98105
Phone: (206) 529-3223

#150
Stoneburner
Cuisines: Pizza, American, Bar
Average Price: Modest
Area: Ballard
Address: 5214 Ballard Ave NW
Seattle, WA 98107
Phone: (206) 695-2051

#151
Market House Meats
Cuisines: Meat Shop, Sandwiches, Deli
Average Price: Inexpensive
Area: Denny Triangle
Address: 1124 Howell St
Seattle, WA 98101
Phone: (206) 624-9248

#152
The Dray
Cuisines: Beer, Wine, Spirits, Sandwiches
Average Price: Modest
Area: Phinney Ridge
Address: 708 NW 65th St
Seattle, WA 98117
Phone: (206) 453-4527

#153
Poppy
Cuisines: American, Tapas
Average Price: Expensive
Area: Capitol Hill
Address: 622 Broadway E
Seattle, WA 98102
Phone: (206) 324-1108

#154
Aladdin Falafel Corner
Cuisines: Falafel
Average Price: Inexpensive
Area: University District
Address: 4541 University Way NE
Seattle, WA 98105
Phone: (206) 548-9539

#155
U:DON Fresh Japanese Noodle Station
Cuisines: Japanese, Soup
Average Price: Inexpensive
Area: University District
Address: 4515 University Way NE
Seattle, WA 98105
Phone: (206) 453-3788

#156
The Fat Hen
Cuisines: Café, Bakery, Breakfast & Brunch
Average Price: Modest
Area: Phinney Ridge
Address: 1418 NW 70th St
Seattle, WA 98117
Phone: (206) 782-5422

#157
Intermezzo Carmine
Cuisines: Cocktail Bar, Italian
Average Price: Modest
Area: Pioneer Square
Address: 409 1st Ave S
Seattle, WA 98104
Phone: (206) 596-8940

#158
Crow
Cuisines: American, European
Average Price: Expensive
Area: Lower Queen Anne
Address: 823 5th Ave N
Seattle, WA 98109
Phone: (206) 283-8800

#159
The Pine Box
Cuisines: Pub, American
Average Price: Modest
Area: Capitol Hill
Address: 1600 Melrose Ave
Seattle, WA 98122
Phone: (206) 588-0375

#160
Cederberg Tea House
Cuisines: Coffee, Tea, Bakery, South African
Average Price: Inexpensive
Area: Queen Anne
Address: 1417 Queen Anne Ave N
Seattle, WA 98109
Phone: (206) 285-1352

#161
Scratch Deli
Cuisines: Sandwiches, Deli, Coffee
Average Price: Inexpensive
Area: Capitol Hill
Address: 1718 12th Ave
Seattle, WA 98122
Phone: (206) 257-4554

#162
Citizen
Cuisines: Crêperie, Coffee, Tea
Average Price: Modest
Area: Lower Queen Anne
Address: 706 Taylor Ave N
Seattle, WA 98109
Phone: (206) 284-1015

#163
Pecos Pit BBQ
Cuisines: Barbeque
Average Price: Inexpensive
Area: Industrial District
Address: 2260 1st Ave S
Seattle, WA 98134
Phone: (206) 623-0629

#164
Café Presse
Cuisines: French, Breakfast & Brunch, Café
Average Price: Modest
Area: First Hill
Address: 1117 12th Ave
Seattle, WA 98122
Phone: (206) 709-7674

#165
Boat Street Cafe & Kitchen
Cuisines: American, French, Breakfast & Brunch
Average Price: Modest
Area: Interbay, Belltown
Address: 3131 Western Ave
Seattle, WA 98121
Phone: (206) 632-4602

#166
Bustle
Cuisines: Coffee, Tea, Sandwiches
Average Price: Inexpensive
Area: Queen Anne
Address: 535 W Mcgraw St
Seattle, WA 98119
Phone: (206) 453-4285

#167
Cafe Munir
Cuisines: Lebanese
Average Price: Modest
Area: Loyal Heights
Address: 2408 NW 80th St
Seattle, WA 98117
Phone: (206) 783-4190

#168
Sitka & Spruce
Cuisines: American
Average Price: Expensive
Area: Capitol Hill
Address: 1531 Melrose Ave
Seattle, WA 98101
Phone: (206) 324-0662

#169
The Crumpet Shop
Cuisines: Bakery, Coffee, Tea, Breakfast & Brunch
Average Price: Inexpensive
Area: Downtown
Address: 1503 1st Ave
Seattle, WA 98101
Phone: (206) 682-1598

#170
Rocco's
Cuisines: Bar, Pizza
Average Price: Modest
Area: Belltown
Address: 2228 2nd Ave
Seattle, WA 98121
Phone: (206) 448-2625

#171
Purple Café And Wine Bar
Cuisines: American, Wine Bar
Average Price: Expensive
Area: Downtown
Address: 1225 4th Ave
Seattle, WA 98101
Phone: (206) 829-2280

#172
Seattle Wood Fired Pizza
Cuisines: Food Truck, Pizza
Average Price: Inexpensive
Area: Queen Anne
Address: 1300 Elliott Ave W
Seattle, WA 98119
Phone: (206) 612-7100

#173
The Zouave Restaurant
Cuisines: Italian, French
Average Price: Modest
Area: Ravenna
Address: 2615 NE 65th St
Seattle, WA 98115
Phone: (206) 525-7747

#174
Uneeda Burger
Cuisines: Burgers, Sandwiches
Average Price: Modest
Area: Fremont
Address: 4302 Fremont Ave N
Seattle, WA 98103
Phone: (206) 547-2600

#175
Red Cow
Cuisines: French, Steakhouse
Average Price: Expensive
Area: Madrona
Address: 1423 34th Ave
Seattle, WA 98122
Phone: (206) 454-7932

#176
Bizzarro Italian Café
Cuisines: Italian
Average Price: Modest
Area: Wallingford
Address: 1307 N 46th St
Seattle, WA 98103
Phone: (206) 632-7277

#177
Five Hooks Fish Grill
Cuisines: Seafood
Average Price: Modest
Area: Queen Anne
Address: 2232 Queen Anne Ave N
Seattle, WA 98109
Phone: (206) 403-1263

#178
Tropicos Breeze
Cuisines: Salvadoran, Seafood
Average Price: Modest
Area: Licton Springs
Address: 9710 Aurora Ave N
Seattle, WA 98103
Phone: (206) 524-3046

#179
Judkins St Cafe
Cuisines: American, Breakfast & Brunch, Burgers
Average Price: Inexpensive
Area: Atlantic
Address: 2608 S Judkins St
Seattle, WA 98144
Phone: (206) 322-1091

#180
La Isla Cuisine
Cuisines: Latin American, Puerto Rican
Average Price: Modest
Area: Ballard
Address: 2320 NW Market St
Seattle, WA 98107
Phone: (206) 789-0516

#181
The Oak
Cuisines: Pub, Burgers
Average Price: Modest
Area: Beacon Hill
Address: 3019 Beacon Ave S
Seattle, WA 98144
Phone: (206) 535-7070

#182
Bar Cotto
Cuisines: Bar, Pizza, Italian
Average Price: Modest
Area: Capitol Hill
Address: 1546 15th Ave
Seattle, WA 98122
Phone: (206) 838-8081

#183
Stumbling Goat Bistro
Cuisines: American
Average Price: Expensive
Area: Phinney Ridge
Address: 6722 Greenwood Ave N
Seattle, WA 98103
Phone: (206) 784-3535

#184
RN74
Cuisines: American, French, Wine Bar
Average Price: Expensive
Area: Downtown
Address: 1433 4th Ave
Seattle, WA 98101
Phone: (206) 456-7474

#185
Fogón Cocina Mexicana
Cuisines: Mexican
Average Price: Modest
Area: Capitol Hill
Address: 600 E Pine St
Seattle, WA 98122
Phone: (206) 320-7777

#186
The Swinery
Cuisines: Meat Shop, Burgers, Sandwiches
Average Price: Modest
Area: Admiral
Address: 3207 California Ave SW
Seattle, WA 98116
Phone: (206) 932-4211

#187
Portage Bay Café & Catering
Cuisines: American, Breakfast & Brunch
Average Price: Modest
Area: University District
Address: 4130 Roosevelt Way NE
Seattle, WA 98105
Phone: (206) 547-8230

#188
Harbor City Restaurant
Cuisines: Barbeque, Dim Sum, Cantonese
Average Price: Inexpensive
Area: International District
Address: 707 S King St
Seattle, WA 98104
Phone: (206) 621-2228

#189
El Quetzal
Cuisines: Mexican
Average Price: Modest
Area: Beacon Hill
Address: 3209 Beacon Ave S
Seattle, WA 98144
Phone: (206) 329-2970

#190
Mezcaleria Oaxaca
Cuisines: Mexican
Average Price: Modest
Area: Queen Anne
Address: 2123 Queen Anne Ave N
Seattle, WA 98109
Phone: (206) 216-4446

#191
The Bear And The Bee
Cuisines: Deli, Breakfast & Brunch, Sandwiches
Average Price: Inexpensive
Area: Belltown
Address: 2211 2nd Ave
Seattle, WA 98121
Phone: (206) 441-7255

#192
Kona Kitchen
Cuisines: Hawaiian, Breakfast & Brunch
Average Price: Modest
Area: Mapleleaf
Address: 8501 5th Ave NE
Seattle, WA 98115
Phone: (206) 517-5662

#193
FOOD At Cortona
Cuisines: Tapas, European
Average Price: Modest
Area: Central District
Address: 2425 E Union St
Seattle, WA 98122
Phone: (206) 696-0991

#194
Bar Del Corso
Cuisines: Italian, Pizza
Average Price: Modest
Area: Beacon Hill
Address: 3057 Beacon Ave S
Seattle, WA 98144
Phone: (206) 395-2069

#195
Blackboard Bistro
Cuisines: American
Average Price: Modest
Area: Admiral
Address: 3247 SW California Ave
Seattle, WA 98116
Phone: (206) 257-4832

#196
La Teranga
Cuisines: Senegalese
Average Price: Modest
Area: Columbia City
Address: 4903 1/2 Rainier Ave S
Seattle, WA 98118
Phone: (206) 725-1188

Seattle Travel Guide 2016 / Shops, Restaurants, Arts, Entertainment & Nightlife

#197
Six Seven
Cuisines: American, Seafood
Average Price: Expensive
Area: Interbay
Address: 2411 Alaskan Way
Seattle, WA 98121
Phone: (206) 269-4575

#198
Blue Heron
Cuisines: Sandwiches
Average Price: Inexpensive
Area: Magnolia
Address: 4001 Gilman Ave W
Seattle, WA 98199
Phone: (206) 285-2171

#199
Bellini Italian Bistro
Cuisines: Italian, Pizza
Average Price: Modest
Area: Belltown
Address: 2302 1st Ave
Seattle, WA 98121
Phone: (206) 441-4480

#200
Umi Sake House
Cuisines: Sushi Bar, Japanese
Average Price: Modest
Area: Belltown
Address: 2230 1st Ave
Seattle, WA 98121
Phone: (206) 374-8717

#201
Chili & Sesame
Cuisines: Korean
Average Price: Modest
Area: Belltown
Address: 2421 2nd Ave
Seattle, WA 98121
Phone: (206) 443-2013

#202
Brass Tacks
Cuisines: Gastropub, Bar
Average Price: Modest
Area: Georgetown
Address: 6031 Airport Way S
Seattle, WA 98108
Phone: (206) 397-3821

#203
Tavern Law
Cuisines: American, Lounge
Average Price: Modest
Area: Capitol Hill
Address: 1406 12th Ave
Seattle, WA 98122
Phone: (206) 322-9734

#204
Nishino
Cuisines: Sushi Bar, Japanese
Average Price: Expensive
Area: Washington Park
Address: 3130 E Madison St
Seattle, WA 98112
Phone: (206) 322-5800

#205
Rumba
Cuisines: Caribbean, Cuban, Lounge
Average Price: Modest
Area: Capitol Hill
Address: 1112 Pike St
Seattle, WA 98101
Phone: (206) 583-7177

#206
Chef Cafe
Cuisines: Ethiopian
Average Price: Inexpensive
Area: Atlantic
Address: 2200 S Jackson St
Seattle, WA 98144
Phone: (206) 568-2681

#207
Local Pho
Cuisines: Vietnamese, Sandwiches
Average Price: Inexpensive
Area: Belltown
Address: 2230 3rd Ave
Seattle, WA 98121
Phone: (206) 441-5995

#208
Piroshki On Madison
Cuisines: Bakery, Russian
Average Price: Inexpensive
Area: First Hill
Address: 1219 Madison St
Seattle, WA 98104
Phone: (206) 624-1295

#209
Sunset Cafe
Cuisines: Ethiopian, Café
Average Price: Modest
Area: Rainier Beach
Address: 8115 Rainier Ave S
Seattle, WA 98118
Phone: (206) 722-0342

#210
Cafe Solstice
Cuisines: Café
Average Price: Inexpensive
Area: Capitol Hill
Address: 925 E Thomas St
Seattle, WA 98102
Phone: (206) 675-0850

#211
DM Cafe & Deli
Cuisines: Vietnamese, Deli
Average Price: Inexpensive
Area: South Lake Union
Address: 230 6th Ave N
Seattle, WA 98109
Phone: (206) 728-5855

#212
Vostok Dumpling House
Cuisines: Russian, Ukrainian
Average Price: Inexpensive
Area: First Hill, Capitol Hill
Address: 1416 Harvard Ave
Seattle, WA 98122
Phone: (206) 687-7865

#213
Dahlia Lounge
Cuisines: American, Seafood, Breakfast & Brunch
Average Price: Expensive
Area: Belltown
Address: 2001 4th Ave
Seattle, WA 98121
Phone: (206) 682-4142

#214
Canon
Cuisines: American, Cocktail Bar
Average Price: Modest
Area: Central District
Address: 928 12th Ave
Seattle, WA 98122
Phone: (206) 552-9755

#215
Chan Seattle
Cuisines: Korean, Seafood, Tapas
Average Price: Modest
Area: Downtown
Address: 86 Pine St
Seattle, WA 98101
Phone: (206) 443-5443

#216
Kau Kau Barbeque
Cuisines: Barbeque, Seafood, Cantonese
Average Price: Inexpensive
Area: International District
Address: 656 S King St
Seattle, WA 98104
Phone: (206) 682-4006

#217
Musashi's
Cuisines: Sushi Bar, Japanese
Average Price: Modest
Area: Wallingford
Address: 1400 N 45th St
Seattle, WA 98103
Phone: (206) 633-0212

#218
Bang Bang Café
Cuisines: Breakfast & Brunch, Vegan, Café
Average Price: Inexpensive
Area: Belltown
Address: 2460 Western Ave
Seattle, WA 98121
Phone: (206) 448-2233

#219
Goldinblack
Cuisines: Sandwiches, Korean, Beer, Wine, Spirits
Average Price: Modest
Area: Lower Queen Anne
Address: 621 Queen Anne Ave N
Seattle, WA 98109
Phone: (206) 466-2737

#220
Zinnia Bistro
Cuisines: American, Sandwiches
Average Price: Modest
Area: Industrial District
Address: 1759 1st Ave S
Seattle, WA 98134
Phone: (206) 682-7955

#221
Gourmet Noodle Bowl
Cuisines: Chinese, Taiwanese, Hot Pot
Average Price: Modest
Area: International District
Address: 707 8th Ave S
Seattle, WA 98104
Phone: (206) 264-8899

#222
Tiko Riko
Cuisines: Salvadoran
Average Price: Inexpensive
Area: Greenwood
Address: 10410 Greenwood Ave N
Seattle, WA 98133
Phone: (206) 784-0203

#223
Thai Curry Simple
Cuisines: Thai
Average Price: Inexpensive
Area: International District
Address: 406 5th Ave S
Seattle, WA 98104
Phone: (206) 327-4838

#224
Feierabend
Cuisines: German, Pub
Average Price: Modest
Area: South Lake Union
Address: 422 Yale Ave N
Seattle, WA 98109
Phone: (206) 340-2528

Seattle Travel Guide 2016 / Shops, Restaurants, Arts, Entertainment & Nightlife

#225
Geraldine's Counter Restaurant
Cuisines: American, Breakfast & Brunch
Average Price: Modest
Area: Columbia City
Address: 4872 Rainier Ave S
Seattle, WA 98118
Phone: (206) 723-2080

#226
Teriyaki 1st
Cuisines: Japanese
Average Price: Inexpensive
Area: University District
Address: 5201 University Way NE
Seattle, WA 98105
Phone: (206) 526-1661

#227
Mad Dawg's Hot Dogs
Cuisines: Hot Dogs, Food Stand
Average Price: Inexpensive
Area: Lower Queen Anne
Address: W Mercer St
Seattle, WA 98119
Phone: (206) 310-3362

#228
Sodo Deli
Cuisines: Deli, Sandwiches
Average Price: Inexpensive
Area: Industrial District
Address: 3228 1st Ave S
Seattle, WA 98134
Phone: (206) 467-0306

#229
La Cocina Oaxaquena
Cuisines: Mexican
Average Price: Modest
Area: Capitol Hill
Address: 1216 Pine St
Seattle, WA 98101
Phone: (206) 623-8226

#230
Subsand
Cuisines: Vietnamese, Sandwiches, Chinese
Average Price: Inexpensive
Area: International District
Address: 419 6th Ave S
Seattle, WA 98104
Phone: (206) 682-1267

#231
Green Leaf Vietnamese Restaurant
Cuisines: Vietnamese, Sandwiches
Average Price: Modest
Area: International District
Address: 418 8th Ave S
Seattle, WA 98104
Phone: (206) 340-1388

#232
Mkt.
Cuisines: American
Average Price: Expensive
Area: Wallingford
Address: 2108 N 55th St
Seattle, WA 98103
Phone: (206) 812-1580

#233
Sichuanese Cuisine
Cuisines: Szechuan, Hot Pot
Average Price: Inexpensive
Area: International District
Address: 1048 S Jackson St
Seattle, WA 98104
Phone: (206) 720-1690

#234
King Noodle
Cuisines: Chinese
Average Price: Inexpensive
Area: International District
Address: 615 S King St
Seattle, WA 98104
Phone: (206) 748-9168

#235
Plaza Garibaldi
Cuisines: Mexican, Karaoke
Average Price: Modest
Area: Lower Queen Anne
Address: 129 1st Ave N
Seattle, WA 98109
Phone: (206) 397-4088

#236
Joe Bar
Cuisines: Coffee, Tea, Crêperie, Bar
Average Price: Inexpensive
Area: Capitol Hill
Address: 810 E Roy St
Seattle, WA 98102
Phone: (206) 324-0407

#237
Cactus
Cuisines: Tex-Mex, Mexican
Average Price: Modest
Area: Madison Park
Address: 4220 E Madison St
Seattle, WA 98112
Phone: (206) 324-4140

#238
Cactus
Cuisines: Tex-Mex, Mexican
Average Price: Modest
Area: South Lake Union
Address: 350 Terry Ave N
Seattle, WA 98109
Phone: (206) 913-2250

#239
Take 5 Urban Market
Cuisines: Deli, Convenience Store, Grocery
Average Price: Inexpensive
Area: Phinney Ridge
Address: 6757 8th Ave NW
Seattle, WA 98117
Phone: (206) 420-8104

#240
Cortona Cafe
Cuisines: Coffee, Tea, Café
Average Price: Inexpensive
Area: Central District
Address: 2425 E Union St
Seattle, WA 98122
Phone: (206) 327-9728

#241
The Blue Glass
Cuisines: American
Average Price: Modest
Area: Phinney Ridge
Address: 704 NW 65th St
Seattle, WA 98117
Phone: (206) 420-1631

#242
Seattle Salads
Cuisines: Salad
Average Price: Modest
Area: Madison Valley
Address: 2711 E Madison St
Seattle, WA 98112
Phone: (206) 324-6445

#243
The Gerald
Cuisines: American, Gastropub, Cocktail Bar
Average Price: Modest
Area: Ballard
Address: 5210 Ballard Ave NW
Seattle, WA 98107
Phone: (206) 432-9280

#244
Delicatus
Cuisines: Deli, Sandwiches, Comfort Food
Average Price: Modest
Area: Pioneer Square
Address: 103 1st Ave S
Seattle, WA 98104
Phone: (206) 623-3780

#245
Lotus Thai Cuisine
Cuisines: Thai
Average Price: Inexpensive
Area: Central District
Address: 2724 East Cherry St
Seattle, WA 98122
Phone: (206) 323-9445

#246
Tilth
Cuisines: American
Average Price: Expensive
Area: Wallingford
Address: 1411 N 45th St
Seattle, WA 98103
Phone: (206) 633-0801

#247
Pecado Bueno
Cuisines: Mexican
Average Price: Inexpensive
Area: Fremont
Address: 4307 Fremont Ave N
Seattle, WA 98103
Phone: (206) 457-8837

#248
Hooverville Bar
Cuisines: Bar, American
Average Price: Inexpensive
Area: Industrial District
Address: 1721 1st Ave S
Seattle, WA 98134
Phone: (206) 264-2428

#249
Serious Pie
Cuisines: Pizza
Average Price: Modest
Area: South Lake Union
Address: 401 Westlake Ave N
Seattle, WA 98109
Phone: (206) 436-0050

#250
Mioposto
Cuisines: Italian, Pizza
Average Price: Modest
Area: Mount Baker
Address: 3601 S Mcclellan St
Seattle, WA 98144
Phone: (206) 760-3400

#251
Mamnoon
Cuisines: Middle Eastern
Average Price: Expensive
Area: Capitol Hill
Address: 1508 Melrose Ave
Seattle, WA 98122
Phone: (206) 906-9606

#252
Crush
Cuisines: American
Average Price: Exclusive
Area: Madison Valley
Address: 2319 E Madison Street
Seattle, WA 98112
Phone: (206) 302-7874

#253
Kokoras Greek Grill
Cuisines: Greek, Mediterranean
Average Price: Modest
Area: Gatewood
Address: 6400 1/2 California Ave SW
Seattle, WA 98136
Phone: (206) 913-0041

#254
Chuck's Hole In The Wall BBQ
Cuisines: Barbeque
Average Price: Inexpensive
Area: Pioneer Square
Address: 215 James St
Seattle, WA 98104
Phone: (206) 622-8717

#255
Vito's
Cuisines: Lounge, Italian
Average Price: Modest
Area: First Hill
Address: 927 9th Ave
Seattle, WA 98104
Phone: (206) 397-4053

#256
Dexter & Hayes Public House
Cuisines: Pub, American
Average Price: Modest
Area: Westlake
Address: 1628 Dexter Ave N
Seattle, WA 98109
Phone: (206) 283-7786

#257
Banh Mi Unwrapped
Cuisines: Vietnamese, Sandwiches
Average Price: Inexpensive
Area: University District
Address: 4725 University Way NE
Seattle, WA 98105
Phone: (206) 456-7192

#258
Loretta's Northwesterner
Cuisines: Bar, American, Burgers
Average Price: Inexpensive
Area: South Park
Address: 8617 14th Ave S
Seattle, WA 98108
Phone: (206) 327-9649

#259
Von's 1000Spirits
Cuisines: American, Burgers, Cocktail Bar
Average Price: Modest
Area: Downtown
Address: 1225 1st Ave
Seattle, WA 98101
Phone: (206) 621-8667

#260
Szechuan Noodle Bowl
Cuisines: Szechuan
Average Price: Inexpensive
Area: International District
Address: 420 8th Ave S
Seattle, WA 98104
Phone: (206) 623-4198

#261
Le Zinc
Cuisines: French, Bar
Average Price: Modest
Area: Capitol Hill
Address: 1449 E Pine St
Seattle, WA 98122
Phone: (206) 257-4151

#262
Vios Café
Cuisines: Greek, Mediterranean, American
Average Price: Modest
Area: Capitol Hill
Address: 903 19th Ave E
Seattle, WA 98112
Phone: (206) 329-3236

#263
Cafe Flora
Cuisines: Vegetarian, Vegan, Gluten-Free
Average Price: Modest
Area: Madison Valley
Address: 2901 E Madison St
Seattle, WA 98112
Phone: (206) 325-9100

#264
The Innkeeper
Cuisines: Pub, Latin American, Caribbean
Average Price: Modest
Area: Belltown
Address: 2510 1st Ave
Seattle, WA 98121
Phone: (206) 441-7817

#265
Ristorante Machiavelli
Cuisines: Italian, Pizza
Average Price: Modest
Area: Capitol Hill
Address: 1215 Pine St
Seattle, WA 98101
Phone: (206) 621-7941

#266
Red Mill Burgers
Cuisines: Burgers
Average Price: Inexpensive
Area: Interbay
Address: 1613 W Dravus St
Seattle, WA 98119
Phone: (206) 284-6300

#267
Sake Nomi
Cuisines: Japanese, Bar
Average Price: Modest
Area: Pioneer Square
Address: 76 S Washington St
Seattle, WA 98104
Phone: (206) 467-7253

#268
Li'l Woody's
Cuisines: Burgers
Average Price: Modest
Area: Capitol Hill
Address: 1211 Pine St
Seattle, WA 98101
Phone: (206) 457-4148

#269
Il Terrazzo Carmine
Cuisines: Italian
Average Price: Expensive
Area: Pioneer Square
Address: 411 1st Ave S
Seattle, WA 98104
Phone: (206) 467-7797

#270
Canlis
Cuisines: American, Seafood
Average Price: Exclusive
Area: Westlake
Address: 2576 Aurora Ave N
Seattle, WA 98109
Phone: (206) 283-3313

#271
Joule
Cuisines: Asian Fusion, Korean, Breakfast & Brunch
Average Price: Expensive
Area: Wallingford
Address: 3506 Stone Way N
Seattle, WA 98103
Phone: (206) 632-5685

#272
The 5 Point Café
Cuisines: Dive Bar, Diner, Breakfast & Brunch
Average Price: Modest
Area: Belltown
Address: 415 Cedar St
Seattle, WA 98121
Phone: (206) 448-9991

#273
Cure
Cuisines: Bar, American
Average Price: Modest
Area: Capitol Hill
Address: 1641 Nagle Pl
Seattle, WA 98122
Phone: (206) 568-5475

#274
Terra Plata
Cuisines: American, Bar
Average Price: Expensive
Area: Capitol Hill
Address: 1501 Melrose Ave
Seattle, WA 98122
Phone: (206) 325-1501

#275
Triumph Bar
Cuisines: Wine Bar, Cocktail Bar, Gastropub
Average Price: Modest
Area: Lower Queen Anne
Address: 114 Republican St
Seattle, WA 98109
Phone: (206) 420-1791

#276
Red Lantern
Cuisines: Chinese, Asian Fusion, Korean
Average Price: Modest
Area: International District
Address: 520 S Jackson St
Seattle, WA 98104
Phone: (206) 682-7211

#277
Smith
Cuisines: Bar, American, Breakfast & Brunch
Average Price: Modest
Area: Capitol Hill
Address: 332 15th Ave E
Seattle, WA 98112
Phone: (206) 709-1900

#278
Canton Wonton House
Cuisines: Cantonese
Average Price: Inexpensive
Area: International District
Address: 608 S Weller St
Seattle, WA 98104
Phone: (206) 682-5080

#279
Runway Cafe
Cuisines: Café, American
Average Price: Modest
Area: Georgetown
Address: 1128 S Albro Pl
Seattle, WA 98108
Phone: (206) 452-7659

#280
The Brooklyn Seafood, Steak & Oyster House
Cuisines: Seafood, Steakhouse
Average Price: Expensive
Area: Downtown
Address: 1212 2nd Ave
Seattle, WA 98101
Phone: (206) 224-7000

#281
Le Rêve Bakery & Café
Cuisines: Bakery, Café, French
Average Price: Modest
Area: Queen Anne
Address: 1805 Queen Anne Ave N
Seattle, WA 98109
Phone: (206) 623-7383

#282
Pinky's Kitchen
Cuisines: Barbeque, Food Truck
Average Price: Inexpensive
Area: Wallingford
Address: 210 NE 45th St
Seattle, WA 98105
Phone: (206) 257-5483

#283
Café Campagne
Cuisines: French, Breakfast & Brunch
Average Price: Modest
Area: Downtown
Address: 1600 Post Alley
Seattle, WA 98101
Phone: (206) 728-2233

#284
Trident Seafoods
Cuisines: Seafood, Seafood Market
Average Price: Inexpensive
Area: Sunset Hill
Address: 2821 NW Market St
Seattle, WA 98107
Phone: (206) 781-7260

#285
Brouwer's Cafe
Cuisines: European, Pub, Belgian
Average Price: Modest
Area: Fremont
Address: 400 N 35th St
Seattle, WA 98103
Phone: (206) 267-2437

#286
Thai Tom
Cuisines: Thai
Average Price: Inexpensive
Area: University District
Address: 4543 University Way NE
Seattle, WA 98105
Phone: (206) 548-9548

#287
Tango
Cuisines: Spanish, Tapas Bar, Basque
Average Price: Modest
Area: Capitol Hill
Address: 1100 Pike St
Seattle, WA 98101
Phone: (206) 583-0382

#288
Ba Bar
Cuisines: Vietnamese, Bar, Bakery
Average Price: Modest
Area: Central District
Address: 550 12th Ave
Seattle, WA 98122
Phone: (206) 328-2030

#289
Sazerac
Cuisines: American
Average Price: Modest
Area: Downtown
Address: 1101 4th Ave
Seattle, WA 98101
Phone: (206) 624-7755

#290
Veggie Grill
Cuisines: American, Vegetarian, Vegan
Average Price: Modest
Area: South Lake Union
Address: 446 Terry Ave N
Seattle, WA 98109
Phone: (206) 623-0336

#291
Bait Shop
Cuisines: Bar, Seafood
Average Price: Modest
Area: Capitol Hill
Address: 606 Broadway E
Seattle, WA 98102
Phone: (206) 420-8742

#292
The Wurst Place
Cuisines: German, American
Average Price: Modest
Area: South Lake Union
Address: 510 Westlake Ave N
Seattle, WA 98102
Phone: (206) 623-3548

#293
Oliver's Twist
Cuisines: Tapas Bar, American
Average Price: Modest
Area: Phinney Ridge
Address: 6822 Greenwood Ave N
Seattle, WA 98103
Phone: (206) 706-6673

#294
Wild Mountain Cafe
Cuisines: American
Average Price: Modest
Area: Crown Hill
Address: 1408 NW 85th St
Seattle, WA 98117
Phone: (206) 297-9453

#295
Pie
Cuisines: Bakery, Desserts, American
Average Price: Inexpensive
Area: Lower Queen Anne
Address: 305 Harrison St
Seattle, WA 98109
Phone: (206) 428-6312

#296
Bell + Whete
Cuisines: European
Average Price: Modest
Area: Belltown
Address: 200 Bell St
Seattle, WA 98121
Phone: (206) 538-0180

#297
Sebi's Bistro
Cuisines: Pizza, Sandwiches, Polish
Average Price: Modest
Area: Portage Bay
Address: 3242 Eastlake Ave E
Seattle, WA 98102
Phone: (206) 420-2199

#298
The Twilight Exit
Cuisines: Dive Bar, American
Average Price: Inexpensive
Area: Central District
Address: 2514 E Cherry St
Seattle, WA 98122
Phone: (206) 324-7462

#299
World Pizza
Cuisines: Pizza, Vegetarian
Average Price: Inexpensive
Area: International District
Address: 672 S King St
Seattle, WA 98104
Phone: (206) 682-4161

#300
Holy Cannoli
Cuisines: Desserts, Italian, Sandwiches
Average Price: Inexpensive
Area: Belltown
Address: 2720 3rd Ave
Seattle, WA 98121
Phone: (206) 841-8205

#301
Café Paloma
Cuisines: Mediterranean, Turkish
Average Price: Modest
Area: Pioneer Square
Address: 93 Yesler Way
Seattle, WA 98104
Phone: (206) 405-1920

#302
Mendoza's Mexican Mercado
Cuisines: Mexican, Grocery, Ethnic Food
Average Price: Inexpensive
Area: Greenwood, Phinney Ridge
Address: 7811 Aurora Ave N
Seattle, WA 98103
Phone: (206) 245-1089

#303
Red Papaya Ale & Spirits
Cuisines: Vietnamese, Tapas Bar
Average Price: Modest
Area: Lower Queen Anne
Address: 530 1st Ave N
Seattle, WA 98109
Phone: (206) 283-6614

#304
Pike Street Fish Fry
Cuisines: Seafood, Fish & Chips
Average Price: Inexpensive
Area: First Hill, Capitol Hill
Address: 925 E Pike St
Seattle, WA 98122
Phone: (206) 329-7453

#305
Cactus
Cuisines: Tex-Mex, Mexican
Average Price: Modest
Area: Alki
Address: 2820 Alki Ave SW
Seattle, WA 98116
Phone: (206) 933-6000

#306
Silver Tray
Cuisines: Thai
Average Price: Modest
Area: Wallingford
Address: 2101 N 45th St
Seattle, WA 98103
Phone: (206) 632-2300

#307
La Carta De Oaxaca
Cuisines: Mexican
Average Price: Modest
Area: Ballard
Address: 5431 Ballard Ave NW
Seattle, WA 98107
Phone: (206) 782-8722

#308
Tamarind Tree
Cuisines: Vietnamese
Average Price: Modest
Area: International District
Address: 1036 S Jackson St
Seattle, WA 98104
Phone: (206) 860-1404

Seattle Travel Guide 2016 / Shops, Restaurants, Arts, Entertainment & Nightlife

#309
Le Fournil
Cuisines: Bakery, French, Café
Average Price: Inexpensive
Area: Portage Bay
Address: 3230 Eastlake Ave E
Seattle, WA 98102
Phone: (206) 328-6523

#310
Sushi Kanpai
Cuisines: Sushi Bar, Japanese
Average Price: Modest
Area: First Hill
Address: 900 8th Ave
Seattle, WA 98104
Phone: (206) 588-2769

#311
Fortuna Cafe
Cuisines: Chinese, Barbeque
Average Price: Inexpensive
Area: International District
Address: 711 S King St
Seattle, WA 98104
Phone: (206) 223-5343

#312
The Octopus Bar
Cuisines: Tapas, Gastropub, Cocktail Bar
Average Price: Inexpensive
Area: Wallingford
Address: 2109 N 45th St
Seattle, WA 98103
Phone: (206) 582-2483

#313
Row House Cafe
Cuisines: Breakfast & Brunch, Comfort Food, Cocktail Bar
Average Price: Modest
Area: South Lake Union
Address: 1170 Republican St
Seattle, WA 98109
Phone: (206) 682-7632

#314
Miyabi 45th
Cuisines: Japanese
Average Price: Modest
Area: Wallingford
Address: 2208 N 45th St
Seattle, WA 98103
Phone: (206) 632-4545

#315
Yong's Tofu House
Cuisines: Korean
Average Price: Modest
Area: Roosevelt
Address: 805 NE 65th St
Seattle, WA 98115
Phone: (206) 557-7391

#316
Bakeman's Restaurant
Cuisines: American, Soup, Sandwiches
Average Price: Inexpensive
Area: Downtown
Address: 122 Cherry St
Seattle, WA 98104
Phone: (206) 622-3375

#317
CJ's Eatery
Cuisines: American, Diner
Average Price: Modest
Area: Belltown
Address: 2619 1st Ave
Seattle, WA 98121
Phone: (206) 728-1648

#318
Staple & Fancy Mercantile
Cuisines: Seafood, Italian
Average Price: Expensive
Area: Ballard
Address: 4739 Ballard Ave NW
Seattle, WA 98107
Phone: (206) 789-1200

#319
Daniel's Broiler
Cuisines: Steakhouse, Seafood
Average Price: Exclusive
Area: South Lake Union, Eastlake
Address: 809 Fairview Pl N
Seattle, WA 98109
Phone: (206) 621-8262

#320
Bakery Nouveau
Cuisines: Bakery, Café, Chocolate Shop
Average Price: Inexpensive
Area: Capitol Hill
Address: 1435 E John St
Seattle, WA 98112
Phone: (206) 858-6957

#321
Mykonos Greek Grill
Cuisines: Greek
Average Price: Modest
Area: Greenlake
Address: 310 NE 72nd St
Seattle, WA 98115
Phone: (206) 523-8929

#322
Pam's Kitchen
Cuisines: Trinidadian
Average Price: Inexpensive
Area: South Lake Union
Address: 609 Eastlake Ave NE
Seattle, WA 98109
Phone: (206) 420-2320

#323
Island Soul Caribbean Cuisine
Cuisines: Caribbean
Average Price: Modest
Area: Columbia City
Address: 4869 Rainier Ave S
Seattle, WA 98118
Phone: (206) 329-1202

#324
The Shanty Cafe
Cuisines: Breakfast & Brunch, American, Café
Average Price: Inexpensive
Area: Lower Queen Anne
Address: 350 Elliott Ave W
Seattle, WA 98119
Phone: (206) 282-1400

#325
Momiji
Cuisines: Japanese, Sushi Bar
Average Price: Expensive
Area: Capitol Hill
Address: 1522 12th Ave
Seattle, WA 98122
Phone: (206) 457-4068

#326
The Sitting Room
Cuisines: Lounge, Wine Bar, Tapas Bar
Average Price: Modest
Area: Lower Queen Anne
Address: 108 W Roy St
Seattle, WA 98119
Phone: (206) 285-2830

#327
Henry's Tavern
Cuisines: American, Seafood, Sports Bar
Average Price: Modest
Area: Sodo
Address: 1518 1st Ave S
Seattle, WA 98134
Phone: (206) 624-0501

#328
Isla Manila Bar & Grill
Cuisines: Filipino
Average Price: Modest
Area: Pinehurst
Address: 11740 15th Ave NE
Seattle, WA 98125
Phone: (206) 365-2500

#329
Caffè Torino
Cuisines: Café, Sandwiches, Breakfast & Brunch
Average Price: Inexpensive
Area: South Lake Union
Address: 422 Yale Ave N
Seattle, WA 98109
Phone: (206) 682-2099

#330
Guanaco's Tacos Pupuseria
Cuisines: Mexican, Salvadoran
Average Price: Inexpensive
Area: University District
Address: 4106 Brooklyn Ave NE
Seattle, WA 98105
Phone: (206) 547-2369

#331
El Camión
Cuisines: Mexican, Food Truck
Average Price: Inexpensive
Area: Ballard
Address: 5314 15th Ave NW
Seattle, WA 98107
Phone: (206) 297-1124

#332
The Neighbor Lady
Cuisines: Bar, American
Average Price: Modest
Area: Central District
Address: 2308 E Union St
Seattle, WA 98122
Phone: (206) 695-2072

#333
Ten Mercer
Cuisines: Bar, American, Gluten-Free
Average Price: Modest
Area: Lower Queen Anne
Address: 10 Mercer St
Seattle, WA 98109
Phone: (206) 691-3723

#334
Mecca Cafe
Cuisines: American, Dive Bar, Breakfast & Brunch
Average Price: Inexpensive
Area: Lower Queen Anne
Address: 526 Queen Anne Ave N
Seattle, WA 98109
Phone: (206) 285-9728

#335
Xplosive Mobile Food Truck
Cuisines: Vietnamese, Food Truck, Filipino
Average Price: Inexpensive
Area: South Lake Union
Address: 425 Terry Ave N
Seattle, WA 98109
Phone: (206) 612-4739

#336
Harbor Café
Cuisines: Thai, Asian Fusion, Café
Average Price: Inexpensive
Area: Downtown
Address: 1411 4th Ave
Seattle, WA 98101
Phone: (206) 340-9908

#337
Home Remedy
Cuisines: Deli, Convenience Store
Average Price: Modest
Area: Denny Triangle
Address: 2121 6th Ave
Seattle, WA 98121
Phone: (206) 812-8407

#338
Metropole American Kitchen & Bar
Cuisines: Bar, American
Average Price: Modest
Area: Downtown
Address: 820 Pike St
Seattle, WA 98101
Phone: (206) 832-5555

#339
Niko's Gyros
Cuisines: Greek, Mediterranean
Average Price: Inexpensive
Area: Magnolia
Address: 2231 32nd Ave W
Seattle, WA 98199
Phone: (206) 285-4778

#340
Ristorante Doria
Cuisines: Italian
Average Price: Modest
Area: University District
Address: 4759 Roosevelt Way NE
Seattle, WA 98105
Phone: (206) 466-2380

#341
Ray's Boathouse
Cuisines: Nightlife, American, Seafood
Average Price: Expensive
Area: Sunset Hill
Address: 6049 Seaview Ave NW
Seattle, WA 98107
Phone: (206) 789-3770

#342
Kisaku
Cuisines: Sushi Bar, Japanese
Average Price: Modest
Area: Wallingford
Address: 2101 N 55th St
Seattle, WA 98103
Phone: (206) 545-9050

#343
Buddha Ruksa
Cuisines: Thai
Average Price: Modest
Area: Genesee
Address: 3520 SW Genesee St
Seattle, WA 98126
Phone: (206) 937-7676

#344
Ocho
Cuisines: Tapas Bar, Lounge, Spanish
Average Price: Modest
Area: Ballard
Address: 2325 NW Market St
Seattle, WA 98107
Phone: (206) 784-0699

#345
The Triple Door
Cuisines: Asian Fusion, Music Venues
Average Price: Expensive
Area: Downtown
Address: 216 Union St
Seattle, WA 98101
Phone: (206) 838-4333

#346
Eureka! Discover American Craft
Cuisines: American, Burgers
Average Price: Modest
Area: University District
Address: 2614 NE 46th St
Seattle, WA 98105
Phone: (206) 812-9655

#347
Phnom Penh Noodle House
Cuisines: Cambodian, Caterer
Average Price: Inexpensive
Area: International District
Address: 660 S King St
Seattle, WA 98104
Phone: (206) 748-9825

#348
MOD Pizza
Cuisines: Pizza, Fast Food
Average Price: Inexpensive
Area: Downtown
Address: 1302 6th Ave
Seattle, WA 98101
Phone: (206) 332-0200

#349
Rancho Bravo Tacos
Cuisines: Mexican, Sandwiches
Average Price: Inexpensive
Area: Capitol Hill
Address: 1001 E Pine St
Seattle, WA 98122
Phone: (206) 322-9399

#350
Veggie Grill
Cuisines: American, Vegan, Vegetarian
Average Price: Modest
Area: Downtown
Address: 1427 4th Ave
Seattle, WA 98101
Phone: (206) 624-1332

Seattle Travel Guide 2016 / Shops, Restaurants, Arts, Entertainment & Nightlife

#351
The Grizzled Wizard
Cuisines: Dive Bar, Sandwiches
Average Price: Inexpensive
Area: Wallingford
Address: 2317 N 45th St
Seattle, WA 98103
Phone: (206) 849-0062

#352
Highliner Public House
Cuisines: Pub, Fish & Chips, Sandwiches
Average Price: Modest
Area: Interbay
Address: 3909 18th Ave W
Seattle, WA 98119
Phone: (206) 216-1254

#353
Coastal Kitchen
Cuisines: American,
Breakfast & Brunch, Seafood
Average Price: Modest
Area: Capitol Hill
Address: 429 15th Ave E
Seattle, WA 98112
Phone: (206) 322-1145

#354
Monster Dogs
Cuisines: Hot Dogs, Caterer, Food Stand
Average Price: Inexpensive
Area: Downtown
Address: 1st&Bell
Seattle, WA 98101
Phone: (888) 571-4447

#355
Serafina
Cuisines: Italian, Bar, Music Venues
Average Price: Expensive
Area: Eastlake
Address: 2043 Eastlake Ave E
Seattle, WA 98102
Phone: (206) 323-0807

#356
Lloydmartin
Cuisines: American, Bar
Average Price: Expensive
Area: Queen Anne
Address: 1525 Queen Anne Ave N
Seattle, WA 98109
Phone: (206) 420-7602

#357
Via Tribunali
Cuisines: Pizza, Italian
Average Price: Modest
Area: First Hill, Capitol Hill
Address: 913 E Pike St
Seattle, WA 98122
Phone: (206) 322-9234

#358
Spur Gastropub
Cuisines: American, Lounge, Gastropub
Average Price: Expensive
Area: Belltown
Address: 113 Blanchard St
Seattle, WA 98121
Phone: (206) 728-6706

#359
Patxi's Pizza
Cuisines: Pizza
Average Price: Modest
Area: Ballard
Address: 5323 Ballard Ave NW
Seattle, WA 98107
Phone: (206) 946-1512

#360
Cantinetta
Cuisines: Italian
Average Price: Expensive
Area: Wallingford
Address: 3650 Wallingford Ave
Seattle, WA 98103
Phone: (206) 632-1000

#361
Lark Restaurant
Cuisines: American, French, Tapas
Average Price: Expensive
Area: Central District
Address: 926 12th Ave
Seattle, WA 98122
Phone: (206) 323-5275

#362
Annapurna Cafe
Cuisines: Indian, Himalayan/Nepalese
Average Price: Modest
Area: Capitol Hill
Address: 1833 Broadway
Seattle, WA 98122
Phone: (206) 320-7770

#363
The Blu Grouse
Cuisines: Bar, American
Average Price: Modest
Area: Georgetown
Address: 412 S Orcas St
Seattle, WA 98108
Phone: (206) 397-4302

#364
Pinkaew Thai Cuisine
Cuisines: Thai, Vegetarian
Average Price: Modest
Area: University District
Address: 5101 25th Ave NE
Seattle, WA 98105
Phone: (206) 522-2200

Seattle Travel Guide 2016 / Shops, Restaurants, Arts, Entertainment & Nightlife

#365
Potbelly Sandwich Shop
Cuisines: Sandwiches, Fast Food
Average Price: Inexpensive
Area: Downtown
Address: 1429 4th Ave
Seattle, WA 98101
Phone: (206) 623-0099

#366
Moonlight Cafe
Cuisines: Vegetarian, Vietnamese
Average Price: Inexpensive
Area: Central District
Address: 1919 S Jackson St
Seattle, WA 98144
Phone: (206) 322-3378

#367
Le Petit Cochon
Cuisines: American, Gastropub
Average Price: Expensive
Area: Fremont
Address: 701 N 36th St
Seattle, WA 98103
Phone: (206) 829-8943

#368
Bamboo
Cuisines: Vietnamese
Average Price: Inexpensive
Area: Capitol Hill
Address: 345 15th Ave E
Seattle, WA 98112
Phone: (206) 567-3399

#369
La Rustica
Cuisines: Italian
Average Price: Expensive
Area: Alki
Address: 4100 Beach Dr SW
Seattle, WA 98116
Phone: (206) 932-3020

#370
Le Panier French Bakery
Cuisines: Bakery, French, Sandwiches
Average Price: Inexpensive
Area: Downtown
Address: 1902 Pike Pl
Seattle, WA 98101
Phone: (206) 441-3669

#371
Bing's
Cuisines: Burgers, American
Average Price: Modest
Area: Madison Park
Address: 4200 E Madison St
Seattle, WA 98112
Phone: (206) 323-8623

#372
Roro BBQ & Grill
Cuisines: Barbeque
Average Price: Modest
Area: Wallingford
Address: 3620 Stone Way N
Seattle, WA 98103
Phone: (206) 954-1100

#373
Daniel's Broiler
Cuisines: Seafood, Steakhouse
Average Price: Expensive
Area: Leschi
Address: 200 Lake Washington Blvd
Seattle, WA 98122
Phone: (206) 329-4191

#374
Kauai Family Restaurant
Cuisines: Hawaiian
Average Price: Inexpensive
Area: Georgetown
Address: 6324 6th Ave S
Seattle, WA 98108
Phone: (206) 762-3469

#375
Porkchop & Co
Cuisines: Sandwiches,
Breakfast & Brunch, Café
Average Price: Modest
Area: Ballard
Address: 5451 Leary Ave NW
Seattle, WA 98107
Phone: (206) 257-5761

#376
Hot Mama's Pizza
Cuisines: Pizza
Average Price: Inexpensive
Area: Capitol Hill
Address: 700 E Pine St
Seattle, WA 98122
Phone: (206) 322-6444

#377
Mo's Sandwiches
Cuisines: Sandwiches
Average Price: Inexpensive
Area: Phinney Ridge
Address: 6108 Phinney Ave N
Seattle, WA 98103
Phone: (206) 257-4084

#378
Barolo Ristorante
Cuisines: Italian, Wine Bar
Average Price: Expensive
Area: Denny Triangle
Address: 1940 Westlake Ave
Seattle, WA 98101
Phone: (206) 770-9000

#379
El Camión Adentro
Cuisines: Mexican
Average Price: Inexpensive
Area: Ballard
Address: 6416 15th Ave NW
Seattle, WA 98107
Phone: (206) 784-5411

#380
Kate's Pub
Cuisines: Pub, American
Average Price: Inexpensive
Area: Wallingford
Address: 309 NE 45th St
Seattle, WA 98127
Phone: (206) 547-6832

#381
Far Eats
Cuisines: Indian
Average Price: Modest
Area: Belltown
Address: 2301 5th Ave
Seattle, WA 98121
Phone: (206) 770-3287

#382
Lunchbox Laboratory
Cuisines: Burgers, American
Average Price: Modest
Area: South Lake Union
Address: 1253 Thomas St
Seattle, WA 98109
Phone: (206) 621-1090

#383
Damn The Weather
Cuisines: Bar, American
Average Price: Modest
Area: Pioneer Square
Address: 116 1st Ave S
Seattle, WA 98104
Phone: (206) 946-1283

#384
Green Leaf Vietnamese Restaurant
Cuisines: Vietnamese, Sandwiches
Average Price: Modest
Area: Belltown
Address: 2800 1st Ave
Seattle, WA 98121
Phone: (206) 448-3318

#385
Alibi Room
Cuisines: American, Lounge, Dance Club
Average Price: Modest
Area: Downtown
Address: 85 Pike St
Seattle, WA 98101
Phone: (206) 623-3180

#386
Smarty Pants
Cuisines: American, Bar
Average Price: Modest
Area: Georgetown
Address: 6017 Airport Way S
Seattle, WA 98108
Phone: (206) 762-4777

#387
El Camión
Cuisines: Mexican, Food Truck
Average Price: Inexpensive
Area: Sodo
Address: 1021 Occidental Ave
Seattle, WA 98134
Phone: (206) 659-0236

#388
Phinney Market Pub & Eatery
Cuisines: Pub, Gastropub, Wine Bar
Average Price: Modest
Area: Phinney Ridge
Address: 5918 Phinney Ave N
Seattle, WA 98103
Phone: (206) 219-9105

#389
Bakery Nouveau
Cuisines: Bakery, Café, Chocolate Shop
Average Price: Modest
Area: Junction
Address: 4737 California Ave SW
Seattle, WA 98116
Phone: (206) 923-0534

#390
Red Mill Burgers
Cuisines: Burgers
Average Price: Inexpensive
Area: Phinney Ridge
Address: 312 N 67th St
Seattle, WA 98103
Phone: (206) 783-6362

#391
Piroshki On 3rd
Cuisines: Russian, Bakery, Café
Average Price: Inexpensive
Area: Downtown
Address: 710 3rd Ave
Seattle, WA 98104
Phone: (206) 322-2820

#392
Araya's Place
Cuisines: Thai, Vegan, Vegetarian
Average Price: Modest
Area: University District
Address: 5240 University Way NE
Seattle, WA 98105
Phone: (206) 524-4332

Seattle Travel Guide 2016 / Shops, Restaurants, Arts, Entertainment & Nightlife

---

#393
Yoroshiku Ramen + Modern Izakaya
Cuisines: Tapas, Ramen
Average Price: Modest
Area: Wallingford
Address: 1913 N 45th St
Seattle, WA 98103
Phone: (206) 547-4649

#394
Beacon Ave Sandwiches
Cuisines: Sandwiches
Average Price: Inexpensive
Area: Beacon Hill
Address: 2505 B Beacon Ave S
Seattle, WA 98144
Phone: (206) 328-5115

#395
Delinomore
Cuisines: Asian Fusion, Fast Food, Deli
Average Price: Inexpensive
Area: Downtown
Address: 1118 5th Ave
Seattle, WA 98101
Phone: (206) 467-5311

#396
Wasabi Bistro Japanese Restaurant & Sushi Bar
Cuisines: Sushi Bar, Japanese
Average Price: Modest
Area: Belltown
Address: 2311 2nd Ave
Seattle, WA 98121
Phone: (206) 441-6044

#397
Cutters Crabhouse
Cuisines: Seafood, Steakhouse, American
Average Price: Modest
Area: Downtown
Address: 2001 Western Ave
Seattle, WA 98121
Phone: (206) 448-4884

#398
Nijo Sushi Bar & Grill
Cuisines: Sushi Bar, Japanese
Average Price: Modest
Area: Downtown
Address: 83 Spring St
Seattle, WA 98104
Phone: (206) 340-8880

#399
Cafe Con Leche
Cuisines: Cuban, Sandwiches
Average Price: Modest
Area: Industrial District
Address: 2901 1st Ave S
Seattle, WA 98134
Phone: (206) 682-7557

#400
@ Cafe
Cuisines: Café, Sandwiches
Average Price: Inexpensive
Area: Central District
Address: 716 Rainier Ave S
Seattle, WA 98144
Phone: (206) 328-5283

#401
Flying Squirrel Pizza Co
Cuisines: Pizza
Average Price: Modest
Area: Seward Park
Address: 4920 S Genesee St
Seattle, WA 98118
Phone: (206) 721-7620

#402
Jewel Box Café
Cuisines: Coffee, Tea, Café, Bubble Tea
Average Price: Inexpensive
Area: Mapleleaf
Address: 321 NE Thornton Pl
Seattle, WA 98125
Phone: (206) 432-9341

#403
Amazing Thai Cuisine
Cuisines: Thai
Average Price: Inexpensive
Area: University District
Address: 5210 Roosevelt Way NE
Seattle, WA 98105
Phone: (206) 528-0102

#404
Rocking Wok Taiwanese Cuisine
Cuisines: Taiwanese
Average Price: Inexpensive
Area: Wallingford
Address: 4301 Interlake Ave N
Seattle, WA 98103
Phone: (206) 545-4878

#405
L'Forno Pizza, Pita & Sweets
Cuisines: Pizza, Diner
Average Price: Inexpensive
Area: Bitter Lake
Address: 13000 Linden Ave N
Seattle, WA 98133
Phone: (206) 402-5474

#406
Pacific Inn Pub
Cuisines: Dive Bar, American
Average Price: Inexpensive
Area: Fremont
Address: 3501 Stone Way N
Seattle, WA 98103
Phone: (206) 547-2967

#407
The Tin Hat
Cuisines: Dive Bar, American
Average Price: Inexpensive
Area: Phinney Ridge
Address: 512 NW 65th St
Seattle, WA 98117
Phone: (206) 782-2770

#408
Huong Duong
Cuisines: Vietnamese
Average Price: Inexpensive
Area: Beacon Hill
Address: 7136 Martin Luther King Junior Way S Seattle, WA 98118
Phone: (206) 849-7794

#409
Ivar's Salmon House
Cuisines: Seafood, Lounge, Breakfast & Brunch
Average Price: Modest
Area: Wallingford
Address: 401 NE Northlake Way
Seattle, WA 98105
Phone: (206) 632-0767

#410
Liberty
Cuisines: Lounge, Coffee, Tea, Sushi Bar
Average Price: Modest
Area: Capitol Hill
Address: 517 15th Ave E
Seattle, WA 98112
Phone: (206) 323-9898

#411
Rub With Love Shack
Cuisines: Deli, Sandwiches
Average Price: Inexpensive
Area: Downtown
Address: 2010 Western Ave
Seattle, WA 98121
Phone: (206) 436-0390

#412
Bistro Turkuaz
Cuisines: Turkish, Mediterranean
Average Price: Modest
Area: Madrona
Address: 1114 34th Ave
Seattle, WA 98122
Phone: (206) 324-3039

#413
Nollie's Cafe
Cuisines: Bakery, Café
Average Price: Inexpensive
Area: South Lake Union
Address: 1165 Harrison St
Seattle, WA 98109
Phone: (206) 402-6724

#414
Cafe Ibex
Cuisines: Ethiopian
Average Price: Modest
Area: Mount Baker
Address: 3219 Martin Luther King Jr Way S
Seattle, WA 98144
Phone: (206) 721-7537

#415
Hallava Falafel
Cuisines: Food Truck, Falafel
Average Price: Inexpensive
Area: Georgetown
Address: 5825 Airport Way S
Seattle, WA 98108
Phone: (206) 307-4769

#416
Mr Gyros
Cuisines: Greek
Average Price: Inexpensive
Area: Ballard
Address: 5522 20th Ave NW
Seattle, WA 98107
Phone: (206) 782-7777

#417
Saint John's Bar & Eatery
Cuisines: American, Gastropub, Breakfast & Brunch
Average Price: Modest
Area: Capitol Hill
Address: 719 E Pike St
Seattle, WA 98122
Phone: (206) 245-1390

#418
Hudson
Cuisines: American, Bar, Breakfast & Brunch
Average Price: Modest
Area: Industrial District
Address: 5000 E Marginal Way S
Seattle, WA 98134
Phone: (206) 767-4777

#419
Owl'n Thistle Irish Pub
Cuisines: Irish, Irish Pub
Average Price: Modest
Area: Downtown
Address: 808 Post Ave
Seattle, WA 98104
Phone: (206) 621-7777

#420
Ada's Technical Books And Cafe
Cuisines: Bookstore, Coffee, Tea, Café
Average Price: Modest
Area: Capitol Hill
Address: 425 15th Ave E
Seattle, WA 98112
Phone: (206) 322-1058

Seattle Travel Guide 2016 / Shops, Restaurants, Arts, Entertainment & Nightlife

#421
Plaka Estiatorio
Cuisines: Greek
Average Price: Modest
Area: Ballard
Address: 5407 20th Ave NW
Seattle, WA 98107
Phone: (206) 829-8934

#422
Homegrown
Cuisines: Sandwiches, Salad
Average Price: Modest
Area: Capitol Hill
Address: 1531 Melrose Ave
Seattle, WA 98122
Phone: (206) 682-0935

#423
The Wandering Goose
Cuisines: Southern, Café, Bakery
Average Price: Modest
Area: Capitol Hill
Address: 403 15th Ave E
Seattle, WA 98112
Phone: (206) 323-9938

#424
Black Bamboo
Cuisines: Chinese, Singaporean
Average Price: Modest
Area: Belltown
Address: 2236 3rd Ave
Seattle, WA 98121
Phone: (206) 443-9898

#425
The Independent Pizzeria
Cuisines: Pizza, Italian
Average Price: Modest
Area: Madison Park
Address: 4235 E Madison St
Seattle, WA 98112
Phone: (206) 860-6110

#426
Beecher's Handmade Cheese
Cuisines: Cheese Shop, Sandwiches, Comfort Food
Average Price: Modest
Area: Downtown
Address: 1600 Pike Pl
Seattle, WA 98101
Phone: (206) 956-1964

#427
Voula's Offshore Cafe
Cuisines: Breakfast & Brunch
Average Price: Inexpensive
Area: University District
Address: 658 NE Northlake Way
Seattle, WA 98105
Phone: (206) 634-0183

#428
Saffron Grill
Cuisines: Indian, Mediterranean
Average Price: Modest
Area: Haller Lake
Address: 2132 N Northgate Way
Seattle, WA 98133
Phone: (206) 417-0707

#429
Little Uncle
Cuisines: Thai, Food Stand
Average Price: Inexpensive
Area: Central District, Capitol Hill
Address: 1509 E Madison St
Seattle, WA 98122
Phone: (206) 329-1503

#430
Aloha Ramen
Cuisines: Ramen
Average Price: Inexpensive
Area: Olympic Hills
Address: 3004 NE 127th St
Seattle, WA 98125
Phone: (206) 838-3837

#431
Delancey
Cuisines: Pizza
Average Price: Modest
Area: Phinney Ridge
Address: 1415 NW 70th St
Seattle, WA 98117
Phone: (206) 838-1960

#432
Vittles Neighborhood Bistro & Bar
Cuisines: Comfort Food
Average Price: Modest
Area: Belltown
Address: 2330 2nd Avenue
Seattle, WA 98121
Phone: (206) 448-3348

#433
Ten Sushi
Cuisines: Japanese, Sushi Bar
Average Price: Modest
Area: Lower Queen Anne
Address: 500 Mercer St
Seattle, WA 98109
Phone: (206) 453-3881

#434
Chef Liao Asian Fusion Cuisine
Cuisines: Asian Fusion, Chinese
Average Price: Inexpensive
Area: Phinney Ridge
Address: 6012 Phinney Ave N
Seattle, WA 98103
Phone: (206) 789-6441

#435
Cocoa Banana
Cuisines: Juice Bar, American
Average Price: Inexpensive
Area: Downtown, Pioneer Square
Address: 118 Cherry St
Seattle, WA 98104
Phone: (206) 903-0224

#436
West Seattle Fish House
Cuisines: Fish & Chips
Average Price: Inexpensive
Area: Fauntleroy
Address: 9005 35th Ave SW
Seattle, WA 98126
Phone: (206) 457-8643

#437
That's Amore! Italian Cafe
Cuisines: Italian, Pizza
Average Price: Modest
Area: Mount Baker
Address: 1425 31st Ave S
Seattle, WA 98144
Phone: (206) 322-3677

#438
In The Bowl Vegetarian Noodle Bistro
Cuisines: Vegetarian, Vegan, Asian Fusion
Average Price: Inexpensive
Area: Capitol Hill
Address: 1554 E Olive Way
Seattle, WA 98102
Phone: (206) 568-2343

#439
Blue Water Taco Grill
Cuisines: Mexican
Average Price: Inexpensive
Area: Lower Queen Anne
Address: 515 Queen Anne Ave N
Seattle, WA 98109
Phone: (206) 352-2407

#440
Pel'Meni Dumpling Tzar
Cuisines: Russian
Average Price: Inexpensive
Area: Fremont
Address: 3516 Fremont Pl
Seattle, WA 98103
Phone: (206) 588-2570

#441
Bookstore Bar & Café
Cuisines: Bar, American
Average Price: Modest
Area: Downtown
Address: 1007 1st Ave
Seattle, WA 98104
Phone: (206) 624-3646

#442
Alibi Room
Cuisines: Pizza, American, Lounge
Average Price: Modest
Area: Greenwood
Address: 10406 Holman Rd N
Seattle, WA 98133
Phone: (206) 783-4880

#443
Zaina Food Drinks & Friends
Cuisines: Mediterranean, Greek
Average Price: Inexpensive
Area: Downtown
Address: 109 Pine St
Seattle, WA 98101
Phone: (206) 623-1730

#444
Pair
Cuisines: American, French, Wine Bar
Average Price: Expensive
Area: Ravenna
Address: 5501 30th Ave NE
Seattle, WA 98105
Phone: (206) 526-7655

#445
Via Tribunali
Cuisines: Pizza, Italian
Average Price: Modest
Area: Lower Queen Anne
Address: 317 W Galer St
Seattle, WA 98119
Phone: (206) 264-7768

#446
Fort St. George
Cuisines: Japanese, Asian Fusion, Sushi Bar
Average Price: Inexpensive
Area: International District
Address: 601 S King St
Seattle, WA 98104
Phone: (206) 382-0662

#447
Señor Moose Café
Cuisines: Mexican
Average Price: Modest
Area: Ballard
Address: 5242 Leary Ave NW
Seattle, WA 98107
Phone: (206) 784-5568

#448
Westcity Sardine Kitchen
Cuisines: American, Italian
Average Price: Modest
Area: Admiral
Address: 3405 California Ave SW
Seattle, WA 98116
Phone: (206) 937-0155

#449
The Whisky Bar
Cuisines: Scottish, British, Pub
Average Price: Modest
Area: Belltown
Address: 2122 2nd Ave
Seattle, WA 98121
Phone: (206) 443-4490

#450
Unicorn
Cuisines: American, Lounge
Average Price: Modest
Area: Capitol Hill
Address: 1118 E Pike St
Seattle, WA 98122
Phone: (206) 325-6492

#451
Cafe Argento
Cuisines: Coffee, Tea, Sandwiches
Average Price: Inexpensive
Area: Capitol Hill
Address: 1125 E Olive St
Seattle, WA 98122
Phone: (206) 383-3295

#452
Ivar's Acres Of Clams
Cuisines: Seafood, Bar, American
Average Price: Modest
Area: Waterfront
Address: 1001 Alaskan Way
Seattle, WA 98104
Phone: (206) 624-6852

#453
Jak's Grill
Cuisines: Steakhouse, American
Average Price: Expensive
Area: Laurelhurst
Address: 3701 NE 45th St
Seattle, WA 98105
Phone: (206) 985-8545

#454
Fonda La Catrina
Cuisines: Mexican
Average Price: Modest
Area: Georgetown
Address: 5905 Airport Way S
Seattle, WA 98108
Phone: (206) 767-2787

#455
The Saint
Cuisines: Mexican, Bar
Average Price: Modest
Area: Capitol Hill
Address: 1416 E Olive Way
Seattle, WA 98122
Phone: (206) 323-9922

#456
Noodle Zone
Cuisines: Chinese, Italian, Thai
Average Price: Inexpensive
Area: Downtown
Address: 400 Pine St
Seattle, WA 98101
Phone: (206) 652-9731

#457
La Crêperie Voilà
Cuisines: Crêperie, Food Stand
Average Price: Inexpensive
Area: Downtown
Address: 707 Pike St
Seattle, WA 98101
Phone: (206) 447-2737

#458
JOEY Kitchen At University Village
Cuisines: American, Lounge
Average Price: Modest
Area: University District
Address: 2603 NE 46th St
Seattle, WA 98105
Phone: (206) 527-6188

#459
Cassis
Cuisines: French
Average Price: Modest
Area: Alki
Address: 2820 Alki Ave SW
Seattle, WA 98116
Phone: (206) 743-8531

#460
Zaina Food Drinks & Friends
Cuisines: Mediterranean
Average Price: Inexpensive
Area: Wedgwood
Address: 8000 Lake City Way NE
Seattle, WA 98115
Phone: (206) 528-3876

#461
Korean Tofu House
Cuisines: Korean
Average Price: Inexpensive
Area: University District
Address: 4142 Brooklyn Ave NE
Seattle, WA 98105
Phone: (206) 632-3119

#462
Shabu Chic
Cuisines: Japanese, Vegetarian, Hot Pot
Average Price: Modest
Area: International District
Address: 1032 S Jackson St
Seattle, WA 98104
Phone: (206) 329-0988

#463
Ray's Café
Cuisines: Seafood
Average Price: Modest
Area: Sunset Hill
Address: 6049 Seaview Ave NW
Seattle, WA 98107
Phone: (206) 782-0094

#464
The Monkey Bridge
Cuisines: Vietnamese, Sandwiches
Average Price: Inexpensive
Area: Ballard
Address: 1723 NW Market St
Seattle, WA 98107
Phone: (206) 297-6048

#465
Pho Viet Anh
Cuisines: Vietnamese
Average Price: Inexpensive
Area: Lower Queen Anne
Address: 372 Roy St
Seattle, WA 98109
Phone: (206) 352-1881

#466
Fat Ducks Deli & Bakery
Cuisines: Deli, Bakery, Sandwiches
Average Price: Inexpensive
Area: University District
Address: 5509 University Way NE
Seattle, WA 98105
Phone: (206) 257-4798

#467
Mr Lu's Burgers & Seafood
Cuisines: Seafood, Burgers
Average Price: Inexpensive
Area: University District
Address: 4752 University Way NE
Seattle, WA 98105
Phone: (206) 525-0365

#468
Saley's Classic
Cuisines: Crêperie, Sandwiches, American
Average Price: Inexpensive
Area: Denny Triangle
Address: 800 Olive Way
Seattle, WA 98101
Phone: (206) 307-4619

#469
Red Mill Totem House
Cuisines: Burgers, Fish & Chips
Average Price: Inexpensive
Area: Sunset Hill
Address: 3058 NW 54th St
Seattle, WA 98107
Phone: (206) 784-1400

#470
Curbside
Cuisines: Food Truck, Vietnamese
Average Price: Inexpensive
Area: Queen Anne
Address: 3 W Nickerson St
Seattle, WA 98119
Phone: (206) 915-2581

#471
Maekawa Bar
Cuisines: Japanese, Pub, Tapas
Average Price: Modest
Area: International District
Address: 601 S King St
Seattle, WA 98104
Phone: (206) 622-0634

#472
Veggie Grill
Cuisines: American, Vegan, Vegetarian
Average Price: Modest
Area: University District
Address: 2681 NE University Village St
Seattle, WA 98105
Phone: (206) 523-1961

#473
Shima
Cuisines: Japanese, Sushi Bar
Average Price: Modest
Area: Wallingford
Address: 4429 Wallingford Ave N
Seattle, WA 98103
Phone: (206) 632-2938

#474
Cocina Esperanza
Cuisines: Mexican
Average Price: Modest
Area: Sunset Hill
Address: 3127 NW 85th St
Seattle, WA 98117
Phone: (206) 783-7020

#475
The Dish
Cuisines: American, Breakfast & Brunch
Average Price: Modest
Area: Fremont
Address: 4358 Leary Way NW
Seattle, WA 98107
Phone: (206) 782-9985

#476
The Other Coast Cafe
Cuisines: Sandwiches, Deli
Average Price: Inexpensive
Area: First Hill, Capitol Hill
Address: 721 E Pike St
Seattle, WA 98122
Phone: (206) 257-5927

#477
La Parisienne French Bakery
Cuisines: French, Bakery, Coffee, Tea
Average Price: Inexpensive
Area: Belltown
Address: 2507 4th Ave
Seattle, WA 98121
Phone: (206) 728-5999

#478
Aladdin Gyro-Cery
Cuisines: Greek, Mediterranean, Halal
Average Price: Inexpensive
Area: University District
Address: 4139 University Way NE
Seattle, WA 98105
Phone: (206) 632-5253

#479
Phayathai Cuisine
Cuisines: Thai
Average Price: Modest
Area: Mapleleaf
Address: 8917 Lake City Way
Seattle, WA 98115
Phone: (206) 729-2295

#480
Duke's Chowder House
Cuisines: Seafood, American, Bar
Average Price: Modest
Area: South Lake Union, Eastlake
Address: 901 Fairview Ave N
Seattle, WA 98109
Phone: (206) 382-9963

#481
Pete's Egg Nest
Cuisines: Breakfast & Brunch
Average Price: Inexpensive
Area: Greenwood, Phinney Ridge
Address: 7717 Greenwood Ave N
Seattle, WA 98103
Phone: (206) 784-5348

#482
Norm's Eatery & Ale House
Cuisines: American, Pub
Average Price: Modest
Area: Fremont
Address: 460 N 36th St
Seattle, WA 98103
Phone: (206) 547-1417

#483
Oddfellows Cafe & Bar
Cuisines: Bar, American, Café
Average Price: Modest
Area: Capitol Hill
Address: 1525 10th Ave
Seattle, WA 98122
Phone: (206) 325-0807

#484
Yard House
Cuisines: American
Average Price: Modest
Area: Downtown
Address: 1501 4th Avenue
Seattle, WA 98101
Phone: (206) 682-2087

#485
Gourmet Dog Japon
Cuisines: Food Stand, Hot Dogs, Japanese
Average Price: Inexpensive
Area: Downtown
Address: 97 Pike St
Seattle, WA 98101
Phone: (425) 503-9017

#486
Voila! Bistrot
Cuisines: French
Average Price: Modest
Area: Madison Valley, Capitol Hill
Address: 2805 E Madison St
Seattle, WA 98112
Phone: (206) 322-5460

#487
Baja Bistro
Cuisines: Mexican, Coffee, Tea, Breakfast & Brunch
Average Price: Inexpensive
Area: Beacon Hill
Address: 2414 Beacon Ave S
Seattle, WA 98144
Phone: (206) 323-0953

#488
Skillet Diner - Ballard
Cuisines: American, Diner
Average Price: Modest
Area: Ballard
Address: 2034 NW 56th St
Seattle, WA 98107
Phone: (206) 922-7981

#489
Steelhead Diner
Cuisines: Diner, Seafood
Average Price: Modest
Area: Downtown
Address: 95 Pine St
Seattle, WA 98101
Phone: (206) 625-0129

#490
Pomodoro Ristorante Italiano
Cuisines: Italian, Spanish, Basque
Average Price: Modest
Area: Eastlake
Address: 2366 Eastlake Ave E
Seattle, WA 98102
Phone: (206) 324-3160

#491
Palomino
Cuisines: American, Mediterranean
Average Price: Modest
Area: Downtown
Address: 1420 5th Ave
Seattle, WA 98101
Phone: (206) 623-1300

#492
Noodle Nation
Cuisines: Thai
Average Price: Inexpensive
Area: University District
Address: 4232 University Way NE
Seattle, WA 98105
Phone: (206) 632-5833

#493
Rendezvous
Cuisines: Bar, Performing Arts, American
Average Price: Modest
Area: Belltown
Address: 2322 2nd Ave
Seattle, WA 98121
Phone: (206) 441-5823

#494
Shuckers
Cuisines: American, Seafood, Live/Raw Food
Average Price: Expensive
Area: Downtown
Address: 411 University St
Seattle, WA 98101
Phone: (206) 621-1984

#495
Magic Dragon
Cuisines: Chinese, Fast Food
Average Price: Inexpensive
Area: Interbay
Address: 1827 15th Ave W
Seattle, WA 98119
Phone: (206) 284-7470

#496
418 Public House
Cuisines: Pub, Mexican
Average Price: Inexpensive
Area: Ballard, Phinney Ridge
Address: 418 NW 65th St
Seattle, WA 98117
Phone: (206) 783-0418

#497
Jade Garden
Cuisines: Dim Sum, Seafood, Cantonese
Average Price: Modest
Area: International District
Address: 424 7th Ave S
Seattle, WA 98104
Phone: (206) 622-8181

#498
Maximilien
Cuisines: French
Average Price: Modest
Area: Downtown
Address: 81A Pike St
Seattle, WA 98101
Phone: (206) 682-7270

#499
La Bodega
Cuisines: Dominican, Sandwiches
Average Price: Modest
Area: Pioneer Square
Address: 100 Prefontaine Pl S
Seattle, WA 98104
Phone: (206) 682-2175

#500
Tutta Bella Neapolitan Pizzeria
Cuisines: Italian, Pizza
Average Price: Modest
Area: Fremont
Address: 4411 Stone Way N
Seattle, WA 98103
Phone: (206) 633-3800

TOP 500
ARTS & ENTERTAINMENT
The Most Recommended by Locals & Trevelers
(From #1 to #500)

Seattle Travel Guide 2016 / Shops, Restaurants, Arts, Entertainment & Nightlife

#1
Chihuly Garden And Glass
Category: Art Gallery, Museum
Average Price: Modest
Area: Lower Queen Anne
Address: 305 Harrison St
Seattle, WA 98109
Phone: (206) 753-4940

#2
Puzzle Break
Category: Arcade
Area: First Hill, Capitol Hill
Address: 1423 10th Ave
Seattle, WA 98122
Phone: (716) 795-2759

#3
Seattle Pinball Museum
Category: Arcade, Museum
Area: International District
Address: 508 Maynard Ave S
Seattle, WA 98104
Phone: (206) 623-0759

#4
Klondike Gold Rush National Historical Park
Category: Museum
Area: Pioneer Square
Address: 319 2nd Ave S
Seattle, WA 98104
Phone: (206) 220-4240

#5
Seattle Cinerama Theater
Category: Cinema
Area: Belltown
Address: 2100 4th Ave
Seattle, WA 98121
Phone: (206) 448-6680

#6
Emerald City Trapeze Arts
Category: Performing Arts, Venues, Event Space
Area: Industrial District
Address: 2702 6th Ave S
Seattle, WA 98134
Phone: (206) 906-9442

#7
Frye Art Museum
Category: Museum, Art Gallery
Average Price: Inexpensive
Area: First Hill
Address: 704 Terry Ave
Seattle, WA 98104
Phone: (206) 622-9250

#8
Seattle Glassblowing Studio & Gallery
Category: Art Gallery,
Average Price: Expensive
Area: Belltown
Address: 2227 5th Ave
Seattle, WA 98121
Phone: (206) 448-2181

#9
John John's Game Room
Category: Arcade
Area: Capitol Hill
Address: 1351 E Olive Way
Seattle, WA 98122
Phone: (206) 696-1613

#10
Paramount Theatre
Category: Performing Arts, Music Venues
Average Price: Expensive
Area: Downtown
Address: 911 Pine St
Seattle, WA 98101
Phone: (206) 682-1414

#11
Shorty's
Category: Dive Bar, Arcade
Average Price: Inexpensive
Area: Belltown
Address: 2222 2nd Ave
Seattle, WA 98121
Phone: (206) 441-5449

#12
EMP Museum
Category: Museum
Area: Lower Queen Anne
Address: 325 5th Ave N
Seattle, WA 98109
Phone: (206) 770-2700

#13
Kubota Garden
Category: Park, Botanical Garden
Area: Rainier Beach
Address: 9817 55th Ave S
Seattle, WA 98118
Phone: (206) 725-4400

#14
Full Tilt Ice Cream
Category: Ice Cream, Arcade
Average Price: Inexpensive
Area: Columbia City
Address: 5041 Rainier Ave S
Seattle, WA 98118
Phone: (206) 226-2740

#15
The Showbox
Category: Music Venues, Bar
Average Price: Modest
Area: Downtown
Address: 1426 1st Ave
Seattle, WA 98101
Phone: (206) 628-3151

#16
Ancient Grounds
Category: Coffee, Tea, Art Gallery
Average Price: Inexpensive
Area: Downtown
Address: 1220 1st Ave
Seattle, WA 98101
Phone: (206) 749-0747

#17
Pacific Science Center
Category: Cinema, Museum, Venues, Event Space
Area: Lower Queen Anne
Address: 200 2nd Ave N
Seattle, WA 98109
Phone: (206) 443-2001

#18
Volunteer Park Conservatory
Category: Park, Botanical Garden
Area: Capitol Hill
Address: 1400 E Galer St
Seattle, WA 98112
Phone: (206) 684-4743

#19
Add-A-Ball
Category: Arcade, Bar
Average Price: Inexpensive
Area: Fremont
Address: 315 N 36th St
Seattle, WA 98103
Phone: (206) 696-1613

#20
Jet City Improv
Category: Performing Arts, Comedy Club, Venues, Event Space
Average Price: Inexpensive
Area: University District
Address: 5510 University Way NE
Seattle, WA 98105
Phone: (206) 352-8291

#21
Big Picture
Category: Cinema, Lounge, Venues, Event Space
Average Price: Modest
Area: Belltown
Address: 2505 1st Ave
Seattle, WA 98121
Phone: (206) 256-0566

#22
The Tasting Room
Category: Winery, Wine Bar
Average Price: Modest
Area: Downtown
Address: 1924 Post Alley
Seattle, WA 98101
Phone: (206) 770-9463

#23
Olympic Sculpture Park
Category: Museum, Park
Area: Belltown
Address: 2901 Western Ave
Seattle, WA 98121
Phone: (206) 654-3100

#24
The Grand Illusion Cinema
Category: Cinema
Area: University District
Address: 1403 NE 50th St
Seattle, WA 98105
Phone: (206) 523-3935

#25
Bill & Melinda Gates Foundation Visitor Center
Category: Museum
Area: Lower Queen Anne
Address: 440 5th Ave N
Seattle, WA 98109
Phone: (206) 709-3100

#26
The Triple Door
Category: Asian Fusion, Music Venues
Average Price: Expensive
Area: Downtown
Address: 216 Union St
Seattle, WA 98101
Phone: (206) 838-4333

#27
The 5th Avenue Theatre
Category: Performing Arts, Cinema
Area: Downtown
Address: 1308 5th Ave
Seattle, WA 98101
Phone: (206) 625-1418

#28
Nordic Heritage Museum
Category: Museum, Cultural Center
Area: Sunset Hill
Address: 3014 NW 67th St
Seattle, WA 98117
Phone: (206) 789-5707

Seattle Travel Guide 2016 / Shops, Restaurants, Arts, Entertainment & Nightlife

#29
Boeing IMAX Theater
Category: Cinema
Area: Lower Queen Anne
Address: 200 2nd Ave N
Seattle, WA 98109
Phone: (206) 443-2001

#30
Gargoyles Statuary
Category: Home Decor, Art Gallery
Average Price: Modest
Area: University District
Address: 4550 University Way NE
Seattle, WA 98105
Phone: (206) 632-4940

#31
The Harvard Exit Theatre
Category: Cinema
Area: Capitol Hill
Address: 807 E Roy St
Seattle, WA 98102
Phone: (206) 323-0587

#32
Can Can
Category: Cabaret, Lounge
Average Price: Modest
Area: Downtown
Address: 94 Pike St
Seattle, WA 98101
Phone: (206) 652-0832

#33
Seattle Center
Category: Amusement Park, Park, Stadium/Arena
Area: Lower Queen Anne
Address: 305 Harrison St
Seattle, WA 98109
Phone: (206) 684-7200

#34
Unexpected Productions
Category: Performing Arts, Lounge, Comedy Club
Average Price: Inexpensive
Area: Queen Anne
Address: 1428 Post Alley
Seattle, WA 98101
Phone: (206) 587-2414

#35
The Center For Wooden Boats
Category: Boating, Museum
Area: South Lake Union, Eastlake
Address: 1010 Valley St
Seattle, WA 98109
Phone: (206) 382-2628

#36
Museum Of History & Industry
Category: Museum
Area: South Lake Union
Address: 860 Terry Ave N
Seattle, WA 98109
Phone: (206) 324-1126

#37
Vermillion
Category: Art Gallery, Bar
Average Price: Inexpensive
Area: Capitol Hill
Address: 1508 11th Ave
Seattle, WA 98122
Phone: (206) 709-9797

#38
Rose Garden At Woodland Park Zoo
Category: Park, Botanical Garden
Area: Phinney Ridge
Address: 750 N 50th St
Seattle, WA 98103
Phone: (206) 233-7272

#39
Seattle Art Museum
Category: Museum
Area: Downtown
Address: 1300 1st Ave
Seattle, WA 98101
Phone: (206) 654-3100

#40
The Comedy Underground
Category: Comedy Club, Performing Arts
Average Price: Modest
Area: Pioneer Square
Address: 109 S Washington St
Seattle, WA 98104
Phone: (206) 628-0303

#41
The Laser Dome At Pacific Science Center
Category: Music Venues, Event Space
Average Price: Inexpensive
Area: Lower Queen Anne
Address: 200 2nd Ave N
Seattle, WA 98109
Phone: (206) 443-2850

#42
Full Tilt Ice Cream
Category: Arcade, Ice Cream
Average Price: Inexpensive
Area: Ballard
Address: 5453 Leary Ave NW
Seattle, WA 98107
Phone: (206) 297-3000

#43
Ark Lodge Cinemas
Category: Cinema, Venues, Event Space
Area: Columbia City
Address: 4816 Rainier Ave S
Seattle, WA 98118
Phone: (206) 721-3156

#44
Seattle Japanese Garden
Category: Botanical Garden
Area: Capitol Hill
Address: 1075 Lake Washington Blvd E
Seattle, WA 98112
Phone: (206) 684-4725

#45
Circus Contraption
Category: Performing Arts
Area: Fremont
Address: 3400 Phinney Ave N
Seattle, WA 98103
Phone: (206) 442-2004

#46
Tractor Tavern
Category: Music Venues
Average Price: Inexpensive
Area: Ballard
Address: 5213 Ballard Ave NW
Seattle, WA 98107
Phone: (206) 789-3599

#47
The Crocodile
Category: Music Venues, Bar
Average Price: Modest
Area: Belltown
Address: 2200 2nd Ave
Seattle, WA 98121
Phone: (206) 441-5611

#48
Dimitriou's Jazz Alley
Category: Jazz, Blues, Music Venues
Average Price: Expensive
Area: Denny Triangle
Address: 2033 6th Ave
Seattle, WA 98121
Phone: (206) 441-9729

#49
Fremont Wine
Category: Winery, Wine Bar
Average Price: Modest
Area: Fremont
Address: 3601 Fremont Ave N
Seattle, WA 98103
Phone: (206) 632-1110

#50
Full Tilt Ice Cream
Category: Arcade, Ice Cream
Average Price: Inexpensive
Area: White Center
Address: 9629 16th Ave SW
Seattle, WA 98106
Phone: (206) 767-4811

#51
Old Seattle Paperworks
Category: Antiques, Home Decor, Art Gallery
Average Price: Modest
Area: Downtown
Address: 1514 Pike Place
Seattle, WA 98101
Phone: (206) 623-2870

#52
Fantagraphics Books
Category: Art Gallery, Comic Books
Average Price: Modest
Area: Georgetown
Address: 1201 S Vale St
Seattle, WA 98108
Phone: (206) 658-0110

#53
Zen Dog Studio & Tea House Gallery
Category: Art Gallery, Tea Room
Average Price: Expensive
Area: Loyal Heights
Address: 2015 N W 85th St
Seattle, WA 98117
Phone: (206) 784-8289

#54
Central Cinema
Category: Cinema, Venues, Event Space, Pizza
Average Price: Modest
Area: Central District
Address: 1411 21st Ave
Seattle, WA 98122
Phone: (206) 686-6684

#55
Comedysportz
Category: Comedy Club, Performing Arts
Average Price: Inexpensive
Area: Fremont
Address: 3509 Fremont Ave N
Seattle, WA 98103
Phone: (425) 954-5618

#56
Le Faux
Category: Performing Arts, Gay Bar
Average Price: Modest
Area: Capitol Hill
Address: 300 Broadway E
Seattle, WA 98122
Phone: (206) 334-0513

#57
Makerhaus
Category: Cultural Center, Education
Area: Fremont
Address: 122 NW 36th St
Seattle, WA 98107
Phone: (206) 457-8968

#58
Seattle Official Bad Art Museum Of Art
Category: Art Gallery
Average Price: Inexpensive
Area: University District
Address: 5828 Roosevelt Way NE
Seattle, WA 98105
Phone: (206) 523-5282

#59
Taproot Theatre Company
Category: Performing Arts
Area: Greenwood
Address: 204 N 85th St
Seattle, WA 98103
Phone: (206) 781-9707

#60
Keys On Main
Category: Bar, Music Venues
Average Price: Modest
Area: Lower Queen Anne
Address: 11 Roy St
Seattle, WA 98109
Phone: (206) 270-4444

#61
SIFF Cinema Uptown
Category: Cinema
Area: Lower Queen Anne
Address: 511 Queen Anne Ave N
Seattle, WA 98109
Phone: (206) 324-9996

#62
Living Computer Museum
Category: Museum
Area: Industrial District
Address: 2245 First Ave S
Seattle, WA 98134
Phone: (206) 342-2020

#63
Neptune Theatre
Category: Cinema, Music Venues, Performing Arts
Average Price: Modest
Area: University District
Address: 1303 NE 45th St
Seattle, WA 98105
Phone: (206) 682-1414

#64
Seamonster Lounge
Category: Jazz, Blues, Lounge, Music Venues
Average Price: Inexpensive
Area: Wallingford
Address: 2202 N 45th St
Seattle, WA 98103
Phone: (206) 992-1120

#65
ACT - A Contemporary Theatre
Category: Performing Arts, Cabaret
Area: Downtown
Address: 700 Union St
Seattle, WA 98101
Phone: (206) 292-7676

#66
Regal Cinemas - Thornton Place Stadium 14 & IMAX
Category: Cinema
Area: Mapleleaf
Address: 301 NE 103rd St
Seattle, WA 98125
Phone: (206) 517-9953

#67
Medina Hookah Lounge
Category: Hookah Bar, Music Venues
Average Price: Inexpensive
Area: International District
Address: 700 S Dearborn St
Seattle, WA 98134
Phone: (206) 856-7660

#68
Artswest
Category: Art Gallery, Performing Arts
Average Price: Modest
Area: Fairmount Park, Junction
Address: 4711 California Ave SW
Seattle, WA 98116
Phone: (206) 938-0339

#69
Northwest Puppet Center
Category: Performing Arts
Area: Mapleleaf
Address: 9123 15th Ave NE
Seattle, WA 98115
Phone: (206) 523-2579

#70
Nectar Lounge
Category: Bar, Music Venues, Event Space
Average Price: Modest
Area: Fremont
Address: 412 N 36th St
Seattle, WA 98103
Phone: (206) 632-2020

#71
Blowing Sands Glass Blowing
Category: Art Gallery
Average Price: Modest
Area: Ballard
Address: 5805 14th Ave NW
Seattle, WA 98107
Phone: (206) 783-5314

#72
The Raygun Lounge
Category: Arcade, Lounge
Average Price: Inexpensive
Area: Capitol Hill
Address: 501 E Pine St
Seattle, WA 98122
Phone: (206) 812-2521

#73
Gameworks
Category: Arcade, American
Average Price: Modest
Area: Downtown
Address: 1511 7th Ave
Seattle, WA 98127
Phone: (206) 521-0952

#74
On The Boards
Category: Performing Arts
Area: Lower Queen Anne
Address: 100 W Roy St
Seattle, WA 98119
Phone: (206) 217-9886

#75
Seafair
Category: Festival
Area: Denny Triangle
Address: 2200 6th Ave
Seattle, WA 98121
Phone: (206) 728-2281

#76
Seattle International Beerfest
Category: Festival
Area: Lower Queen Anne
Address: 305 Harrison St
Seattle, WA 98109
Phone: (206) 979-3830

#77
Comedy Womb
Category: Performing Arts
Area: Belltown
Address: 2322 2nd Ave
Seattle, WA 98121
Phone: (206) 441-5823

#78
Greenstage
Category: Performing Arts
Area: Sand Point
Address: 7400 Sandpoint Way
Seattle, WA 98115
Phone: (206) 748-1551

#79
Tamara The Trapeze Lady Presents The Columbia City Cabaret
Category: Performing Arts, Cabaret
Area: Columbia City
Address: 4916 Rainier Ave S
Seattle, WA 98118
Phone: (206) 605-9920

#80
Seattle Public Theatre At The Bathhouse
Category: Performing Arts
Area: Greenlake
Address: 7312 W Green Lake Dr N
Seattle, WA 98103
Phone: (206) 524-1300

#81
The Moore Theatre
Category: Performing Arts, Music Venues
Average Price: Modest
Area: Belltown
Address: 1932 2nd Ave
Seattle, WA 98101
Phone: (206) 467-5510

#82
Rainier Glass Studio
Category: Art Gallery, Art Classes
Average Price: Modest
Area: Industrial District
Address: 3200 Airport WY S
Seattle, WA 98134
Phone: (206) 557-7883

#83
The Burke Museum
Category: Museum
Area: University District
Address: 17th Ave NE & NE 45th St
Seattle, WA 98105
Phone: (206) 543-5590

#84
Northwest Film Forum
Category: Cinema
Area: Capitol Hill
Address: 1515 12th Ave
Seattle, WA 98122
Phone: (206) 329-2629

#85
The Central Saloon
Category: Bar, Music Venues, American
Average Price: Inexpensive
Area: Pioneer Square
Address: 207 1st Ave S
Seattle, WA 98127
Phone: (206) 622-0209

#86
Wing-It Productions
Category: Performing Arts
Area: University District
Address: 5510 University Way NE
Seattle, WA 98105
Phone: (206) 352-8291

#87
Westlake Dance Center
Category: Performing Arts
Area: Northgate
Address: 10703 8th Ave NE
Seattle, WA 98125
Phone: (206) 621-7378

#88
Far4
Category: Home Decor, Art Gallery, Interior Design
Average Price: Expensive
Area: Downtown
Address: 1020 1st Ave
Seattle, WA 98104
Phone: (206) 621-8831

#89
Showbox Sodo
Category: Music Venues, Burgers, Pizza
Average Price: Modest
Area: Industrial District
Address: 1700 1st Ave S
Seattle, WA 98104
Phone: (206) 652-0444

#90
Ace Of Illusions
Category: Performing Arts, Magicians
Area: Downtown
Address: 701 5th Ave
Seattle, WA 98104
Phone: (206) 695-2194

#91
The Royal Room
Category: Music Venues, Lounge
Average Price: Modest
Area: Columbia City
Address: 5000 Rainier Ave S
Seattle, WA 98118
Phone: (206) 906-9920

#92
Varsity Theatre
Category: Cinema
Area: University District
Address: 4329 University Way NE
Seattle, WA 98105
Phone: (206) 781-5755

#93
Miss Indigo Blue's Academy Of Burlesque
Category: Dance School, Performing Arts
Area: Capitol Hill
Address: 915 E Pine St, 2nd Fl
Seattle, WA 98122
Phone: (206) 478-9475

#94
Monster Art And Clothing
Category: Art Gallery, Women's Clothing
Average Price: Modest
Area: Ballard
Address: 5000 20th Ave NW
Seattle, WA 98107
Phone: (206) 789-0037

#95
The Fremont Fair
Category: Festival
Area: Fremont
Address: N 35th St
Seattle, WA 98103
Phone: (206) 633-0422

#96
The Curious Nest
Category: Antiques, Jewelry, Art Gallery
Average Price: Expensive
Area: Ravenna
Address: 2916 NE 55th St
Seattle, WA 98105
Phone: (206) 729-6378

#97
Northwest African American Museum
Category: Museum
Area: Atlantic
Address: 2300 S Massachusetts St
Seattle, WA 98144
Phone: (206) 518-6000

#98
Tula's
Category: Jazz, Blues, Greek, Mediterranean
Average Price: Modest
Area: Belltown
Address: 2214 2nd Ave
Seattle, WA 98121
Phone: (206) 443-4221

#99
Teatro Zinzanni
Category: Performing Arts, American
Average Price: Exclusive
Area: Lower Queen Anne
Address: 222 Mercer St
Seattle, WA 98109
Phone: (206) 802-0015

#100
Columbia City Theater
Category: Performing Arts, Music Venues, Karaoke
Average Price: Modest
Area: Columbia City
Address: 4916 Rainier Ave S
Seattle, WA 98118
Phone: (206) 722-3009

#101
Guild 45th Theatre
Category: Cinema
Area: Wallingford
Address: 2115 N 45th St
Seattle, WA 98103
Phone: (206) 547-2127

#102
Serafina
Category: Italian, Bar, Music Venues
Average Price: Expensive
Area: Eastlake
Address: 2043 Eastlake Ave E
Seattle, WA 98102
Phone: (206) 323-0807

#103
Seattle International Film Festival
Category: Festival, Cinema
Area: Lower Queen Anne
Address: 305 Harrison St
Seattle, WA 98109
Phone: (206) 382-2434

#104
Theatre Off Jackson
Category: Performing Arts
Area: International District
Address: 409 7th Ave S
Seattle, WA 98104
Phone: (206) 340-1049

#105
University District Street Fair
Category: Festival
Area: University District
Address: 4710 University Way N.E.
Seattle, WA 98105
Phone: (206) 632-9084

#106
Admiral Theatres
Category: Cinema
Area: Admiral
Address: 2343 California Ave SW
Seattle, WA 98116
Phone: (206) 938-0360

#107
Great Pumpkin Beer Festival
Category: Festival
Area: Industrial District
Address: 5510 Airport Way S
Seattle, WA 98108
Phone: (206) 860-3977

#108
Virginia V Foundation
Category: Boat Charter, Venues, Event Space, Museum, Music Venues
Average Price: Modest
Area: South Lake Union, Westlake
Address: 860 Terry Ave N
Seattle, WA 98109
Phone: (206) 624-9119

#109
Roq La Rue Gallery
Category: Art Gallery
Average Price: Exclusive
Area: Sodo
Address: 532 1st Ave S
Seattle, WA 98104
Phone: (206) 374-8977

#110
Center For Urban Horticulture
Category: Botanical Garden
Area: University District
Address: 3501 NE 41st St
Seattle, WA 98105
Phone: (206) 543-8616

#111
Ballard Seafoodfest
Category: Local Flavor, Festival
Area: Ballard
Address: 2208 NW Market St
Seattle, WA 98107
Phone: (206) 784-9705

#112
Seven Gables Theatre
Category: Cinema
Area: University District
Address: 911 NE 50th St
Seattle, WA 98105
Phone: (206) 781-5755

Seattle Travel Guide 2016 / Shops, Restaurants, Arts, Entertainment & Nightlife

#113
Glasshouse Studio
Category: Art Gallery
Area: Pioneer Square
Address: 311 Occidental Avenue South
Seattle, WA 98104
Phone: (206) 682-9939

#114
Youngstown Cultural Arts Center
Category: Arts, Entertainment,
Venues, Event Space
Area: Cottage Grove
Address: 4408 Delridge Way SW
Seattle, WA 98106
Phone: (206) 935-2999

#115
Fremont Outdoor Movies
Category: Cinema
Area: Fremont
Address: N 35th And Phinney Ave
Seattle, WA 98103
Phone: (206) 781-4230

#116
Foundation Nightclub
Category: Dance Club, Music Venues
Average Price: Modest
Area: Belltown
Address: 2218 Western Ave
Seattle, WA 98121
Phone: (206) 535-7285

#117
Dragon Fest
Category: Festival
Area: International District
Address: Chinatown-International District
Seattle, WA 98104
Phone: (206) 382-1197

#118
Voracious Tasting & Food Awards
Category: Festival
Area: Downtown
Address: Paramount Theatre
Seattle, WA
Phone: (206) 467-4500

#119
Columbia City Beatwalk
Category: Music Venues
Average Price: Inexpensive
Area: Columbia City
Address: 4914 Rainier Ave S
Seattle, WA 98118
Phone: (206) 963-8599

#120
The Josephine
Category: Music Venues
Average Price: Inexpensive
Area: Phinney Ridge
Address: 608 NW 65th St
Seattle, WA 98117
Phone: (206) 543-0065

#121
The Fireside Room
Category: Lounge, Tea Room, Music Venues
Average Price: Modest
Area: First Hill
Address: 900 Madison St
Seattle, WA 98104
Phone: (206) 622-6400

#122
AMC Loews Oak Tree 6
Category: Cinema
Area: Licton Springs
Address: 10006 Aurora Ave N
Seattle, WA 98133
Phone: (206) 527-3117

#123
Bon Odori Festival
Category: Festival
Area: Central District
Address: 1427 S Main St
Seattle, WA 98144
Phone: (206) 329-0800

#124
Pacific Galleries,
Antique Mall & Auction House.
Category: Antiques,
Shopping Center, Art Gallery
Average Price: Expensive
Area: Industrial District
Address: 241 S Lander St
Seattle, WA 98134
Phone: (206) 292-3999

#125
Annex Theatre
Category: Performing Arts
Area: Capitol Hill
Address: 1100 E Pike St
Seattle, WA 98122
Phone: (206) 728-0933

#126
Highway 99 Blues Club
Category: Jazz, Blues, Music Venues
Average Price: Modest
Area: Downtown
Address: 1414 Alaskan Way
Seattle, WA 98101
Phone: (206) 382-2171

#127
Wing Luke Museum Of The Asian Pacific American Experience
Category: Museum
Area: International District
Address: 719 S King St
Seattle, WA 98104
Phone: (206) 623-5124

#128
Henry Art Gallery
Category: Art Gallery, Museum
Average Price: Inexpensive
Area: University District
Address: 15th Ave NE & NE 41st St
Seattle, WA 98195
Phone: (206) 543-2280

#129
Spectrum Dance Theater
Category: Performing Arts, Dance School
Area: Madrona
Address: 800 Lake Washington Blvd
Seattle, WA 98122
Phone: (206) 325-4161

#130
Medicinal Herb Garden
Category: Botanical Garden
Area: University District
Address: Stevens Way
Seattle, WA 98105
Phone: (206) 543-0436

#131
Aladdin Hookah Lounge
Category: Hookah Bar, Music Venues
Average Price: Modest
Area: South Lake Union
Address: 1314 Denny Way
Seattle, WA 98109
Phone: (206) 261-7592

#132
Volume
Category: Bar, Dance Club, Music Venues
Average Price: Modest
Area: Pioneer Square
Address: 172 S Washington St
Seattle, WA 98104
Phone: (206) 486-0805

#133
Careening Cat Dance
Category: Performing Arts, Dance School
Area: Capitol Hill
Address: 1014 E John St
Seattle, WA 98102
Phone: (206) 419-0055

#134
Frida: Fineries & Frocks
Category: Art Gallery, Fashion
Average Price: Modest
Area: Georgetown
Address: 5905 Airport Way S
Seattle, WA 98108
Phone: (206) 767-0331

#135
The Museum Of Communications
Category: Local Flavor, Museum
Area: Georgetown
Address: 7000 E Marginal Way S
Seattle, WA 98144
Phone: (206) 767-3012

#136
Bumbershoot: Seattle's Music & Arts Festival
Category: Festival
Area: Lower Queen Anne
Address: 305 Harrison St
Seattle, WA 98109
Phone: (206) 281-7788

#137
Dennis Moss
Category: Jazz, Blues, Performing Arts
Area: Greenwood, Phinney Ridge
Address: 634 NW 80th St
Seattle, WA 98117
Phone: (206) 349-0758

#138
619 Western
Category: Art Gallery
Area: Downtown, Pioneer Square
Address: 619 Western Ave
Seattle, WA 98104
Phone: (206) 447-9667

#139
Eastlake P-Patch Community Gardens
Category: Botanical Garden
Area: Eastlake
Address: 2900 Fairview Ave E
Seattle, WA 98102
Phone: (206) 684-0264

#140
The Ballard Underground
Category: Performing Arts
Area: Ballard
Address: 2220 NW Market St
Seattle, WA 98107
Phone: (206) 395-5458

#141
Mimosas With Mama
Category: Cabaret, Performing Arts
Area: Capitol Hill
Address: 1118 E Pike St
Seattle, WA 98122
Phone: (206) 437-2532

#142
Stretch And Staple
Category: Art Gallery
Area: Greenwood, Phinney Ridge
Address: 8005 Greenwood Ave N
Seattle, WA 98133
Phone: (206) 607-9277

#143
Erickson Theater Off Broadway
Category: Performing Arts, Cinema
Area: Capitol Hill
Address: 1524 Harvard Ave
Seattle, WA 98122
Phone: (206) 329-1050

#144
Rendezvous
Category: Bar, Performing Arts, American
Average Price: Modest
Area: Belltown
Address: 2322 2nd Ave
Seattle, WA 98121
Phone: (206) 441-5823

#145
AMC Pacific Place 11
Category: Cinema
Area: Downtown
Address: 600 Pine S
Seattle, WA 98101
Phone: (206) 652-8908

#146
Nena
Category: Art Gallery, Gift Shop
Average Price: Modest
Area: Madrona
Address: 1105 34th Ave
Seattle, WA 98122
Phone: (206) 860-4282

#147
The Vera Project
Category: Music Venues,
Average Price: Inexpensive
Area: Lower Queen Anne
Address: 305 Harrison St
Seattle, WA 98109
Phone: (206) 956-8372

#148
Stir
Category: Art Gallery
Average Price: Modest
Area: Pioneer Square
Address: 216 Alaskan Way S
Seattle, WA 98104
Phone: (206) 264-0200

#149
Bartholomew Winery
Category: Winery
Average Price: Modest
Area: Industrial District
Address: 3100 Airport Way S
Seattle, WA 98134
Phone: (206) 755-5296

#150
Vetri Glass
Category: Art Gallery
Average Price: Exclusive
Area: Downtown
Address: 1404 1st Ave
Seattle, WA 98101
Phone: (206) 667-9608

#151
Versatile Arts
Category: Fitness & Instruction, Performing Arts
Area: Greenwood, Phinney Ridge
Address: 7601 Greenwood Ave N
Seattle, WA 98103
Phone: (866) 887-5256

#152
Barboza
Category: Music Venues, Event Space
Average Price: Inexpensive
Area: First Hill, Capitol Hill
Address: 925 E Pike St
Seattle, WA 98122
Phone: (206) 709-9442

#153
Intiman Theatre
Category: Performing Arts
Area: Lower Queen Anne
Address: 201 Mercer St
Seattle, WA 98109
Phone: (206) 441-7178

#154
Sundance Cinemas
Category: Cinema
Area: University District
Address: 4500 9th Ave NE
Seattle, WA 98105
Phone: (206) 633-0059

#155
Moe Bar
Category: Bar, Music Venues
Average Price: Inexpensive
Area: First Hill, Capitol Hill
Address: 1425 10th Ave
Seattle, WA 98122
Phone: (206) 709-9951

#156
Skylark Café & Club
Category: Music Venues, American, Bar
Average Price: Modest
Area: Youngstown
Address: 3803 Delridge Way SW
Seattle, WA 98106
Phone: (206) 935-2111

#157
Kremwerk
Category: Dance Club,
Music Venues, Cocktail Bar
Average Price: Modest
Area: Denny Triangle
Address: 1809 Minor Ave
Seattle, WA 98101
Phone: (206) 682-2935

#158
**School Of Acrobatics
And New Circus Arts**
Category: Performing Arts
Area: Georgetown
Address: 674 S Orcas St
Seattle, WA 98108
Phone: (206) 652-4433

#159
Friesen Gallery Of Fine Art
Category: Art Gallery
Area: Downtown
Address: 1200 2nd Ave
Seattle, WA 98101
Phone: (208) 726-4174

#160
Flip Flip, Ding Ding
Category: Arcade
Area: Georgetown
Address: 6012 12th Ave S
Seattle, WA 98108
Phone: (206) 297-8330

#161
Live Girls! Theater
Category: Performing Arts
Area: Ballard
Address: 2220 NW Market
Seattle, WA 98107
Phone: (206) 783-1698

#162
Eight Bells Winery
Category: Winery
Average Price: Modest
Area: Roosevelt
Address: 6213 Roosevelt Way NE
Seattle, WA 98115
Phone: (206) 947-9692

#163
Seattle Asian Art Museum
Category: Museum, Venues,
Event Space, Art Gallery
Average Price: Inexpensive
Area: Capitol Hill
Address: 1400 E Prospect St
Seattle, WA 98112
Phone: (206) 654-3100

#164
Northwest Woodworkers Gallery
Category: Furniture Store, Art Gallery
Average Price: Exclusive
Area: Belltown
Address: 2111 1st Ave
Seattle, WA 98121
Phone: (206) 625-0542

#165
Crackerjack Contemporary Crafts
Category: Jewelry, Arts, Crafts, Art Gallery
Average Price: Modest
Area: Wallingford
Address: 1815 N 45th St
Seattle, WA 98103
Phone: (206) 547-4983

#166
Trinity Nightclub
Category: Dance Club, Music Venues
Average Price: Modest
Area: Pioneer Square
Address: 111 Yesler Way
Seattle, WA 98104
Phone: (206) 697-7702

#167
High Dive
Category: Music Venues, Dive Bar, American
Average Price: Inexpensive
Area: Fremont
Address: 513 N 36th St
Seattle, WA 98103
Phone: (206) 632-0212

#168
**BECU Zoo Tunes
At Woodland Park Zoo**
Category: Arts, Entertainment, Zoo
Area: Phinney Ridge
Address: 5500 Phinney Ave N.
Seattle, WA 98103
Phone: (206) 548-2500

#169
**Emerald City Fired
Arts Studio & Gallery**
Category: Art Gallery, Arts, Crafts,
Average Price: Modest
Area: Mount Baker
Address: 3333 Rainier Ave S
Seattle, WA 98144
Phone: (206) 721-0450

Seattle Travel Guide 2016 / Shops, Restaurants, Arts, Entertainment & Nightlife

#170
Benaroya Hall
Category: Performing Arts, Music Venues
Average Price: Modest
Area: Downtown
Address: 200 University St
Seattle, WA 98101
Phone: (206) 215-4700

#171
Raven's Nest Treasure
Category: Jewelry, Antiques, Art Gallery
Average Price: Expensive
Area: Downtown
Address: 85 Pike St Ste B
Seattle, WA 98101
Phone: (206) 343-0890

#172
Lake Union Wooden Boat Festival
Category: Festival
Area: South Lake Union, Westlake
Address: 1010 Valley St
Seattle, WA 98109
Phone: (206) 382-2628

#173
Tuck Seattle
Category: Dance Club, Performing Arts, Gay Bar
Average Price: Inexpensive
Area: Central District, Capitol Hill
Address: 1325 E Madison St
Seattle, WA 98122
Phone: (206) 324-8005

#174
Columbia City Gallery
Category: Art Gallery
Average Price: Inexpensive
Area: Columbia City
Address: 4864 Rainier Ave S
Seattle, WA 98118
Phone: (206) 760-9843

#175
Keyarena At Seattle Center
Category: Stadium/Arena, Music Venues
Average Price: Modest
Area: Lower Queen Anne
Address: 305 Harrison Street
Seattle, WA 98109
Phone: (206) 684-7200

#176
Seattle Waterfront Arcade
Category: Arcade
Area: Waterfront
Address: 1301 Alaskan Way
Seattle, WA 98101
Phone: (206) 903-1081

#177
Kobo At Higo
Category: Home Decor, Furniture Store, Art Gallery
Average Price: Modest
Area: International District
Address: 602-608 S Jackson St
Seattle, WA 98104
Phone: (206) 381-3000

#178
Twelfth Night Productions
Category: Performing Arts
Area: Riverview
Address: 4408 Delridge Ave SW
Seattle, WA 98106
Phone: (206) 937-1394

#179
Mcquesten Framing And Fine Art Services
Category: Framing, Art Gallery
Average Price: Exclusive
Area: Madison Park
Address: 2460 Canterbury Lane East
Seattle, WA 98112
Phone: (206) 650-5508

#180
Tim's Tavern On 105th
Category: Bar, Barbeque, Music Venues
Average Price: Inexpensive
Area: Greenwood, Bitter Lake
Address: 602 N 105th St
Seattle, WA 98133
Phone: (206) 789-9005

#181
Seattle Metropolitan Police Museum
Category: Museum
Area: Pioneer Square
Address: 317 3rd Ave S
Seattle, WA 98104
Phone: (206) 748-9991

#182
Stomani Cellars And Winery
Category: Winery
Average Price: Modest
Area: Westlake
Address: 1403 Dexter Ave N
Seattle, WA 98109
Phone: (206) 340-6137

#183
Walker Rock Garden
Category: Botanical Garden
Area: Fairmount Park
Address: 5407 37th Ave SW
Seattle, WA 98126
Phone: (206) 935-3036

#184
Canlis Glass
Category: Art Gallery
Average Price: Modest
Area: Interbay, Belltown
Address: 3131 Western Ave
Seattle, WA 98121
Phone: (206) 282-4428

#185
The Piranha Shop
Category: Arts, Entertainment, Venues, Event Space
Area: Sodo
Address: 1022 1st Ave S
Seattle, WA 98134
Phone: (612) 205-1573

#186
West Of Lenin
Category: Performing Arts
Area: Fremont
Address: 203 N 36th St
Seattle, WA 98103
Phone: (206) 352-1777

#187
Local Color
Category: Coffee, Tea, Art Gallery
Average Price: Inexpensive
Area: Downtown
Address: 1600 Pike Pl
Seattle, WA 98101
Phone: (206) 728-1717

#188
Salsa N' Seattle
Category: Performing Arts, Dance Studio, Dance School, Venues, Event Space
Area: Denny Triangle
Address: 1200 Stewart St
Seattle, WA 98101
Phone: (206) 910-6318

#189
Cornish Playhouse
Category: Performing Arts
Area: Lower Queen Anne
Address: 201 Mercer St
Seattle, WA 98109
Phone: (206) 726-5133

#190
HUMP
Category: Cinema
Area: Lower Queen Anne
Address: 100 W Roy St
Seattle, WA 98109
Phone: (206) 111-1111

#191
Patterson Cellars
Category: Winery
Average Price: Modest
Area: Downtown
Address: 1427 Western Ave
Seattle, WA 98101
Phone: (206) 724-0664

#192
The Reading Room
Category: Art Gallery, Beer, Wine, Spirits, Bookstore
Average Price: Modest
Area: Pioneer Square
Address: 308 1st Ave S
Seattle, WA 98104
Phone: (206) 682-6664

#193
Majestic Bay Theatres
Category: Cinema
Area: Ballard
Address: 2044 NW Market St
Seattle, WA 98107
Phone: (206) 781-2229

#194
Twilight Artist Collective
Category: Art Gallery
Average Price: Inexpensive
Area: Downtown
Address: 1530 Post Alley
Seattle, WA 98101
Phone: (206) 933-2444

#195
The Art Study
Category: Art Gallery
Average Price: Modest
Area: Ravenna
Address: 4630 Village Ct NE
Seattle, WA 98105
Phone: (206) 525-2400

#196
Belltown Ballet Studio
Category: Performing Arts
Area: Belltown
Address: 2306 4th Ave
Seattle, WA 98121
Phone: (206) 441-6071

#197
Langston Hughes Performing Arts Center
Category: Performing Arts
Area: Central District
Address: 104 17th Ave S
Seattle, WA 98144
Phone: (206) 684-4757

Seattle Travel Guide 2016 / Shops, Restaurants, Arts, Entertainment & Nightlife

#198
Regal Meridian 16
Category: Cinema
Area: Downtown
Address: 1501 7th Ave
Seattle, WA 98101
Phone: (206) 223-9600

#199
King's Hookah Lounge
Category: Hookah Bar, Music Venues
Average Price: Modest
Area: International District
Address: 814 S Lane St
Seattle, WA 98104
Phone: (206) 518-8320

#200
US Coffee Championships
Category: Festival
Area: Downtown
Address: 800 Convention Pl
Seattle, WA 98101
Phone: (562) 624-4100

#201
Sisko Gallery
Category: Art Gallery
Average Price: Exclusive
Area: Interbay, Belltown
Address: 3126 Elliot Ave
Seattle, WA 98121
Phone: (206) 283-2998

#202
Nancy Schutt
Category: Art Gallery
Area: Madrona
Address: 911 32nd Ave
Seattle, WA 98122
Phone: (206) 324-1855

#203
Bemis Building
Category: Art Gallery, Venues, Event Space
Area: Sodo
Address: 55 S Atlantic St
Seattle, WA 98134
Phone: (206) 587-4036

#204
Studio Seven
Category: Music Venues
Average Price: Inexpensive
Area: Industrial District
Address: 110 S Horton St
Seattle, WA 98134
Phone: (206) 286-1312

#205
Omnivorous
Category: Festival, Local Flavor
Area: Capitol Hill
Address: 420 E Pike
Seattle, WA 98122
Phone: (206) 329-7303

#206
Daybreak Star Art & Cultural Center
Category: Performing Arts,
Venues, Event Space
Area: Magnolia
Address: 3801 W Government Way
Seattle, WA 98139
Phone: (206) 285-4425

#207
Tin Can Studio
Category: Dance Studio, Performing Arts
Area: Industrial District
Address: 3130 Airport Way S
Seattle, WA 98134
Phone: (206) 909-5744

#208
Jet City Stream
Category: Music Venues
Area: Industrial District
Address: 3200 Airport Way S
Seattle, WA 98134
Phone: (206) 682-3055

#209
Empty Sea Studios
Category: Music Venues, Tutoring Center
Average Price: Modest
Area: Phinney Ridge
Address: 6300 Phinney Ave N
Seattle, WA 98103
Phone: (206) 228-2483

#210
Liquid Lounge
At Experience Music Project
Category: Museum
Area: Lower Queen Anne
Address: 325 5th Ave N
Seattle, WA 98109
Phone: (206) 770-2779

#211
Mural Amphitheatre
Category: Music Venues
Average Price: Inexpensive
Area: Lower Queen Anne
Address: 305 Harrison Street
Seattle, WA 98109
Phone: (206) 684-7200

#212
Emerald City Comicon
Category: Festival
Area: Downtown
Address: 800 Convention Pl
Seattle, WA 98101
Phone: (425) 744-2767

#213
The Kraken Bar & Lounge
Category: Dive Bar, American, Music Venues
Average Price: Inexpensive
Area: University District
Address: 5257 University Way NE
Seattle, WA 98105
Phone: (206) 522-5334

#214
Eclectic Theater
Category: Performing Arts
Area: First Hill
Address: 1214 10th Ave
Seattle, WA 98122
Phone: (206) 679-3271

#215
Arcade Lights
Category: Festival, Food
Area: Downtown
Address: 85 Pike St
Seattle, WA 98101
Phone: (206) 682-7453

#216
Venue Work Studio + Boutique
Category: Jewelry, Home Decor, Art Gallery
Average Price: Expensive
Area: Ballard
Address: 5408 22nd Ave NW
Seattle, WA 98107
Phone: (206) 789-3335

#217
Ward Johnson Winery
Category: Winery
Average Price: Modest
Address: 1445 Elliott Avenue W
Seattle, WA 98119
Phone: (206) 284-2635

#218
The Pocket Theater
Category: Performing Arts
Area: Greenwood, Phinney Ridge
Address: 8312 Greenwood Ave N
Seattle, WA 98103
Phone: (303) 803-4589

#219
Gasworks Gallery
Category: Art Gallery, Venues, Event Space
Area: Wallingford
Address: 3815 4th Ave NE
Seattle, WA 98103
Phone: (206) 632-6442

#220
Wamu Theater
Category: Music Venues, Event Space
Average Price: Expensive
Area: Sodo
Address: 800 Occidental Ave S
Seattle, WA 98134
Phone: (206) 381-7555

#221
Arc School Of Ballet
Category: Performing Arts
Area: Crown Hill
Address: 9250 14th Avenue NW
Seattle, WA 98117
Phone: (206) 352-0799

#222
Husky Stadium
Category: Stadium/Arena
Area: University District
Address: 3800 Montlake Blvd
Seattle, WA 98105
Phone: (206) 543-2200

#223
Bazaz Studios
Category: Jewelry, Art Gallery,
Average Price: Expensive
Area: Ballard
Address: 4604 14th Ave NW
Seattle, WA 98107
Phone: (206) 783-8090

#224
Stone Soup Theatre
Category: Performing Arts,
Venues, Event Space
Area: Fremont
Address: 4029 Stone Way N
Seattle, WA 98103
Phone: (206) 633-1883

#225
Michelle Badion - Dance Instructor
Category: Performing Arts, Dance School
Area: Roosevelt
Address: 1320 NE 63rd St
Seattle, WA 98115
Phone: (206) 334-7496

#226
Halogen
Category: Art Gallery
Area: Belltown
Address: 2316 2nd Ave
Seattle, WA 98121
Phone: (206) 905-7775

#227
88 Keys Dueling Piano And Sports Bar
Category: Music Venues, Piano Bar
Average Price: Modest
Area: Pioneer Square
Address: 315 2nd Ave S
Seattle, WA 98104
Phone: (206) 839-1300

#228
Live Aloha Hawaiian Cultural Festival
Category: Festival
Area: Lower Queen Anne
Address: 305 Harrison St
Seattle, WA 98109
Phone: (206) 650-4882

#229
Northwest Tribal Art
Category: Art Gallery
Area: Downtown
Address: 1417 1st Avenue
Seattle, WA 98101
Phone: (206) 467-9330

#230
Orbit Audio
Category: Performing Arts
Area: Pioneer Square
Address: 219 1st Ave S
Seattle, WA 98104
Phone: (206) 381-1244

#231
Seattle Talent
Category: Performing Arts
Area: Downtown
Address: 300 Pine St
Seattle, WA 98181
Phone: (206) 903-6900

#232
Centurylink Field Event Center
Category: Stadium/Arena
Area: Sodo
Address: 1000 Occidental Ave
Seattle, WA 98134
Phone: (800) 745-3000

#233
Twilight Gallery & Boutique
Category: Art Gallery, Jewelry
Average Price: Modest
Area: Junction
Address: 4306 SW Alaska St
Seattle, WA 98116
Phone: (206) 933-2444

#234
Balagan Theatre
Category: Performing Arts
Area: Capitol Hill
Address: 1524 Harvard Ave
Seattle, WA 98122
Phone: (206) 718-3245

#235
Seattle Drum School
Category: Music Venues
Average Price: Modest
Area: Olympic Hills
Address: 12510 15th Ave NE
Seattle, WA 98125
Phone: (206) 364-8815

#236
Snow Goose Associates Inc
Category: Art Gallery
Area: Mapleleaf
Address: 8806 Roosevelt Way NE
Seattle, WA 98115
Phone: (206) 523-6223

#237
Greg Kucera Gallery
Category: Art Gallery
Average Price: Exclusive
Area: Pioneer Square
Address: 212 3rd Ave S
Seattle, WA 98104
Phone: (206) 624-0770

#238
Jules Maes Saloon
Category: Bar, Music Venues
Average Price: Modest
Area: Georgetown
Address: 5919 Airport Way S
Seattle, WA 98127
Phone: (206) 957-7766

#239
Lo-Fi Performance Gallery
Category: Music Venues, Bar, Dance Club
Average Price: Inexpensive
Area: South Lake Union
Address: 429 Eastlake Ave E
Seattle, WA 98109
Phone: (206) 254-2824

#240
Almquist Family Vintners
Category: Winery
Average Price: Modest
Area: Queen Anne
Address: 198 Nickerson St
Seattle, WA 98109
Phone: (206) 859-9400

#241
True Love Art Gallery
Category: Art Gallery, Tattoo
Average Price: Modest
Area: Capitol Hill
Address: 1525 Summit Ave
Seattle, WA 98122
Phone: (206) 227-3572

#242
Style Of Russia
Category: Art Gallery
Area: Downtown
Address: 400 Pine St
Seattle, WA 98101
Phone: (206) 682-3020

#243
All That Dance
Category: Performing Arts
Area: Wedgwood
Address: 8507 35th Ave NE
Seattle, WA 98115
Phone: (206) 524-8944

#244
Chop Suey
Category: Music Venues
Average Price: Modest
Area: Central District, Capitol Hill
Address: 1325 E Madison St
Seattle, WA 98122
Phone: (206) 324-8005

#245
Red Star Press
Category: Art Gallery
Area: Fremont
Address: PO Box 31407
Seattle, WA 98103
Phone: (206) 453-0060

#246
Platform Gallery
Category: Art Gallery
Average Price: Inexpensive
Area: Pioneer Square
Address: 114 3rd Ave S
Seattle, WA 98104
Phone: (206) 323-2808

#247
Laurelhurst Cellars Winery
Category: Winery
Average Price: Modest
Area: Georgetown
Address: 5608 7th Ave S
Seattle, WA 98108
Phone: (206) 992-2875

#248
Polish Festival Seattle
Category: Festival
Area: Lower Queen Anne
Address: 305 Harrison St
Seattle, WA 98109
Phone: (206) 948-8064

#249
Quetzalcoatl Gallery
Category: Art Gallery
Area: Beacon Hill
Address: 3209 Beacon Ave S
Seattle, WA 98144
Phone: (206) 334-0749

#250
Dance Fremont
Category: Performing Arts
Area: Fremont
Address: 4015 Stone Way N
Seattle, WA 98103
Phone: (206) 633-0812

#251
Seattle Chinese Garden
Category: Botanical Garden
Area: Riverview
Address: 6000 16th Ave SW
Seattle, WA 98106
Phone: (206) 934-5219

#252
Lawrimore Project
Category: Art Gallery
Area: Sodo
Address: 831 Airport Way S
Seattle, WA 98134
Phone: (206) 264-1455

#253
Experience Karaoke Project
Category: Performing Arts, Djs
Area: Rainier Beach
Address: 9803 Rainier Ave S
Seattle, WA 98118
Phone: (206) 317-4417

#254
Whirligig Festival
Category: Festival
Area: Lower Queen Anne
Address: 305 Harrison St
Seattle, WA 98109
Phone: (206) 684-7200

#255
Sunset Tavern
Category: Dive Bar, Music Venues, Pizza
Average Price: Inexpensive
Area: Ballard
Address: 5433 Ballard Ave NW
Seattle, WA 98107
Phone: (206) 784-4880

#256
Log House Museum
Category: Museum
Area: Alki
Address: 3003 61st Ave SW
Seattle, WA 98116
Phone: (206) 938-5293

#257
LUCID
Category: Jazz, Blues, Lounge
Average Price: Modest
Area: University District
Address: 5241 University Way NE
Seattle, WA 98105
Phone: (206) 402-3042

#258
Hard Rock Café
Category: Music Venues, American, Burgers
Average Price: Modest
Area: Downtown
Address: 116 Pike Street
Seattle, WA 98101
Phone: (206) 204-2233

#259
Super Smash Games Ballard
Category: Hobby Shop, Electronics, Arcade
Average Price: Modest
Area: Ballard
Address: 5500 8th Ave Nw
Seattle, WA 98107
Phone: (206) 257-1566

#260
O S Winery
Category: Winery
Average Price: Modest
Area: South Park
Address: 1501 S 92nd Pl
Seattle, WA 98108
Phone: (206) 243-3427

#261
Art On The Ridge
Category: Art Gallery
Average Price: Exclusive
Area: Greenwood, Phinney Ridge
Address: 8005 Greenwood Ave N
Seattle, WA 98103
Phone: (206) 510-3421

#262
Click Imports
Category: Winery
Area: Denny Triangle
Address: 808 Howell Street
Seattle, WA 98101
Phone: (206) 443-1996

#263
Massai Ethnic Treasures
Category: Art Gallery
Average Price: Inexpensive
Area: Capitol Hill
Address: 217 Broadway E
Seattle, WA 98102
Phone: (206) 323-0768

#264
Precept Wine Brands
Category: Winery, Beer, Wine, Spirits
Area: Eastlake
Address: 1910 Fairview Ave E
Seattle, WA 98102
Phone: (206) 267-5252

#265
Can't Look Away
The Lure Of Horror Film Exhibit
Category: Museum
Area: Lower Queen Anne
Address: 325 5th Avenue N
Seattle, WA 98109
Phone: (206) 770-2702

#266
In The Groove DJ Academy
Category: Performing Arts,
Vocational & Technical School
Area: First Hill, Capitol Hill
Address: 500 E Pike St
Seattle, WA 98122
Phone: (206) 369-0108

#267
Sacred Muse Face Painting
Category: Performing Arts, Makeup Artists
Area: Eastlake
Address: 100 E Boston St
Seattle, WA 98102
Phone: (415) 368-7994

#268
Facere Jewelry Art Gallery
Category: Jewelry, Art Gallery, Antiques
Average Price: Modest
Area: Downtown
Address: 1420 5th Ave
Seattle, WA 98101
Phone: (206) 624-6768

#269
Pacini Lubel Gallery
Category: Art Gallery
Average Price: Expensive
Area: Pioneer Square
Address: 207 2nd Avenue S
Seattle, WA 98104
Phone: (206) 326-5555

#270
Next Stage
Category: Performing Arts
Area: Capitol Hill
Address: 1634 11th Ave
Seattle, WA 98122
Phone: (206) 322-7030

#271
Steinbrueck Native Gallery
Category: Art Gallery
Average Price: Expensive
Area: Downtown
Address: 2030 Western Ave
Seattle, WA 98121
Phone: (206) 441-3821

#272
Gallery Mack
Category: Art Gallery
Average Price: Expensive
Area: Downtown
Address: 2003 Western Avenue
Seattle, WA 98121
Phone: (206) 448-1616

#273
Cry Baby Studios
Category: Performing Arts
Area: Capitol Hill
Address: 1514 11th Ave
Seattle, WA 98122
Phone: (206) 660-0117

#274
Three Dollar Bill Cinema
Category: Cinema
Area: Capitol Hill
Address: 1515 12th Ave
Seattle, WA 98122
Phone: (206) 323-4274

#275
Art Stall Gallery
Category: Art Gallery
Average Price: Inexpensive
Area: Downtown
Address: 97 Pike Street
Seattle, WA 98101
Phone: (206) 623-7538

#276
Reflecting On Seattle
Category: Art Gallery
Average Price: Modest
Area: Downtown
Address: 1501 Pike Pl
Seattle, WA 98101
Phone: (206) 250-2390

#277
Market Cellars Tasting Room
Category: Winery
Average Price: Modest
Area: Downtown
Address: 1432 Western Ave
Seattle, WA 98101
Phone: (206) 384-8583

#278
Seattle Pops
Category: Performing Arts
Area: Downtown
Address: 200 Universtiy St
Seattle, WA 98101
Phone: (206) 215-4895

#279
Benaroya Hall - Bh Music Center
Category: Performing Arts
Area: Downtown
Address: 200 University Street
Seattle, WA 98101
Phone: (206) 215-4800

#280
The Legacy Ltd
Category: Art Gallery
Area: Downtown
Address: 1003 1st Avenue
Seattle, WA 98104
Phone: (206) 624-6350

#281
Natsu Matsuri
Category: Festival
Area: International District
Address: 600 5th Ave S
Seattle, WA 98104
Phone: (206) 624-6248

#282
La Familia Gallery
Category: Art Gallery
Average Price: Exclusive
Area: Pioneer Square
Address: 117 Prefontaine Place South
Seattle, WA 98104
Phone: (206) 291-4608

#283
G Gibson Gallery
Category: Art Gallery
Average Price: Expensive
Area: Pioneer Square
Address: 300 South Washington St
Seattle, WA 98104
Phone: (206) 587-4033

Seattle Travel Guide 2016 / Shops, Restaurants, Arts, Entertainment & Nightlife

#284
F H & Company
Category: Art Gallery
Average Price: Modest
Area: Pioneer Square
Address: 309 Occidental Ave
Seattle, WA 98104
Phone: (206) 682-0166

#285
Art Of The Dragon
Category: Museum
Area: Pioneer Square
Address: 313B 1st Avenue South
Seattle, WA 98104
Phone: (206) 652-2445

#286
Washington Foundation James W & Jamie Rogella
Category: Museum
Area: Central District
Address: 1816 26th Avenue
Seattle, WA 98122
Phone: (206) 709-4241

#287
Kibo Gallery African Art
Category: Art Gallery
Area: Pioneer Square
Address: 323 Occidental Ave S
Seattle, WA 98104
Phone: (206) 442-2100

#288
Gallery IMA
Category: Art Gallery, Venues, Event Space
Average Price: Exclusive
Area: Pioneer Square
Address: 123 S Jackson St
Seattle, WA 98104
Phone: (206) 625-0055

#289
Walrus Dance
Category: Performing Arts
Area: Queen Anne
Address: 89 Yesler, 3rd Floor
Seattle, WA 98119
Phone: (206) 331-6673

#290
Art Wolfe
Category: Art Gallery
Average Price: Modest
Area: Sodo
Address: 520 1st Ave S
Seattle, WA 98104
Phone: (206) 332-0993

#291
Artfx
Category: Art Gallery, Arts, Crafts
Average Price: Modest
Area: Fremont
Address: 420 N 35th St
Seattle, WA 98103
Phone: (206) 545-7459

#292
Omnivorous
Category: Festival
Area: Central District
Address: 915 E Pine St
Seattle, WA 98122
Phone: (206) 204-3841

#293
Chong Wa Benevolent Association
Category: Cultural Center, Language School
Area: International District
Address: 522 7th Ave S
Seattle, WA 98104
Phone: (206) 623-2527

#294
Continuum, Heart In Motion
Category: Art Gallery
Area: Sodo
Address: 570 1st Ave S
Seattle, WA 98104
Phone: (206) 478-8342

#295
Plaza Dome El Obrero
Category: Coffee, Tea, Lounge, Music Venues
Average Price: Modest
Area: Central District
Address: 1712 S Jackson St
Seattle, WA 98144
Phone: (206) 323-9247

#296
Café Nordo
Category: Performing Arts
Area: Central District
Address: 135 14th Ave
Seattle, WA 98122
Phone: (206) 790-5166

#297
Between Cultures
Category: Art Gallery
Average Price: Modest
Area: Mapleleaf
Address: 8809 Roosevelt Way NE
Seattle, WA 98115
Phone: (206) 523-0053

#298
Visionary Dance Productions
Category: Performing Arts, Dance Studio
Area: Fremont
Address: 4128 Fremont Ave N
Seattle, WA 98103
Phone: (206) 632-2353

#299
Roosevelt High School Jazz Band
Category: Performing Arts
Area: Wallingford
Address: 4400 Interlake Avenue N.
Seattle, WA 98103
Phone: (206) 252-4810

#300
Samba Dance
Category: Dance Studio, Performing Arts
Area: Fremont
Address: 4272 Fremont Ave N
Seattle, WA 98103
Phone: (206) 354-9433

#301
The Vineyard Table
Category: Winery, Local Flavor, Venues, Event Space
Average Price: Modest
Area: Sodo
Address: 85 S Atlantic St
Seattle, WA 98134
Phone: (206) 420-5564

#302
Galaxy Lounge
Category: Leisure Center, Music Venues
Area: Beacon Hill
Address: 2329 Rainier Ave S
Seattle, WA 98144
Phone: (206) 325-6555

#303
University Of Washington School Of Music
Category: Performing Arts
Area: University District
Address: University Of Washington
Seattle, WA 98195
Phone: (206) 543-1201

#304
Chapel Performance Space
Category: Music Venues
Average Price: Inexpensive
Area: Wallingford
Address: 4649 Sunnyside Ave N
Seattle, WA 98103
Phone: (206) 789-1939

#305
Last Resort Fire Department
Category: Museum,
Area: Ballard
Address: 1433 NW 51st Street
Seattle, WA 98107
Phone: (206) 783-4474

#306
Porcelain Gallery
Category: Art Gallery
Area: Magnolia
Address: 2426 32nd Avenue W
Seattle, WA 98199
Phone: (206) 284-5893

#307
Pottery Time
Category: Art Gallery
Area: Industrial District
Address: 2700 4th Ave S
Seattle, WA 98124
Phone: (206) 224-9815

#308
Plasteel Frames & Gallery
Category: Art Gallery, Framing
Average Price: Modest
Area: Industrial District
Address: 3300 1st Ave S
Seattle, WA 98134
Phone: (206) 324-3379

#309
Night Market & Moon Festival
Category: Festival
Area: International District
Address: 401 S Jackson St
Seattle, WA 98104
Phone: (206) 382-1197

#310
Young At Art
Category: Art Gallery
Average Price: Inexpensive
Area: Gatewood
Address: 5962 Fauntleroy Way SW
Seattle, WA 98116
Phone: (206) 937-0736

#311
Volunteer Park Dahlia Garden
Category: Botanical Garden
Address: 1247 15th Ave E
Seattle, WA 98103
Phone: (206) 684-4555

#312
Imusic
Category: Music Venues, Event Space, Lounge
Average Price: Expensive
Area: Lower Queen Anne
Address: 332 5th Ave N
Seattle, WA 98109
Phone: (206) 391-5413

Seattle Travel Guide 2016 / Shops, Restaurants, Arts, Entertainment & Nightlife

#313
Puget Sound Strings
Category: Performing Arts,
Area: Ravenna
Address: NE 65th And 31st NE
Seattle, WA 98115
Phone: (425) 210-9262

#314
Space To Create
Category: Art Gallery
Average Price: Inexpensive
Area: Phinney Ridge
Address: 1414 NW 70th St
Seattle, WA 98117
Phone: (206) 784-0401

#315
Fine Impressions Gallery
Category: Art Gallery
Average Price: Modest
Area: Mapleleaf
Address: 8300 5th Ave NE
Seattle, WA 98115
Phone: (206) 784-5270

#316
The Civetta Dance Space
Category: Performing Arts, Dance Studio
Area: Greenwood
Address: 124 N 103rd St
Seattle, WA 98133
Phone: (206) 781-1111

#317
El Corazón
Category: Music Venues, Dive Bar
Average Price: Modest
Area: South Lake Union
Address: 109 Eastlake Ave E
Seattle, WA 98109
Phone: (206) 262-0482

#318
Kobo
Category: Art Gallery, Home Decor
Average Price: Modest
Area: Capitol Hill
Address: 814 E Roy
Seattle, WA 98102
Phone: (206) 726-0704

#319
The Bite Of Seattle
Category: Festival
Area: Lower Queen Anne
Address: 305 Harrison St
Seattle, WA 98109
Phone: (425) 283-5050

#320
Densho's Sushi & Sake Fest
Category: Festival
Area: Denny Triangle
Address: 1900 5th Ave
Seattle, WA 98101
Phone: (206) 320-0095

#321
Mercury At Machinewerks
Category: Lounge, Music Venues, Dance Club
Average Price: Inexpensive
Area: First Hill
Address: 1009 E Union St
Seattle, WA 98122
Phone: (206) 328-9481

#322
School Of Rock
Category: Performing Arts
Average Price: Exclusive
Area: Greenwood
Address: 106 N 85th St
Seattle, WA 98103
Phone: (206) 417-7625

#323
King Cat Theatre
Category: Performing Arts,
Cinema, Music Venues
Area: Denny Triangle
Address: 2130 6th Ave
Seattle, WA 98121
Phone: (206) 269-7444

#324
**Ballard Academy
Of Music And Dance**
Category: Dance School, Performing Arts
Area: Loyal Heights
Address: 2404 NW 80th St
Seattle, WA 98117
Phone: (206) 240-3408

#325
Kate Alkarni Gallery
Category: Art Gallery
Area: Georgetown
Address: 5701 6th Ave S
Seattle, WA 98108
Phone: (206) 453-0043

#326
Seattle's Littlest Performers
Category: Performing Arts
Area: Greenwood
Address: 5510 University Way NE
Seattle, WA 98105
Phone: (206) 473-9580

#327
Parnassus Cafe & Art Gallery
Category: Coffee, Tea, Art Gallery
Average Price: Inexpensive
Area: University District
Address: University Of Washington Art Building
Seattle, WA 98105
Phone: (206) 543-7033

#328
Richard Hugo House
Category: Performing Arts,
Area: Capitol Hill
Address: 1634 11th Ave
Seattle, WA 98122
Phone: (206) 322-7030

#329
The Miller School Of Art
Category: Art Gallery
Average Price: Inexpensive
Area: Georgetown
Address: 1226 S Bailey St
Seattle, WA 98108
Phone: (206) 861-9265

#330
Frame It
Category: Framing, Art Gallery, Home Decor
Average Price: Modest
Area: Northgate
Address: 10712 5th Ave NE
Seattle, WA 98125
Phone: (206) 364-7477

#331
Hop Scotch Festival
Category: Festival
Area: Fremont
Address: 155 N 35th St
Seattle, WA 98103
Phone: (206) 633-0422

#332
Seattle Musical Theatre
Category: Performing Arts
Area: Sand Point
Address: 7400 Sand Point Way NE
Seattle, WA 98115
Phone: (206) 363-2809

#333
Grand Central Arcade
Category: Museum, Shopping Center
Area: Pioneer Square
Address: 214 1st Avenue South
Seattle, WA 98104
Phone: (206) 623-7417

#334
Winter Beer Festival
Category: Festival
Area: Fremont
Address: 4301 Leary Way NW
Seattle, WA 98107
Phone: (206) 787-1989

#335
Kirsten Gallery
Category: Art Gallery
Average Price: Inexpensive
Area: University District
Address: 5320 Roosevelt Way NE
Seattle, WA 98105
Phone: (206) 522-2011

#336
Domanico Cellars
Category: Winery, Venues, Event Space
Average Price: Modest
Area: Ballard
Address: 825 NW 49th St
Seattle, WA 98107
Phone: (206) 465-9406

#337
Lost River Winery
Category: Winery
Average Price: Modest
Area: Downtown
Address: 2003 Western Ave
Seattle, WA 98121
Phone: (206) 448-2124

#338
La Tienda Folk Art Gallery
Category: Jewelry, Art Gallery, Cards, Stationery
Average Price: Modest
Area: Ballard
Address: 2050 NW Market St
Seattle, WA 98107
Phone: (206) 297-3605

#339
Dunn Gardens
Category: Botanical Garden
Area: Broadview
Address: 13533 Northshire Rd NW
Seattle, WA 98177
Phone: (206) 362-0933

#340
Balorico
Category: Dance Studio, Performing Arts
Area: Roxhill
Address: 7904 35th Ave SW
Seattle, WA 98126
Phone: (206) 679-7229

Seattle Travel Guide 2016 / Shops, Restaurants, Arts, Entertainment & Nightlife

#341
Theater Schmeater
Category: Performing Arts
Area: Belltown
Address: 2125 3rd Ave
Seattle, WA 98121
Phone: (206) 324-5801

#342
Seattle Cherry Blossom & Japanese Cultural Festival
Category: Festival
Area: South Lake Union
Address: 305 Harrison St
Seattle, WA 98109
Phone: (206) 723-2003

#343
Belltown Artwalk
Category: Art Gallery
Area: Belltown
Address: 2302 4th Ave
Seattle, WA 98121
Phone: (206) 420-7057

#344
Taste Of Main Old Bellevue
Category: Festival
Area: Belltown
Address: 1904 3rd Ave, Ste 339
Seattle, WA 98101
Phone: (206) 464-0826

#345
Movies On The Pedestal
Category: Cinema
Area: Downtown
Address: 1301 5th Ave.
Seattle, WA 98101
Phone: (206) 628-5050

#346
Narwhal
Category: Arcade, Pub
Average Price: Inexpensive
Area: Capitol Hill
Address: 1118 E Pike St
Seattle, WA 98122
Phone: (206) 325-6492

#347
Robert Ramsay Cellars
Category: Beer, Wine, Spirits, Winery
Area: Queen Anne
Address: 1697-1769 Queen Anne Ave N
Seattle, WA 98109
Phone: (425) 686-9463

#348
R E Welch Art Galleries
Category: Art Gallery
Average Price: Exclusive
Address: 1214 1st Ave
Seattle, WA 98101
Phone: (206) 264-8141

#349
Wyland Galleries-Northwest
Category: Art Gallery
Average Price: Exclusive
Area: Downtown
Address: 1211 1st Ave
Seattle, WA 98101
Phone: (206) 342-9400

#350
Giant Shoe Museum
Category: Local Flavor, Museum
Area: Downtown
Address: Pikes Place Market
Seattle, WA 98101
Phone: (206) 623-2870

#351
Rogues Gallery
Category: Art Gallery
Area: Pioneer Square
Address: 608 First Ave
Seattle, WA 98104
Phone: (206) 682-4646

#352
Noble Horse Gallery
Category: Art Gallery
Area: Pioneer Square
Address: 216 1st Ave S
Seattle, WA 98104
Phone: (206) 382-8566

#353
Juan Alonso Studio
Category: Art Gallery
Area: Pioneer Square
Address: 214 1st Ave S, Ste B15
Seattle, WA 98104
Phone: (206) 390-4882

#354
History House
Category: Museum
Area: Fremont
Address: 790 N 34th St
Seattle, WA 98103
Phone: (206) 675-8875

#355
Seattle Sculpture And Statuary
Category: Art Gallery
Area: Pioneer Square
Address: 85 South Main Street
Seattle, WA 98104
Phone: (206) 624-1443

#356
Sam Day Gallery And Studio
Category: Art Gallery
Area: Pioneer Square
Address: 79 S Main St
Seattle, WA 98104
Phone: (206) 382-7413

#357
Patrick Howe Gallery
Category: Art Gallery
Average Price: Inexpensive
Area: Portage Bay
Address: 3200 Harvard Avenue E
Seattle, WA 98102
Phone: (206) 322-5540

#358
Artxchange
Category: Art Gallery
Average Price: Modest
Area: Sodo
Address: 512 1st Ave S
Seattle, WA 98104
Phone: (206) 839-0377

#359
Infinite One Wellness Center
Category: Art Gallery
Area: Fremont
Address: 3519 Fremont Pl N
Seattle, WA 98103
Phone: (206) 708-1789

#360
Azuma Gallery
Category: Antiques, Art Gallery
Average Price: Expensive
Area: Sodo
Address: 530 1st Avenue S
Seattle, WA 98104
Phone: (206) 622-5599

#361
The Reiki Fellowship
Category: Performing Arts
Area: Highland Park
Address: 7709 8th Ave SW
Seattle, WA 98106
Phone: (206) 947-7687

#362
SIFF Cinema At The Film Center
Category: Cinema
Area: Lower Queen Anne
Address: 305 Harrison St
Seattle, WA 98109
Phone: (206) 633-7151

#363
My World Dance And Fitness
Category: Dance Studio, Arts, Entertainment
Area: Central District
Address: 849 Hiawatha Pl S
Seattle, WA 98144
Phone: (206) 861-2500

#364
Cadence Winery
Category: Winery
Area: South Park
Address: 9320 15th Ave S
Seattle, WA 98108
Phone: (206) 381-9507

#365
Thistle Theatre
Category: Performing Arts
Area: Sand Point
Address: 6344 NE 74th St
Seattle, WA 98115
Phone: (206) 524-3388

#366
Afishionado Gallery
Category: Art Gallery
Average Price: Modest
Area: Interbay
Address: 1900 W Nickerson St
Seattle, WA 98119
Phone: (206) 283-5078

#367
Bank Of America Arena
Category: Stadium/Arena
Area: Interbay
Address: 1900 W Nickerson St
Seattle, WA 98195
Phone: (206) 543-2200

#368
A/NT Gallery
Category: Art Gallery
Average Price: Inexpensive
Area: Denny Triangle
Address: 2045 Westlake Ave
Seattle, WA 98121
Phone: (206) 233-0680

#369
Falling Rain Wines
Category: Winery
Area: Westlake
Address: 1403 Dexter Ave N
Seattle, WA 98109
Phone: (206) 390-2567

#370
Foster/White Gallery
Category: Art Gallery
Area: Pioneer Square
Address: 220 3rd Ave S
Seattle, WA 98104
Phone: (206) 622-2833

#371
The Sound Asylum
Category: Performing Arts
Area: Interbay
Address: 1107 Elliott Ave W
Seattle, WA 98119
Phone: (206) 788-0524

#372
Soll Artist Cooperative
Category: Art Gallery
Average Price: Inexpensive
Area: Pioneer Square
Address: 112 3rd Ave S
Seattle, WA 98104
Phone: (206) 264-8061

#373
SAM Shop
Category: Art Gallery
Average Price: Expensive
Area: Washington Park
Address: 1400 E Prospect St
Seattle, WA 98112
Phone: (206) 654-3160

#374
Carlson Audio Systems
Category: Performing Arts
Area: Industrial District
Address: 2250 1st Ave S
Seattle, WA 98134
Phone: (206) 340-8811

#375
Book-It Repertory Theatre
Category: Performing Arts
Area: Lower Queen Anne
Address: 305 Harrison St
Seattle, WA 98109
Phone: (206) 216-0833

#376
Beyond The Ink Tattoo In Fremont
Category: Art Gallery, Tattoo
Average Price: Modest
Area: Fremont
Address: 469 N 36th St
Seattle, WA 98103
Phone: (206) 659-4012

#377
Seattle Opera
Category: Performing Arts, Opera, Ballet
Area: Lower Queen Anne
Address: 321 Mercer St
Seattle, WA 98109
Phone: (206) 389-7676

#378
Viking Days
Category: Festival
Area: Sunset Hill
Address: 3014 NW 67th St
Seattle, WA 98117
Phone: (206) 789-5707

#379
Carmona Flamenco
Category: Performing Arts
Area: Admiral
Address: 3634 48th Avenue SW
Seattle, WA 98116
Phone: (206) 932-4067

#380
Davidson Galleries
Category: Art Gallery
Area: Pioneer Square
Address: 313 Occidental Avenue S
Seattle, WA 98104
Phone: (206) 624-1324

#381
Lisa Harris Gallery
Category: Art Gallery
Average Price: Modest
Area: Downtown
Address: 1922 Pike Pl
Seattle, WA 98101
Phone: (206) 443-3315

#382
Rainier Valley Cultural Center
Category: Performing Arts
Area: Columbia City
Address: 3515 S Alaska St
Seattle, WA 98118
Phone: (206) 725-7517

#383
Fall Line Winery
Category: Winery
Average Price: Modest
Area: Georgetown
Address: 6122 6th Avenue S
Seattle, WA 98108
Phone: (206) 768-9463

#384
Toshiro Kaplan Lofts
Category: Art Gallery
Average Price: Modest
Area: Pioneer Square
Address: 115 South Prefontaine Place
Seattle, WA 98104
Phone: (206) 223-1160

#385
Steven Fey Photography Gallery
Category: Art Gallery, Framing, Session Photography
Area: Belltown, Denny Triangle
Address: 2615 Fifth Ave
Seattle, WA 98121
Phone: (206) 443-6003

#386
San Gennaro Festival
Category: Festival
Area: Georgetown
Address: S Angelo St
Seattle, WA 98108
Phone: (253) 872-1900

#387
Lunar New Year Festival
Category: Festival
Area: International District
Address: 423 Maynard Ave S
Seattle, WA 98104
Phone: (206) 382-1197

#388
Bokrosh Studio
Category: Art Gallery
Average Price: Inexpensive
Area: Beacon Hill
Address: 1905 22nd Avenue S
Seattle, WA 98144
Phone: (206) 860-9748

#389
**Lisa Lamoureaux,
Systems Theory Collection**
Category: Art Gallery
Average Price: Exclusive
Area: Denny Triangle
Address: 2326 Sixth Avenue
Seattle, WA 98121
Phone: (206) 772-0012

#390
**Seattle International
Children's Friendship Festival**
Category: Festival
Area: Lower Queen Anne
Address: 305 Harrison St
Seattle, WA 98109
Phone: (206) 684-7338

#391
Safeco Field
Category: Stadium/Arena
Area: Sodo
Address: 1250 1st Ave S
Seattle, WA 98134
Phone: (206) 346-4001

#392
Thai Exotic Importers
Category: Art Gallery
Average Price: Modest
Area: Pioneer Square
Address: 85 Yesler Wy
Seattle, WA 98104
Phone: (206) 682-2190

#393
Wilridge Winery
Category: Winery
Area: Madrona
Address: 1416 34th Ave
Seattle, WA 98122
Phone: (206) 325-3051

#394
Kenyon Hall
Category: Performing Arts
Area: Roxhill
Address: 7904 35th Ave SW
Seattle, WA 98126
Phone: (206) 937-3613

#395
Creative Dance Center
Category: Performing Arts
Area: Haller Lake
Address: 12577 Densmore Ave N
Seattle, WA 98133
Phone: (206) 363-7281

#396
Center House Theatre
Category: Performing Arts
Area: Lower Queen Anne
Address: 305 Harrison St
Seattle, WA 98109
Phone: (206) 684-7200

#397
Belltown Ballet & Conditioning Studio
Category: Performing Arts, Dance Studio
Area: Belltown
Address: 2306 4th Ave
Seattle, WA 98121
Phone: (206) 851-6526

#398
Flamenco Danzarte
Category: Dance Studio, Performing Arts
Area: Belltown
Address: 2306 4th Ave
Seattle, WA 98121
Phone: (206) 781-4256

#399
The Ballet Studio
Category: Dance Studio,
Performing Arts, Opera, Ballet
Area: University District
Address: 4556 University Way NE
Seattle, WA 98105
Phone: (206) 329-9166

#400
Affordable Art Fair Seattle
Category: Art Gallery, Festival
Average Price: Exclusive
Area: Lower Queen Anne
Address: 3rd Ave N And Mercer St
Seattle, WA 98109
Phone: (212) 255-2003

#401
Cambodian Cultural Museum And Killing Field Memorial
Category: Museum
Area: White Center
Address: 9809 16th Avenue SW
Seattle, WA 98106
Phone: (206) 763-8088

#402
The L.A.B.
Category: Jazz, Blues, Music Venues
Area: Olympic Hills
Address: 12510 15th Ave NE
Seattle, WA 98125
Phone: (206) 364-8815

#403
White Sage Studio
Category: Art Gallery
Average Price: Exclusive
Area: Ballard
Address: 5317 Ballard Ave NW
Seattle, WA 98107
Phone: (206) 784-7243

#404
Visionary Dance Productions
Category: Performing Arts
Area: Fremont
Address: 4115 Fremont Ave N
Seattle, WA 98103
Phone: (206) 632-2353

#405
Suicide Squeeze Records
Category: Performing Arts
Area: Ballard
Address: 2221 NW 56th St
Seattle, WA 98107
Phone: (206) 789-3359

#406
Jacob Lawrence
Category: Art Gallery
Area: First Hill
Address: University Of Washington, Art Building, Room 132 Seattle, WA
Phone: (206) 685-1805

#407
Artforte Gallery
Category: Art Gallery
Area: Pioneer Square
Address: 307 Occidental Ave S
Seattle, WA 98104
Phone: (206) 748-0187

#408
The Nautilus Studio
Category: Art Gallery
Average Price: Expensive
Address: 5913 B Airport Way S
Seattle, WA 98108
Phone: (612) 655-6463

#409
Neumos Crystal Ball Reading Room
Category: Music Venues
Average Price: Modest
Area: First Hill, Capitol Hill
Address: 925 E Pike St
Seattle, WA 98122
Phone: (206) 709-9442

#410
Winston Wachter Fine Art
Category: Art Gallery
Average Price: Expensive
Area: South Lake Union
Address: 203 Dexter Ave N
Seattle, WA 98109
Phone: (206) 652-5855

#411
Rainier Dance Center
Category: Performing Arts
Area: Rainier Beach
Address: 9264 57th Ave S
Seattle, WA 98118
Phone: (206) 721-3133

#412
Northwest Seaport Maritime Heritage Center
Category: Museum, Boating, Boat Charter
Area: South Lake Union, Westlake
Address: 860 Terry Ave N
Seattle, WA 98109
Phone: (206) 447-9800

#413
Hodges Linda
Category: Art Gallery
Average Price: Exclusive
Area: Pioneer Square
Address: 316 1st Ave S
Seattle, WA 98104
Phone: (206) 624-3034

#414
Abmeyer + Wood Fine Art
Category: Art Gallery
Area: Downtown
Address: 1210 2nd Ave
Seattle, WA 98101
Phone: (206) 628-9501

#415
Marion Oliver Mccaw Hall
Category: Performing Arts, Music Venues, Event Space
Average Price: Expensive
Area: Lower Queen Anne
Address: 321 Mercer St
Seattle, WA 98109
Phone: (206) 733-9725

#416
The Dinner Detective Murder Mystery Show
Category: Comedy Club, Performing Arts
Average Price: Expensive
Area: University District
Address: 4507 Brooklyn Ave Ne
Seattle, WA 98105
Phone: (866) 496-0535

#417
Seattle Repertory Theatre
Category: Performing Arts
Area: Lower Queen Anne
Address: 155 Mercer St
Seattle, WA 98109
Phone: (206) 443-2222

#418
Seattle Pro Musica
Category: Performing Arts
Area: Ballard
Address: 1770 NW 58th St
Seattle, WA 98107
Phone: (206) 781-2766

#419
Mariner Moose
Category: Local Flavor, Professional Sports Team
Area: Downtown
Address: Safeco Field
Seattle, WA 98101
Phone: (206) 101-2345

#420
Seattle Shakespeare Company
Category: Performing Arts
Area: Queen Anne
Address: Seattle Center-Center House Theatre Seattle, WA 98109
Phone: (206) 733-8222

#421
7 Ate 9 Clothing
Category: Art Gallery, Women's Clothing, Used, Vintage
Area: Pioneer Square
Address: 214 1st Ave S
Seattle, WA 98104
Phone: (206) 660-5158

#422
Flatcolor Gallery
Category: Art Gallery
Area: Pioneer Square
Address: 77 Main St
Seattle, WA 98104
Phone: (206) 390-6537

#423
Tether Design Gallery
Category: Art Gallery
Area: Pioneer Square
Address: 323 Occidental Ave S
Seattle, WA 98104
Phone: (206) 518-6300

#424
Cullom Gallery
Category: Art Gallery
Area: International District
Address: 603 S Main St
Seattle, WA 98104
Phone: (206) 340-8000

#425
Seattle Girls' Choir
Category: Performing Arts
Area: Central District
Address: 1910 E Spruce St
Seattle, WA 98122
Phone: (206) 526-1900

#426
Studio SODO
Category: Art Gallery, Art Classes
Average Price: Modest
Area: Sodo
Address: 85 S Atlantic
Seattle, WA 98134
Phone: (206) 200-4141

#427
The Wet Paint Studio
Category: Art Gallery
Average Price: Modest
Area: Fremont
Address: 819 N 49th St
Seattle, WA 98103
Phone: (206) 355-4382

#428
Seattle Models Guild
Category: Performing Arts
Area: South Lake Union, Eastlake
Address: 1264 Eastlake Ave E
Seattle, WA 98102
Phone: (206) 622-1406

#429
Blindfold Gallery
Category: Art Gallery
Area: Capitol Hill
Address: 1718 E Olive Way
Seattle, WA 98102
Phone: (206) 328-5100

#430
Kristopher Jenkins Voice Studio
Category: Performing Arts, Private Tutor
Area: Capitol Hill
Address: 1610 Belmont Ave
Seattle, WA 98122
Phone: (206) 588-6810

Seattle Travel Guide 2016 / Shops, Restaurants, Arts, Entertainment & Nightlife

---

#431
Frye Art Museum Store
Category: Art Gallery
Area: First Hill
Address: 704 Terry Ave
Seattle, WA 98104
Phone: (206) 432-8201

#432
Seattle Symphony
Category: Performing Arts
Area: Downtown
Address: 200 University St
Seattle, WA 98127
Phone: (206) 215-4747

#433
Stallman Studio Gallery
Category: Art Gallery
Area: Madison Valley
Address: 2331 E Madison St
Seattle, WA 98112
Phone: (206) 947-4422

#434
Efflux Creations
Category: Art Gallery
Area: Pioneer Square
Address: 201 Yesler Way
Seattle, WA 98104
Phone: (206) 922-2249

#435
Fictilis
Category: Art Gallery, Performing Arts
Area: Pioneer Square
Address: 210 S Washington St
Seattle, WA 98104
Phone: (206) 552-0210

#436
Bryan Ohno Gallery
Category: Art Gallery
Area: International District
Address: 521 S Main St
Seattle, WA 98104
Phone: (206) 459-6857

#437
4Culture
Category: Art Gallery, Cultural Center
Area: International District
Address: 101 Prefontaine Place S
Seattle, WA 98127
Phone: (206) 296-7580

#438
Enigma Studio - Chainber Break
Category: Arcade
Area: Fremont
Address: 4000 Aurora Ave N
Seattle, WA 98103
Phone: (202) 550-3870

#439
Seattle Art Loft
Category: Art Gallery
Area: Sodo
Address: 55 S Atlantic St
Seattle, WA 98134
Phone: (206) 417-9972

#440
Flamenco Seattle Music And Dance School
Category: Performing Arts, Dance School
Area: Wallingford
Address: 408 NE 44th St
Seattle, WA 98105
Phone: (206) 347-4583

#441
Glass Eye Studio
Category: Art Gallery
Area: Fremont, Ballard
Address: 600 NW 40th St
Seattle, WA 98107
Phone: (206) 782-6548

#442
South Lake Union Block Party
Category: Festival
Area: South Lake Union
Address: 101 Westlake Ave N
Seattle, WA 98109
Phone: (206) 342-5900

#443
Woodside Braseth Gallery
Category: Art Gallery
Area: Denny Triangle
Address: 2101 9th Ave
Seattle, WA 98121
Phone: (206) 622-7243

#444
Fantasy Unlimited Arcade
Category: Cinema, Adult Entertainment
Area: Denny Triangle
Address: 2027 Westlake Ave
Seattle, WA 98121
Phone: (206) 622-4669

#445
Crawl Space
Category: Art Gallery
Area: Capitol Hill
Address: 504 E Denny Way
Seattle, WA 98122
Phone: (206) 201-2441

#446
Level Up!
Category: Comedy Club, Performing Arts
Area: Capitol Hill
Address: 414 E Pine St
Seattle, WA 98122
Phone: (206) 325-2149

#447
Festa Italiana
Category: Festival
Area: Lower Queen Anne
Address: 305 Harrison St
Seattle, WA 98109
Phone: (206) 282-0627

#448
Warren Knapp Gallery
Category: Art Gallery
Area: Capitol Hill
Address: 1530 Melrose Ave
Seattle, WA 98122
Phone: (206) 381-3335

#449
Moonlight Tango
Category: Performing Arts
Area: Westlake
Address: 655 Crockett St A105
Seattle, WA 98109
Phone: (206) 484-7287

#450
Najla Seattle Belly Dancer
Category: Dance Studio, Performing Arts, Event Planning, Service
Area: Ballard
Address: 1138 NW Market St
Seattle, WA 98107
Phone: (206) 427-7790

#451
Seattle Chamber Music Society
Category: Performing Arts
Area: Lower Queen Anne
Address: 10 Harrison St
Seattle, WA 98109
Phone: (206) 283-8710

#452
Yoga Unique
Category: Yoga, Music Venues
Area: First Hill, Capitol Hill
Address: 1426 Broadway
Seattle, WA 98122
Phone: (206) 240-4125

#453
Velocity Art And Design
Category: Art Gallery
Area: Downtown
Address: 1411 4th Ave
Seattle, WA 98101
Phone: (206) 624-1772

#454
Sound And Smoke Presents
Category: Performing Arts
Area: Capitol Hill
Address: 1118 E Pike St
Seattle, WA 98122
Phone: (206) 351-9464

#455
BEHR Watercolor Paintings Gallery
Category: Art Gallery
Area: Downtown
Address: 1516 Western Ave
Seattle, WA 98101
Phone: (206) 446-0225

#456
Dwyer Gallery
Category: Art Gallery
Area: Downtown
Address: 1518 Western Ave
Seattle, WA 98101
Phone: (425) 681-6123

#457
The Crow$Nest
Category: Art Gallery
Area: Capitol Hill
Address: 1205 E Pike St
Seattle, WA 98122
Phone: (206) 579-7780

#458
The Rainier Valley
Category: Performing Arts, Shopping, Local Services
Area: First Hill
Address: 1011 Boren Ave #823
Seattle, WA 98104
Phone: (206) 355-5141

#459
The Black Box Theatre
Category: Performing Arts, Music Venues, Cinema
Area: Capitol Hill
Address: 20310 68th Ave W
Seattle, WA 98102
Phone: (425) 640-1448

#460
Seattle Baroque Orchestra
Category: Performing Arts
Area: Eastlake
Address: 2366 Eastlake Ave E
Seattle, WA 98102
Phone: (206) 325-7066

#461
The Cabiri
Category: Dance Studio, Performing Arts
Area: Downtown
Address: PO Box 21186
Seattle, WA 98111
Phone: (206) 632-1673

#462
M.I.A Gallery
Category: Art Gallery
Area: Downtown
Address: 1203 A Second Ave
Seattle, WA 98101
Phone: (206) 467-4297

#463
Rainy Night Productions
Category: Performing Arts
Area: First Hill
Address: PO Box 30808
Seattle, WA 98113
Phone: (206) 697-0276

#464
509 Wine Company
Category: Winery
Area: Wallingford
Address: 1300 N Northlake Way
Seattle, WA 98103
Phone: (206) 632-7516

#465
Da Projectz Music Recording Studio
Category: Music Venues,
Area: Pioneer Square
Address: 114 Alaskan Way S
Seattle, WA 98104
Phone: (206) 397-6094

#466
Millstream
Category: Jewelry, Art Gallery
Area: Pioneer Square
Address: 112 1st Ave S
Seattle, WA 98104
Phone: (206) 623-1960

#467
Punch Gallery
Category: Art Gallery
Area: Pioneer Square
Address: 119 Prefontaine Pl S
Seattle, WA 98104
Phone: (206) 621-1945

#468
Core Gallery
Category: Art Gallery
Area: Pioneer Square
Address: 117 Prefontaine Pl S
Seattle, WA 98104
Phone: (206) 467-4444

#469
Siren Song Wines
Category: Inexpensive Winery
Area: Queen Anne
Address: 4521 California Ave SW
Seattle, WA 98116
Phone: (206) 465-1047

#470
Flury & Company
Category: Art Gallery
Area: Pioneer Square
Address: 322 1st Avenue S
Seattle, WA 98104
Phone: (206) 748-9072

#471
Musicians' Association Of Seattle
Category: Performing Arts, Musicians
Area: Portage Bay
Address: 3209 Eastlake Ave E
Seattle, WA 98102
Phone: (206) 441-7600

#472
206 Zulu
Category: Music Venues
Area: Central District
Address: 153 14th Ave
Seattle, WA 98122
Phone: (206) 322-1151

#473
Neptune Gallery
Category: Art Gallery
Area: Central District
Address: 1708 Martin Luther King Jr Way
Seattle, WA 98144
Phone: (206) 913-1411

#474
The Green Chair Project
Category: Flowers, Gifts, Art Gallery
Area: University District
Address: 1001 NE Boat St
Seattle, WA 98105
Phone: (503) 580-0629

#475
West Coast Entertainment
Category: Casino
Area: Admiral
Address: 2705 California Ave SW
Seattle, WA 98116
Phone: (206) 938-0569

#476
Gallery 63 Eleven
Category: Art Gallery
Area: Ballard
Address: 6311 24th NW
Seattle, WA 98107
Phone: (206) 478-2238

#477
Sakura-Con
Category: Festival
Area: Downtown
Address: 800 Convention Pl
Seattle, WA 98101
Phone: (206) 447-5000

#478
Roxbury Lanes & Roxy's Casino
Category: Bowling, Casino, Bar
Average Price: Modest
Area: White Center
Address: 2823 SW Roxbury St
Seattle, WA 98126
Phone: (206) 935-7400

#479
Grand Image
Category: Art Gallery, Framing
Area: Industrial District
Address: 4730 Ohio Ave S
Seattle, WA 98134
Phone: (206) 624-0444

#480
Madart
Category: Art Gallery
Area: South Lake Union
Address: 325 Westlake Ave N
Seattle, WA 98109
Phone: (206) 623-1180

#481
Third & Wall Art Group
Category: Art Gallery
Area: South Lake Union
Address: 312 9th Ave N
Seattle, WA 98109
Phone: (206) 443-8452

#482
Wall Space Gallery
Category: Art Gallery,
Photography Store, Services
Area: South Lake Union
Address: 509 Dexter Ave
Seattle, WA 98109
Phone: (206) 330-9137

#483
Drop City Gallery
Category: Art Gallery
Area: South Lake Union
Address: 964 Denny Way
Seattle, WA 98109
Phone: (206) 624-2150

#484
Seattle Glass Galary
Category: Art Gallery
Area: Denny Triangle
Address: 900 Lenora St
Seattle, WA 98121
Phone: (206) 708-6711

#485
Heartsinspyre Entertainment
Category: Performing Arts
Area: Capitol Hill
Address: 700 E Mercer
Seattle, WA 98102
Phone: (206) 992-7935

#486
The King Kat Theater
Category: Music Venues
Area: Denny Triangle
Address: 2130 6th Ave
Seattle, WA 98121
Phone: (206) 269-7444

#487
Artattack Theater
Category: Performing Arts
Area: Capitol Hill
Address: 1715 Olive Way East
Seattle, WA 98112
Phone: (206) 905-9835

#488
Seattle School
Category: Performing Arts
Area: Lower Queen Anne
Address: 301 Mercer St
Seattle, WA 98109
Phone: (206) 441-2435

#489
One Reel
Category: Performing Arts,
Opera, Ballet, Music Venues
Area: Lower Queen Anne
Address: 222 Mercer St
Seattle, WA 98109
Phone: (206) 285-1718

#490
Dead End Press
Category: Art Gallery
Area: Ballard
Address: 1518 NW 52nd St
Seattle, WA 98107
Phone: (302) 743-5474

#491
Firesteed Corporation
Category: Winery
Area: Denny Triangle
Address: 1809 7th Avenue
Seattle, WA 98101
Phone: (206) 233-0683

#492
Dueling Pianos With Jeff & Rhiannon
Category: Performing Arts
Area: Downtown
Address: 737 Olive Way 2404
Seattle, WA 98101
Phone: (206) 724-2782

#493
Paramount Defined
Category: Performing Arts
Area: Downtown
Address: 911 Pine Street
Seattle, WA 98101
Phone: (206) 902-5500

#494
The Enematic Cinematic: Lives!!
Category: Cinema
Area: Belltown
Address: 2322 2nd Ave
Seattle, WA 98121
Phone: (206) 441-5823

#495
Wine Shots: Comedy's Happiest Hour!
Category: Comedy Club, Cabaret
Area: Belltown
Address: 2322 2nd Ave
Seattle, WA 98121
Phone: (206) 441-5823

#496
Theater Puget Sound
Category: Performing Arts
Area: Lower Queen Anne
Address: 305 Harrison St
Seattle, WA 98109
Phone: (206) 770-0370

#497
Cineplex Odeon Theatres
Category: Cinema
Area: Downtown
Address: 1501 7th Ave
Seattle, WA 98101
Phone: (206) 223-9600

#498
SIFF Cinema
Category: Cinema
Area: Capitol Hill
Address: 805 E Pine St
Seattle, WA 98122
Phone: (206) 720-4560

#499
Westlake Gallery
Category: Art Gallery
Area: Downtown
Address: 400 Pine Street
Seattle, WA 98101
Phone: (206) 625-0084

#500
Broadway Management Group
Category: Performing Arts, Cinema
Area: Capitol Hill
Address: 1625 Broadway
Seattle, WA 98122
Phone: (206) 325-3113

TOP 500 NIGHTLIFE
The Most Recommended by Locals & Trevelers
(From #1 to #500)

#1
The Backdoor At Roxy's
Category: Lounge, American
Average Price: Modest
Area: Fremont
Address: 462 N 36th St
Seattle, WA 98103
Phone: (206) 632-7322

#2
Bathtub Gin & Co
Category: Cocktail Bar
Average Price: Modest
Area: Belltown
Address: 2205 2nd Ave
Seattle, WA 98121
Phone: (206) 728-6069

#3
Q Nightclub
Category: Dance Club, Lounge, Venues, Event Space
Average Price: Modest
Area: First Hill, Capitol Hill
Address: 1426 Broadway
Seattle, WA 98122
Phone: (206) 432-9306

#4
Moe Bar
Category: Bar, Music Venues
Average Price: Inexpensive
Area: First Hill, Capitol Hill
Address: 1425 10th Ave
Seattle, WA 98122
Phone: (206) 709-9951

#5
Volume
Category: Bar, Dance Club, Music Venues
Average Price: Modest
Area: Pioneer Square
Address: 172 S Washington St
Seattle, WA 98104
Phone: (206) 486-0805

#6
The Sitting Room
Category: Lounge, Wine Bar, Tapas Bar
Average Price: Modest
Area: Lower Queen Anne
Address: 108 W Roy St
Seattle, WA 98119
Phone: (206) 285-2830

#7
Nitelite Lounge
Category: Dive Bar, American
Average Price: Inexpensive
Area: Belltown
Address: 1920 2nd Ave
Seattle, WA 98101
Phone: (206) 443-0899

#8
Unicorn
Category: American, Lounge
Average Price: Modest
Area: Capitol Hill
Address: 1118 E Pike St
Seattle, WA 98122
Phone: (206) 325-6492

#9
Rock Box
Category: Karaoke, Lounge
Average Price: Modest
Area: Capitol Hill
Address: 1603 Nagle Pl
Seattle, WA 98122
Phone: (206) 302-7625

#10
The Diller Room
Category: Bar
Average Price: Modest
Area: Downtown
Address: 1224 1st Ave
Seattle, WA 98101
Phone: (206) 467-4042

#11
Cha Cha Lounge
Category: Lounge
Average Price: Inexpensive
Area: Capitol Hill
Address: 1013 E Pike St
Seattle, WA 98122
Phone: (206) 322-0703

#12
Unexpected Productions
Category: Performing Arts, Lounge, Comedy Club
Average Price: Inexpensive
Area: Queen Anne
Address: 1428 Post Alley
Seattle, WA 98101
Phone: (206) 587-2414

#13
Aston Manor
Category: Dance Club, Bar
Average Price: Modest
Area: Industrial District
Address: 2946 1st Ave S
Seattle, WA 98134
Phone: (206) 382-7866

#14
Knee High Stocking Co.
Category: American, Cocktail Bar
Average Price: Modest
Area: Capitol Hill
Address: 1356 E Olive Way
Seattle, WA 98122
Phone: (206) 979-7049

#15
Foundation Nightclub
Category: Dance Club, Music Venues
Average Price: Modest
Area: Belltown
Address: 2218 Western Ave
Seattle, WA 98121
Phone: (206) 535-7285

#16
The Tasting Room
Category: Winery, Wine Bar
Average Price: Modest
Area: Downtown
Address: 1924 Post Alley
Seattle, WA 98101
Phone: (206) 770-9463

#17
Diesel Seattle
Category: Gay Bar
Average Price: Inexpensive
Area: Central District
Address: 1413 14th Ave
Seattle, WA 98122
Phone: (206) 322-1080

#18
Tia Lou
Category: Lounge, Mexican, Dance Club
Average Price: Modest
Area: Belltown
Address: 2218 1st Ave
Seattle, WA 98121
Phone: (206) 733-8226

#19
Can Can
Category: Cabaret, Lounge
Average Price: Modest
Area: Downtown
Address: 94 Pike St
Seattle, WA 98101
Phone: (206) 652-0832

#20
Suite 410
Category: Lounge
Average Price: Modest
Area: Belltown
Address: 410 Stewart St
Seattle, WA 98101
Phone: (206) 682-4101

#21
Rob Roy
Category: Lounge, Cocktail Bar
Average Price: Modest
Area: Belltown
Address: 2332 2nd Ave
Seattle, WA 98121
Phone: (206) 956-8423

#22
Nectar Lounge
Category: Bar, Music Venues, Event Space
Average Price: Modest
Area: Fremont
Address: 412 N 36th St
Seattle, WA 98103
Phone: (206) 632-2020

#23
Honeyhole
Category: Bar, Sandwiches
Average Price: Inexpensive
Area: First Hill, Capitol Hill
Address: 703 E Pike St
Seattle, WA 98122
Phone: (206) 709-1399

#24
College Inn Pub
Category: Pub
Average Price: Inexpensive
Area: University District
Address: 4006 University Way NE
Seattle, WA 98105
Phone: (206) 634-2307

#25
High Dive
Category: Music Venues, Dive Bar, American
Average Price: Inexpensive
Area: Fremont
Address: 513 N 36th St
Seattle, WA 98103
Phone: (206) 632-0212

#26
Bookstore Bar & Café
Category: Bar, American
Average Price: Modest
Area: Downtown
Address: 1007 1st Ave
Seattle, WA 98104
Phone: (206) 624-3646

#27
Barca
Category: Venues, Event Space, Cocktail Bar
Average Price: Modest
Area: Capitol Hill
Address: 1510 11th Ave
Seattle, WA 98122
Phone: (206) 325-8263

#28
Grim's
Category: Bar, American, Breakfast & Brunch
Average Price: Modest
Area: Capitol Hill
Address: 1512 11th Ave
Seattle, WA 98122
Phone: (206) 324-7467

Seattle Travel Guide 2016 / Shops, Restaurants, Arts, Entertainment & Nightlife

#29
Tavern Law
Category: American, Lounge
Average Price: Modest
Area: Capitol Hill
Address: 1406 12th Ave
Seattle, WA 98122
Phone: (206) 322-9734

#30
Contour
Category: Dance Club, American, Bar
Average Price: Inexpensive
Area: Downtown
Address: 807 1st Ave
Seattle, WA 98104
Phone: (206) 447-7704

#31
Shelter Lounge
Category: Lounge
Average Price: Modest
Area: Ballard
Address: 4910 Leary Ave NW
Seattle, WA 98107
Phone: (206) 829-8568

#32
Balmar
Category: American, Lounge, Dance Club
Average Price: Modest
Area: Ballard
Address: 5449 Ballard Ave NW
Seattle, WA 98107
Phone: (206) 486-5449

#33
Needle And Thread
Category: Lounge, Cocktail Bar
Average Price: Expensive
Area: Central District, Capitol Hill
Address: 1406 12th Ave
Seattle, WA 98122
Phone: (206) 325-0133

#34
West 5
Category: American, Lounge
Average Price: Modest
Area: Junction
Address: 4539 California Ave SW
Seattle, WA 98116
Phone: (206) 935-1966

#35
Highline
Category: Vegan, Bar, Music Venues
Average Price: Modest
Area: Capitol Hill
Address: 210 Broadway E
Seattle, WA 98102
Phone: (206) 328-7837

#36
The Ballroom
Category: Pool Hall, Lounge, Pizza
Average Price: Modest
Area: Fremont
Address: 456 N 36th St
Seattle, WA 98103
Phone: (206) 634-2575

#37
Some Random Bar
Category: Pub, American
Average Price: Modest
Area: Belltown
Address: 2604 1st Ave
Seattle, WA 98121
Phone: (206) 745-2185

#38
Garage
Category: Pool Hall, Bowling, Bar
Average Price: Modest
Area: First Hill
Address: 1130 Broadway
Seattle, WA 98122
Phone: (206) 322-2296

#39
The Hideout
Category: Lounge
Average Price: Modest
Area: First Hill
Address: 1005 Boren Ave
Seattle, WA 98127
Phone: (206) 903-8480

#40
Mulleady's Irish Pub
Category: Pub, Irish, Breakfast & Brunch
Average Price: Modest
Area: Magnolia
Address: 3055 21st Ave W
Seattle, WA 98199
Phone: (206) 283-8843

#41
Paragon Restaurant And Bar
Category: American, Pub, Music Venues
Average Price: Modest
Area: Queen Anne
Address: 2125 Queen Anne Ave N
Seattle, WA 98109
Phone: (206) 283-4548

#42
LUCID
Category: Jazz, Blues, Lounge
Average Price: Modest
Area: University District
Address: 5241 University Way NE
Seattle, WA 98105
Phone: (206) 402-3042

#43
The Beer Junction
Category: Beer, Wine, Spirits, Bar
Average Price: Modest
Area: Junction
Address: 4511 California Ave SW
Seattle, WA 98116
Phone: (206) 938-2337

#44
Vito's
Category: Lounge, Italian
Average Price: Modest
Area: First Hill
Address: 927 9th Ave
Seattle, WA 98104
Phone: (206) 397-4053

#45
Hazlewood
Category: Lounge
Average Price: Modest
Area: Ballard
Address: 2311 NW Market St
Seattle, WA 98107
Phone: (206) 783-0478

#46
Alibi Room
Category: American, Lounge, Dance Club
Average Price: Modest
Area: Downtown
Address: 85 Pike St
Seattle, WA 98101
Phone: (206) 623-3180

#47
Neighbours
Category: Dance Club, Gay Bar
Average Price: Modest
Area: Capitol Hill
Address: 1509 Broadway
Seattle, WA 98122
Phone: (206) 324-5358

#48
Havana
Category: Lounge, Dance Club
Average Price: Modest
Area: Capitol Hill
Address: 1010 E Pike St
Seattle, WA 98122
Phone: (206) 323-2822

#49
The Showbox
Category: Music Venues, Bar
Average Price: Modest
Area: Downtown
Address: 1426 1st Ave
Seattle, WA 98101
Phone: (206) 628-3151

#50
Amber
Category: Bar, American, Dance Club
Average Price: Modest
Area: Belltown
Address: 2214 1st Ave
Seattle, WA 98121
Phone: (206) 728-8500

#51
Witness
Category: Southern, Cocktail Bar
Average Price: Modest
Area: Capitol Hill
Address: 410 Broadway E
Seattle, WA 98102
Phone: (206) 329-0248

#52
Ballard Loft
Category: Sports Bar, American
Average Price: Modest
Area: Ballard
Address: 5105 Ballard Ave NW
Seattle, WA 98107
Phone: (206) 420-2737

#53
Über Tavern
Category: Bar
Average Price: Modest
Area: Greenwood, Phinney Ridge
Address: 7517 Aurora Ave N
Seattle, WA 98103
Phone: (206) 782-2337

#54
Babirusa
Category: Bar, American
Average Price: Modest
Area: Eastlake
Address: 2236 Eastlake Ave E
Seattle, WA 98102
Phone: (206) 329-2744

#55
White Horse Trading Company
Category: Pub, Beer, Wine, Spirits
Average Price: Modest
Area: Downtown
Address: 1908 Post Alley
Seattle, WA 98101
Phone: (206) 441-7767

#56
Big Picture
Category: Cinema, Lounge, Venues, Event Space
Average Price: Modest
Area: Belltown
Address: 2505 1st Ave
Seattle, WA 98121
Phone: (206) 256-0566

#57
Bottlehouse
Category: Wine Bar, Tapas
Average Price: Modest
Area: Madrona
Address: 1416 34th Ave
Seattle, WA 98122
Phone: (206) 708-7164

#58
Montana
Category: Dive Bar, Cocktail Bar
Average Price: Inexpensive
Area: Capitol Hill
Address: 1506 E Olive Way
Seattle, WA 98122
Phone: (206) 422-4647

#59
Pie Bar
Category: Cocktail Bar, Desserts
Average Price: Modest
Area: Capitol Hill
Address: 1361 E Olive Way
Seattle, WA 98122
Phone: (206) 257-1459

#60
The Crocodile
Category: Music Venues, Bar
Average Price: Modest
Area: Belltown
Address: 2200 2nd Ave
Seattle, WA 98121
Phone: (206) 441-5611

#61
Rhein Haus
Category: German, Pub
Average Price: Modest
Area: Central District
Address: 912 12th Ave
Seattle, WA 98122
Phone: (206) 325-5409

#62
The Stumbling Monk
Category: Pub
Average Price: Modest
Area: Capitol Hill
Address: 1635 E Olive Way
Seattle, WA 98102
Phone: (206) 860-0916

#63
The Forge Lounge
Category: Lounge
Average Price: Inexpensive
Area: Downtown
Address: 65 Marion St
Seattle, WA 98104
Phone: (206) 623-5107

#64
Re:Public
Category: American, Bar
Average Price: Modest
Area: South Lake Union
Address: 429 Westlake Ave N
Seattle, WA 98109
Phone: (206) 467-5300

#65
Radiator Whiskey
Category: American, Cocktail Bar
Average Price: Modest
Area: Downtown
Address: 94 Pike St
Seattle, WA 98101
Phone: (206) 467-4268

#66
Shorty's
Category: Dive Bar, Arcade
Average Price: Inexpensive
Area: Belltown
Address: 2222 2nd Ave
Seattle, WA 98121
Phone: (206) 441-5449

#67
The Whisky Bar
Category: Scottish, British, Pub
Average Price: Modest
Area: Belltown
Address: 2122 2nd Ave
Seattle, WA 98121
Phone: (206) 443-4490

#68
Latona Pub
Category: Pub
Average Price: Modest
Area: Greenlake
Address: 6423 Latona Ave NE
Seattle, WA 98115
Phone: (206) 525-2238

#69
The Zig Zag Café
Category: American, Cocktail Bar
Average Price: Modest
Area: Downtown
Address: 1501 Western Ave
Seattle, WA 98101
Phone: (206) 625-1146

#70
The Upstairs
Category: Lounge, Cocktail Bar
Average Price: Modest
Area: Belltown
Address: 2209 2nd Ave
Seattle, WA 98121
Phone: (206) 441-4013

#71
Canon
Category: American, Cocktail Bar
Average Price: Modest
Area: Central District
Address: 928 12th Ave
Seattle, WA 98122
Phone: (206) 552-9755

#72
Sunset Tavern
Category: Dive Bar, Music Venues, Pizza
Average Price: Inexpensive
Area: Ballard
Address: 5433 Ballard Ave NW
Seattle, WA 98107
Phone: (206) 784-4880

#73
Seamonster Lounge
Category: Jazz, Blues, Lounge, Music Venues
Average Price: Inexpensive
Area: Wallingford
Address: 2202 N 45th St
Seattle, WA 98103
Phone: (206) 992-1120

#74
The Twilight Exit
Category: Dive Bar, American
Average Price: Inexpensive
Area: Central District
Address: 2514 E Cherry St
Seattle, WA 98122
Phone: (206) 324-7462

#75
Lava Lounge
Category: Lounge, Dive Bar
Average Price: Inexpensive
Area: Belltown
Address: 2226 2nd Ave
Seattle, WA 98121
Phone: (206) 441-5660

#76
Smith
Category: Bar, American, Breakfast & Brunch
Average Price: Modest
Area: Capitol Hill
Address: 332 15th Ave E
Seattle, WA 98112
Phone: (206) 709-1900

#77
The Grizzled Wizard
Category: Dive Bar, Sandwiches
Average Price: Inexpensive
Area: Wallingford
Address: 2317 N 45th St
Seattle, WA 98103
Phone: (206) 849-0062

#78
The Octopus Bar
Category: Tapas, Gastropub, Cocktail Bar
Average Price: Inexpensive
Area: Wallingford
Address: 2109 N 45th St
Seattle, WA 98103
Phone: (206) 582-2483

#79
The Bottleneck Lounge
Category: Lounge
Average Price: Modest
Area: Madison Valley, Capitol Hill
Address: 2328 E Madison St
Seattle, WA 98138
Phone: (206) 323-1098

#80
Red Door
Category: Pub, American
Average Price: Modest
Area: Fremont
Address: 3401 Evanston Ave N
Seattle, WA 98103
Phone: (206) 547-7521

#81
Fremont Brewing
Category: Brewerie, Bar
Average Price: Inexpensive
Area: Fremont
Address: 1050 N 34th St
Seattle, WA 98103
Phone: (206) 420-2407

#82
Trinity Nightclub
Category: Dance Club, Music Venues
Average Price: Modest
Area: Pioneer Square
Address: 111 Yesler Way
Seattle, WA 98104
Phone: (206) 697-7702

#83
The Sixgill
Category: American, Tapas, Pub
Average Price: Modest
Area: Fremont
Address: 3417 Evanston Ave N
Seattle, WA 98103
Phone: (206) 466-2846

#84
Medina Hookah Lounge
Category: Hookah Bar, Music Venues
Average Price: Inexpensive
Area: International District
Address: 700 S Dearborn St
Seattle, WA 98134
Phone: (206) 856-7660

#85
Sun Liquor
Category: Lounge, Cocktail Bar
Average Price: Modest
Area: Capitol Hill
Address: 607 Summit Ave E
Seattle, WA 98102
Phone: (206) 860-1130

#86
Teachers Lounge
Category: Lounge
Average Price: Modest
Area: Greenwood
Address: 8505 Greenwood Ave N
Seattle, WA 98103
Phone: (206) 706-2880

#87
Tippe And Drague Alehouse
Category: American, Pub
Average Price: Modest
Area: Beacon Hill
Address: 3315 Beacon Ave S
Seattle, WA 98144
Phone: (206) 538-0094

#88
Beveridge Place Pub
Category: Pub
Average Price: Modest
Area: Seaview
Address: 6413 California Ave SW
Seattle, WA 98136
Phone: (206) 932-9906

#89
Liberty
Category: Lounge, Coffee, Tea, Sushi Bar
Average Price: Modest
Area: Capitol Hill
Address: 517 15th Ave E
Seattle, WA 98112
Phone: (206) 323-9898

#90
Le Faux
Category: Performing Arts, Gay Bar
Average Price: Modest
Area: Capitol Hill
Address: 300 Broadway E
Seattle, WA 98122
Phone: (206) 334-0513

#91
Fuel
Category: Sports Bar, American
Average Price: Inexpensive
Area: Pioneer Square
Address: 164 Washington St
Seattle, WA 98104
Phone: (206) 405-3835

#92
Barnacle
Category: Wine Bar, Seafood, Tapas
Average Price: Modest
Area: Ballard
Address: 4743 Ballard Ave NW
Seattle, WA 98107
Phone: (206) 706-3379

#93
Palace Kitchen
Category: American, Bar, Desserts
Average Price: Modest
Area: Denny Triangle
Address: 2030 5th Ave
Seattle, WA 98121
Phone: (206) 448-2001

#94
Triumph Bar
Category: Wine Bar, Cocktail Bar, Gastropub
Average Price: Modest
Area: Lower Queen Anne
Address: 114 Republican St
Seattle, WA 98109
Phone: (206) 420-1791

#95
Skylark Café & Club
Category: Music Venues, American, Bar
Average Price: Modest
Area: Youngstown
Address: 3803 Delridge Way SW
Seattle, WA 98106
Phone: (206) 935-2111

#96
Sake Nomi
Category: Japanese, Bar
Average Price: Modest
Area: Pioneer Square
Address: 76 S Washington St
Seattle, WA 98104
Phone: (206) 467-7253

#97
The Mix Martini Lounge
Category: Lounge, American
Average Price: Modest
Area: Belltown
Address: 2318 2nd Ave
Seattle, WA 98121
Phone: (206) 448-2656

#98
The Kraken Bar & Lounge
Category: Dive Bar, American, Music Venues
Average Price: Inexpensive
Area: University District
Address: 5257 University Way NE
Seattle, WA 98105
Phone: (206) 522-5004

#99
Phoenecia
Category: Tapas Bar, Wine Bar, Pizza
Average Price: Modest
Area: Alki
Address: 2716 Alki Ave SW
Seattle, WA 98116
Phone: (206) 935-6550

#100
The Pine Box
Category: Pub, American
Average Price: Modest
Area: Capitol Hill
Address: 1600 Melrose Ave
Seattle, WA 98122
Phone: (206) 588-0375

#101
Bar Cantinetta
Category: Bar, Tapas, Italian
Average Price: Modest
Area: Madison Valley
Address: 2811 E Madison St
Seattle, WA 98112
Phone: (206) 329-1501

#102
Rendezvous
Category: Bar, Performing Arts, American
Average Price: Modest
Area: Belltown
Address: 2322 2nd Ave
Seattle, WA 98121
Phone: (206) 441-5823

#103
Rabbit Hole
Category: Dive Bar
Average Price: Inexpensive
Area: Belltown
Address: 2222 2nd Ave
Seattle, WA 98121
Phone: (206) 956-4653

#104
Keys On Main
Category: Bar, Music Venues
Average Price: Modest
Area: Lower Queen Anne
Address: 11 Roy St
Seattle, WA 98109
Phone: (206) 270-4444

#105
Purr Cocktail Lounge
Category: Gay Bar, Lounge
Average Price: Modest
Area: Capitol Hill
Address: 1518 11th Ave
Seattle, WA 98122
Phone: (206) 325-3112

#106
Hooverville Bar
Category: Bar, American
Average Price: Inexpensive
Area: Industrial District
Address: 1721 1st Ave S
Seattle, WA 98134
Phone: (206) 264-2428

#107
Bait Shop
Category: Bar, Seafood
Average Price: Modest
Area: Capitol Hill
Address: 606 Broadway E
Seattle, WA 98102
Phone: (206) 420-8742

#108
Clever Bottle
Category: Wine Bar, Lounge
Average Price: Modest
Area: Belltown
Address: 2222 2nd Ave
Seattle, WA 98121
Phone: (206) 915-2220

#109
Streamline Tavern
Category: Bar
Average Price: Inexpensive
Area: Lower Queen Anne
Address: 121 W Mercer St
Seattle, WA 98119
Phone: (206) 283-0519

#110
Essex
Category: Bar
Average Price: Modest
Area: Phinney Ridge
Address: 1421 NW 70th St
Seattle, WA 98117
Phone: (206) 838-1960

#111
The Tin Hat
Category: Dive Bar, American
Average Price: Inexpensive
Area: Phinney Ridge
Address: 512 NW 65th St
Seattle, WA 98117
Phone: (206) 782-2770

#112
Conor Byrne Pub
Category: Pub, Irish
Average Price: Inexpensive
Area: Ballard
Address: 5140 Ballard Ave NW
Seattle, WA 98107
Phone: (206) 784-3640

#113
Add-A-Ball
Category: Arcade, Bar
Average Price: Inexpensive
Area: Fremont
Address: 315 N 36th St
Seattle, WA 98103
Phone: (206) 696-1613

#114
Comet Tavern
Category: Dive Bar, American
Average Price: Inexpensive
Area: First Hill, Capitol Hill
Address: 922 E Pike St
Seattle, WA 98122
Phone: (206) 322-9272

#115
Targy's Tavern
Category: Dive Bar
Average Price: Inexpensive
Area: Queen Anne
Address: 600 W Crockett St
Seattle, WA 98119
Phone: (206) 352-8882

#116
Quarter Lounge
Category: Dive Bar
Average Price: Inexpensive
Area: First Hill
Address: 909 Madison St
Seattle, WA 98104
Phone: (206) 332-0772

#117
The Neighbor Lady
Category: Bar, American
Average Price: Modest
Area: Central District
Address: 2308 E Union St
Seattle, WA 98122
Phone: (206) 695-2072

#118
The Great Nabob
Category: Bar
Average Price: Modest
Area: Lower Queen Anne
Address: 819 5th Ave N
Seattle, WA 98109
Phone: (206) 281-9850

#119
The Noble Fir
Category: Bar, Tapas
Average Price: Modest
Area: Ballard
Address: 5316 Ballard Ave NW
Seattle, WA 98107
Phone: (206) 420-7425

#120
Polar Bar
Category: Lounge, Venues, Event Space
Average Price: Modest
Area: Downtown
Address: 700 3rd Ave
Seattle, WA 98104
Phone: (206) 340-0340

#121
Peso's Kitchen & Lounge
Category: Mexican, Lounge
Average Price: Modest
Area: Lower Queen Anne
Address: 605 Queen Anne Ave N
Seattle, WA 98109
Phone: (206) 283-9353

#122
Maekawa Bar
Category: Japanese, Pub, Tapas
Average Price: Modest
Area: International District
Address: 601 S King St
Seattle, WA 98104
Phone: (206) 622-0634

#123
Hot Cakes Molten Chocolate Cakery
Category: Desserts, Coffee, Tea, Bar
Average Price: Modest
Area: Ballard
Address: 5427 Ballard Ave NW
Seattle, WA 98107
Phone: (206) 420-3431

#124
Feedback Lounge
Category: Lounge
Average Price: Modest
Area: Seaview
Address: 6451 California Ave SW
Seattle, WA 98136
Phone: (206) 453-3259

#125
Purple Café And Wine Bar
Category: American, Wine Bar
Average Price: Expensive
Area: Downtown
Address: 1225 4th Ave
Seattle, WA 98101
Phone: (206) 829-2280

#126
Owl'n Thistle Irish Pub
Category: Irish, Irish Pub
Average Price: Modest
Area: Downtown
Address: 808 Post Ave
Seattle, WA 98104
Phone: (206) 621 7777

Seattle Travel Guide 2016 / Shops, Restaurants, Arts, Entertainment & Nightlife

#127
A Terrible Beauty
Category: Irish, Irish Pub
Average Price: Modest
Area: South Lake Union, Eastlake
Address: 1001 Fairview Ave N
Seattle, WA 98109
Phone: (206) 420-4498

#128
Baranof
Category: Dive Bar,
Breakfast & Brunch, Karaoke
Average Price: Inexpensive
Area: Greenwood
Address: 8549 Greenwood Ave N
Seattle, WA 98103
Phone: (206) 782-9260

#129
E Smith Mercantile
Category: Cocktail Bar, Gift Shop
Average Price: Modest
Area: Pioneer Square
Address: 208 1st Ave S
Seattle, WA 98104
Phone: (206) 641-7250

#130
Eastlake Zoo Tavern
Category: Sports Bar, Dive Bar, Pool Hall
Average Price: Inexpensive
Area: Eastlake
Address: 2301 Eastlake Ave E
Seattle, WA 98102
Phone: (206) 329-3277

#131
9 LB Hammer
Category: Dive Bar
Average Price: Inexpensive
Area: Georgetown
Address: 6009 Airport Way S
Seattle, WA 98108
Phone: (206) 762-3373

#132
Lo-Fi Performance Gallery
Category: Music Venues, Bar, Dance Club
Average Price: Inexpensive
Area: South Lake Union
Address: 429 Eastlake Ave E
Seattle, WA 98109
Phone: (206) 254-2824

#133
The 5 Point Café
Category: Dive Bar, Diner
Average Price: Modest
Area: Belltown
Address: 415 Cedar St
Seattle, WA 98121
Phone: (206) 448-9991

#134
Sully's Lounge
Category: Pub, Sports Bar
Average Price: Modest
Area: Queen Anne
Address: 1625 Queen Anne Ave N
Seattle, WA 98109
Phone: (206) 283-3900

#135
Pioneer Square Saloon
Category: Bar
Average Price: Inexpensive
Area: Pioneer Square
Address: 77 Yesler Way
Seattle, WA 98104
Phone: (206) 628-6444

#136
Jules Maes Saloon
Category: Bar, Music Venues
Average Price: Modest
Area: Georgetown
Address: 5919 Airport Way S
Seattle, WA 98127
Phone: (206) 957-7766

#137
Jolly Roger Taproom
Category: Brewerie, Pub
Average Price: Modest
Area: Ballard
Address: 1111 NW Ballard Way
Seattle, WA 98107
Phone: (206) 782-6181

#138
Dexter & Hayes Public House
Category: Pub, American
Average Price: Modest
Area: Westlake
Address: 1628 Dexter Ave N
Seattle, WA 98109
Phone: (206) 283-7786

#139
Le Caviste
Category: Wine Bar, French
Average Price: Modest
Area: Denny Triangle
Address: 1919 7th Ave
Seattle, WA 98101
Phone: (206) 728-2657

#140
The Monkey Pub
Category: Pub
Average Price: Inexpensive
Area: University District
Address: 5305 Roosevelt Way NE
Seattle, WA 98105
Phone: (206) 523-6457

Seattle Travel Guide 2016 / Shops, Restaurants, Arts, Entertainment & Nightlife

#141
Dante's
Category: Bar, American, Dance Club
Average Price: Inexpensive
Area: University District
Address: 5300 Roosevelt Way NE
Seattle, WA 98105
Phone: (206) 525-1300

#142
Mercury At Machinewerks
Category: Lounge, Music Venues, Dance Club
Average Price: Inexpensive
Area: First Hill
Address: 1009 E Union St
Seattle, WA 98122
Phone: (206) 328-9481

#143
Talarico's Pizzeria & Lounge
Category: Pizza, Lounge, Karaoke
Average Price: Modest
Area: Fairmount Park, Junction
Address: 4718 California Ave SW
Seattle, WA 98116
Phone: (206) 937-3463

#144
Rumba
Category: Caribbean, Cuban, Lounge
Average Price: Modest
Area: Capitol Hill
Address: 1112 Pike St
Seattle, WA 98101
Phone: (206) 583-7177

#145
Von's 1000Spirits
Category: American, Burgers, Cocktail Bar
Average Price: Modest
Area: Downtown
Address: 1225 1st Ave
Seattle, WA 98101
Phone: (206) 621-8667

#146
Tini Bigs Lounge
Category: Lounge, Cocktail Bar, Sandwiches
Average Price: Modest
Area: Lower Queen Anne
Address: 100 Denny Way
Seattle, WA 98109
Phone: (206) 284-0931

#147
Acquabar
Category: Dance Club, Lounge, Seafood
Average Price: Modest
Area: Belltown
Address: 305 Bell St
Seattle, WA 98121
Phone: (206) 728-6583

#148
The Leary Traveler
Category: Pub, American
Average Price: Modest
Area: Fremont
Address: 4356 Leary Way NW
Seattle, WA 98107
Phone: (206) 783-4805

#149
Tap House Grill
Category: Pub, American
Average Price: Modest
Area: Downtown
Address: 1506 6th Ave
Seattle, WA 98101
Phone: (206) 816-3314

#150
The Pub At Third Place
Category: Pub, American
Average Price: Modest
Area: Ravenna
Address: 6504 20th Ave NE
Seattle, WA 98115
Phone: (206) 523-0217

#151
Waterwheel Lounge
Category: Bar, Karaoke
Average Price: Inexpensive
Area: Loyal Heights
Address: 7034 15th Ave NW
Seattle, WA 98117
Phone: (206) 784-5701

#152
Serafina
Category: Italian, Bar, Music Venues
Average Price: Expensive
Area: Eastlake
Address: 2043 Eastlake Ave E
Seattle, WA 98102
Phone: (206) 323-0807

#153
El Norte Lounge
Category: Lounge, Mexican
Average Price: Modest
Area: Olympic Hills
Address: 13717 Lake City Way NE
Seattle, WA 98125
Phone: (206) 954-1349

#154
Ten Mercer
Category: Bar, American, Gluten-Free
Average Price: Modest
Area: Lower Queen Anne
Address: 10 Mercer St
Seattle, WA 98109
Phone: (206) 691-3723

#155
Duchess Tavern
Category: Dive Bar
Average Price: Inexpensive
Area: Ravenna
Address: 2827 NE 55th St
Seattle, WA 98105
Phone: (206) 527-8606

#156
The Royal Room
Category: Music Venues, Lounge
Average Price: Modest
Area: Columbia City
Address: 5000 Rainier Ave S
Seattle, WA 98118
Phone: (206) 906-9920

#157
Brouwer's Cafe
Category: European, Pub, Belgian
Average Price: Modest
Area: Fremont
Address: 400 N 35th St
Seattle, WA 98103
Phone: (206) 267-2437

#158
Naked City Brewery & Taphouse
Category: Brewerie, Pub, American
Average Price: Modest
Area: Greenwood
Address: 8564 Greenwood Ave N
Seattle, WA 98103
Phone: (206) 838-6299

#159
Blue Moon Tavern
Category: Dive Bar
Average Price: Inexpensive
Area: University District
Address: 712 NE 45th St
Seattle, WA 98105
Phone: (206) 675-9116

#160
Oliver's Lounge
Category: Lounge
Average Price: Modest
Area: Downtown
Address: 405 Olive Way
Seattle, WA 98101
Phone: (206) 623-8700

#161
Pony
Category: Gay Bar, Dive Bar
Average Price: Inexpensive
Area: Central District, Capitol Hill
Address: 1221 E Madison St
Seattle, WA 98122
Phone: (206) 324-2854

#162
The Redwood
Category: Dive Bar
Average Price: Inexpensive
Area: Capitol Hill
Address: 514 E Howell St
Seattle, WA 98102
Phone: (206) 329-1952

#163
The Hillside Bar
Category: Bar
Average Price: Inexpensive
Area: Capitol Hill
Address: 1520 E Olive Way
Seattle, WA 98122
Phone: (206) 324-0154

#164
The Benbow Room
Category: Dive Bar
Average Price: Modest
Area: Admiral
Address: 4210 SW Admiral Way
Seattle, WA 98116
Phone: (206) 922-3313

#165
Hilltop Ale House
Category: Pub, American
Average Price: Modest
Area: Queen Anne
Address: 2129 Queen Anne Ave N
Seattle, WA 98109
Phone: (206) 285-3877

#166
The Mix
Category: Lounge, Cajun, Creole
Average Price: Inexpensive
Area: Georgetown
Address: 6006 12th Ave S
Seattle, WA 98108
Phone: (206) 767-0280

#167
Harry's Bar
Category: Pub, Pizza, Greek
Average Price: Modest
Area: Capitol Hill
Address: 514 15th Ave E
Seattle, WA 98112
Phone: (206) 329-4500

#168
Triangle Pub
Category: Pub, American
Average Price: Inexpensive
Area: Sodo
Address: 553 1st Ave S
Seattle, WA 98104
Phone: (206) 628-0474

#169
Georgetown Liquor Company
Category: Vegetarian, Pub, Breakfast & Brunch
Average Price: Modest
Area: Industrial District
Address: 5501 Airport Way S
Seattle, WA 98108
Phone: (206) 763-6764

#170
Pair
Category: American, French, Wine Bar
Average Price: Expensive
Area: Ravenna
Address: 5501 30th Ave NE
Seattle, WA 98105
Phone: (206) 526-7655

#171
Gainsbourg
Category: French, Lounge
Average Price: Modest
Area: Greenwood
Address: 8550 Greenwood Ave N
Seattle, WA 98103
Phone: (206) 783-4004

#172
The Barrel Thief
Category: Coffee, Tea, Lounge, Wine Bar
Average Price: Modest
Area: Fremont
Address: 3417 Evanston Ave N
Seattle, WA 98103
Phone: (206) 402-5492

#173
Mecca Cafe
Category: American, Dive Bar,
Breakfast & Brunch
Average Price: Inexpensive
Area: Lower Queen Anne
Address: 526 Queen Anne Ave N
Seattle, WA 98109
Phone: (206) 285-9728

#174
Woodsky's
Category: Bar
Average Price: Inexpensive
Area: Fremont
Address: 303 N 36th St
Seattle, WA 98103
Phone: (206) 547-9662

#175
Smarty Pants
Category: American, Bar
Average Price: Modest
Area: Georgetown
Address: 6017 Airport Way S
Seattle, WA 98108
Phone: (206) 762-4777

#176
The Oak
Category: Pub, Burgers
Average Price: Modest
Area: Beacon Hill
Address: 3019 Beacon Ave S
Seattle, WA 98144
Phone: (206) 535-7070

#177
Ballard Station Public House
Category: Pub, Sports Bar
Average Price: Modest
Area: Ballard
Address: 2236 NW Market St
Seattle, WA 98107
Phone: (206) 906-9040

#178
Intermezzo Carmine
Category: Cocktail Bar, Italian
Average Price: Modest
Area: Pioneer Square
Address: 409 1st Ave S
Seattle, WA 98104
Phone: (206) 596-8940

#179
The Matador
Category: Bar, Mexican
Average Price: Modest
Area: Junction
Address: 4546 California Ave SW
Seattle, WA 98116
Phone: (206) 932-9988

#180
The District Lounge
Category: Lounge
Average Price: Modest
Area: University District
Address: 4507 Brooklyn Ave NE
Seattle, WA 98127
Phone: (206) 634-2000

#181
Die Bierstube
Category: German, Pub
Average Price: Modest
Area: Roosevelt
Address: 6106 Roosevelt Way NE
Seattle, WA 98115
Phone: (206) 527-7019

#182
The Blu Grouse
Category: Bar, American
Average Price: Modest
Area: Georgetown
Address: 412 S Orcas St
Seattle, WA 98108
Phone: (206) 397-4302

#183
Red Onion Tavern
Category: Bar, American
Average Price: Modest
Area: Madison Park
Address: 4210 E Madison St
Seattle, WA 98112
Phone: (206) 323-1611

#184
Frank's Oyster House & Champagne Parlor
Category: Seafood, Champagne Bar
Average Price: Expensive
Area: Ravenna
Address: 2616 NE 55th St
Seattle, WA 98105
Phone: (206) 525-0220

#185
Quoin
Category: Bar
Average Price: Modest
Area: Fremont
Address: 403 N 36th St
Seattle, WA 98103
Phone: (206) 547-2040

#186
Tim's Tavern On 105th
Category: Bar, Barbeque, Music Venues
Average Price: Inexpensive
Area: Greenwood, Bitter Lake
Address: 602 N 105th St
Seattle, WA 98133
Phone: (206) 789-9005

#187
Summit Public House
Category: Dive Bar, Pub
Average Price: Inexpensive
Area: Capitol Hill
Address: 601 Summit Ave E
Seattle, WA 98102
Phone: (206) 324-7611

#188
Solo
Category: Bar
Average Price: Modest
Area: Lower Queen Anne
Address: 200 Roy St
Seattle, WA 98109
Phone: (206) 213-0080

#189
The Crescent Lounge
Category: Karaoke, Gay Bar, Dive Bar
Average Price: Inexpensive
Area: Capitol Hill
Address: 1413 E Olive Way
Seattle, WA 98122
Phone: (206) 659-4476

#190
Joe Bar
Category: Coffee, Tea, Crêperie, Bar
Average Price: Inexpensive
Area: Capitol Hill
Address: 810 E Roy St
Seattle, WA 98102
Phone: (206) 324-0407

#191
Lloydmartin
Category: American, Bar
Average Price: Expensive
Area: Queen Anne
Address: 1525 Queen Anne Ave N
Seattle, WA 98109
Phone: (206) 420-7602

#192
Treehouse Lounge
Category: Wine Bar, Lounge
Average Price: Modest
Area: Admiral
Address: 2206 California Ave SW
Seattle, WA 98116
Phone: (206) 293-5719

#193
Vermillion
Category: Art Gallery, Bar
Average Price: Inexpensive
Area: Capitol Hill
Address: 1508 11th Ave
Seattle, WA 98122
Phone: (206) 709-9797

#194
Boud's Pinehurst Pub
Category: Dive Bar, American, Breakfast & Brunch
Average Price: Inexpensive
Area: Pinehurst
Address: 11753 15th Ave NE
Seattle, WA 98125
Phone: (206) 363-0542

#195
Fremont Wine
Category: Winery, Wine Bar
Average Price: Modest
Area: Fremont
Address: 3601 Fremont Ave N
Seattle, WA 98103
Phone: (206) 632-1110

#196
Burgundian
Category: Bar, American
Average Price: Modest
Area: Wallingford
Address: 2253 N 56th St
Seattle, WA 98103
Phone: (206) 420-8943

#197
Bandits Bar
Category: Bar
Average Price: Inexpensive
Area: Belltown
Address: 159 Denny Way
Seattle, WA 98109
Phone: (206) 443-5447

#198
Company
Category: Bar, American
Average Price: Modest
Area: White Center
Address: 9608 16th Ave SW
Seattle, WA 98106
Phone: (206) 257-1162

#199
Elliott Bay Public House & Brewery
Category: Brewerie, Pub
Average Price: Modest
Area: Olympic Hills
Address: 12537 Lake City Way NE
Seattle, WA 98125
Phone: (206) 365-2337

#200
Brass Tacks
Category: Gastropub, Bar
Average Price: Modest
Area: Georgetown
Address: 6031 Airport Way S
Seattle, WA 98108
Phone: (206) 397-3821

#201
POCO Wine + Spirits
Category: Wine Bar, American, Lounge
Average Price: Modest
Area: Capitol Hill
Address: 1408 E Pine St
Seattle, WA 98122
Phone: (206) 322-9463

#202
The J&M Cafe
Category: American, Pub
Average Price: Modest
Area: Pioneer Square
Address: 201 1st Ave S
Seattle, WA 98104
Phone: (206) 402-6654

#203
Ha!
Category: Comfort Food, Bar
Average Price: Modest
Area: Fremont
Address: 4256 Fremont Ave N
Seattle, WA 98103
Phone: (206) 588-1169

#204
Sarajevo Restaurant & Lounge
Category: Lounge, European, American
Average Price: Modest
Area: Downtown
Address: 2332 1st Ave
Seattle, WA 98121
Phone: (206) 448-9000

#205
The Angry Beaver
Category: Bar
Average Price: Modest
Area: Greenwood, Phinney Ridge
Address: 8412 Greenwood Ave N
Seattle, WA 98103
Phone: (206) 782-6044

#206
The Sexton
Category: Bar, Tapas
Average Price: Modest
Area: Ballard
Address: 5327 Ballard Ave NW
Seattle, WA 98107
Phone: (206) 829-8645

#207
The Central Saloon
Category: Bar, Music Venues, American
Average Price: Inexpensive
Area: Pioneer Square
Address: 207 1st Ave S
Seattle, WA 98127
Phone: (206) 622-0209

#208
Kangaroo & Kiwi Pub
Category: Pub, Australian
Average Price: Modest
Area: Ballard
Address: 2026 NW Market St
Seattle, WA 98107
Phone: (206) 297-0507

#209
Pies & Pints
Category: Pub, American
Average Price: Modest
Area: Roosevelt
Address: 1215 NE 65th St
Seattle, WA 98115
Phone: (206) 524-7082

#210
The Terrace Lounge
Category: Lounge, Piano Bar
Average Price: Expensive
Area: Downtown
Address: 411 University St
Seattle, WA 98101
Phone: (200) 021-7000

#211
Union Bar - Hillman City
Category: American, Pub
Average Price: Modest
Area: Columbia City
Address: 5609 Rainier Ave S
Seattle, WA 98118
Phone: (206) 258-4377

#212
Bastille Cafe & Bar
Category: Bar, French, Breakfast & Brunch
Average Price: Modest
Area: Ballard
Address: 5307 Ballard Ave NW
Seattle, WA 98107
Phone: (206) 453-5014

#213
Corner Pocket
Category: Dive Bar, Pool Hall, Sports Bar
Average Price: Inexpensive
Area: Junction
Address: 4302 Alaska St SW
Seattle, WA 98116
Phone: (206) 933-0320

#214
Hopvine Pub
Category: Pub, American, Sandwiches
Average Price: Modest
Area: Capitol Hill
Address: 507 15th Ave E
Seattle, WA 98102
Phone: (206) 328-3120

#215
Two Bells Tavern
Category: Restaurant, Bar
Average Price: Modest
Area: Belltown
Address: 2313 4th Ave
Seattle, WA 98121
Phone: (206) 441-3050

#216
The People's Pub
Category: German, Pub
Average Price: Modest
Area: Ballard
Address: 5429 Ballard Ave NW
Seattle, WA 98107
Phone: (206) 783-6521

#217
Lottie's Lounge
Category: Breakfast & Brunch, American, Lounge
Average Price: Modest
Area: Columbia City
Address: 4900 Rainier Ave S
Seattle, WA 98118
Phone: (206) 725-0519

#218
The Tin Table
Category: American, Lounge
Average Price: Modest
Area: Capitol Hill
Address: 915 E Pine St
Seattle, WA 98122
Phone: (206) 320-8458

#219
Cooper's Alehouse
Category: Pub, American
Average Price: Modest
Area: Mapleleaf
Address: 8065 Lake City Way NE
Seattle, WA 98115
Phone: (206) 522-2923

#220
Ravenna Alehouse
Category: Bar
Average Price: Inexpensive
Area: Ravenna
Address: 2258 NE 65th St
Seattle, WA 98115
Phone: (206) 729-9083

#221
Greenlake Bar & Grill
Category: American, Bar
Average Price: Modest
Area: Greenlake
Address: 7200 E Green Lake Dr N
Seattle, WA 98115
Phone: (206) 729-6179

#222
Elysian Brewing Co
Category: Brewerie, Bar, American
Average Price: Modest
Area: Capitol Hill
Address: 1221 E Pike St
Seattle, WA 98122
Phone: (206) 860-1920

#223
Rocco's
Category: Bar, Pizza
Average Price: Modest
Area: Belltown
Address: 2228 2nd Ave
Seattle, WA 98121
Phone: (206) 448-2625

#224
The Ridge
Category: Pizza, Pub, Sandwiches
Average Price: Modest
Area: Phinney Ridge
Address: 7217 Greenwood Ave N
Seattle, WA 98103
Phone: (206) 687-7621

Seattle Travel Guide 2016 / Shops, Restaurants, Arts, Entertainment & Nightlife

#225
Highliner Public House
Category: Pub, Fish & Chips, Sandwiches
Average Price: Modest
Area: Interbay
Address: 3909 18th Ave W
Seattle, WA 98119
Phone: (206) 216-1254

#226
Paddy Coyne's Irish Pub
Category: Irish, Irish Pub
Average Price: Modest
Area: South Lake Union
Address: 1190 Thomas St
Seattle, WA 98109
Phone: (206) 405-1548

#227
Cloud 9 Hookah Lounge
Category: Hookah Bar
Average Price: Inexpensive
Area: Central District
Address: 2522 E Cherry St
Seattle, WA 98122
Phone: (206) 457-3263

#228
The Raygun Lounge
Category: Arcade, Lounge
Average Price: Inexpensive
Area: Capitol Hill
Address: 501 E Pine St
Seattle, WA 98122
Phone: (206) 812-2521

#229
Stoneburner
Category: Pizza, American, Bar
Average Price: Modest
Area: Ballard
Address: 5214 Ballard Ave NW
Seattle, WA 98107
Phone: (206) 695-2051

#230
Roosevelt Ale House
Category: American, Pub
Average Price: Modest
Area: Mapleleaf
Address: 8824 Roosevelt Way NE
Seattle, WA 98115
Phone: (206) 527-5480

#231
The Hummingbird Saloon
Category: Bar, American
Average Price: Modest
Area: Columbia City
Address: 5041 Rainier Ave S
Seattle, WA 98118
Phone: (206) 349-1731

#232
Smash Wine Bar & Bistro
Category: Wine Bar, American
Average Price: Modest
Area: Wallingford
Address: 1401 N 45th St
Seattle, WA 98103
Phone: (206) 535-6772

#233
Roanoke Park Place Tavern
Category: Sports Bar
Average Price: Modest
Area: Capitol Hill
Address: 2409 10th Ave E
Seattle, WA 98102
Phone: (206) 324-5882

#234
Toulouse Petit
Category: Cajun, Creole, Breakfast & Brunch, Bar
Average Price: Modest
Area: Lower Queen Anne
Address: 601 Queen Anne Ave N
Seattle, WA 98109
Phone: (206) 432-9069

#235
Marco Polo Bar & Grill
Category: Dive Bar, Karaoke, American
Average Price: Inexpensive
Area: Georgetown
Address: 5613 4th Ave S
Seattle, WA 98108
Phone: (206) 762-3964

#236
Artusi
Category: Bar, Italian
Average Price: Modest
Area: Capitol Hill
Address: 1535 14th Ave
Seattle, WA 98122
Phone: (206) 678-2516

#237
Ravish
Category: American, Breakfast & Brunch, Cocktail Bar
Average Price: Modest
Area: Eastlake
Address: 2956 Eastlake Ave E
Seattle, WA 98102
Phone: (206) 913-2497

#238
Magnolia Village Pub
Category: Pub, Gastropub
Average Price: Modest
Area: Magnolia
Address: 3221 W Mcgraw St
Seattle, WA 98199
Phone: (206) 285-9756

#239
Le Zinc
Category: French, Bar
Average Price: Modest
Area: Capitol Hill
Address: 1449 E Pine St
Seattle, WA 98122
Phone: (206) 257-4151

#240
Duck Island Ale House
Category: Pub
Average Price: Inexpensive
Area: Phinney Ridge
Address: 7317 Aurora Ave N
Seattle, WA 98103
Phone: (206) 783-3360

#241
El Chupacabra
Category: Bar, Mexican
Average Price: Modest
Area: Alki
Address: 2620 Alki Ave SW
Seattle, WA 98116
Phone: (206) 933-7344

#242
Hudson
Category: Bar, Breakfast & Brunch
Average Price: Modest
Area: Industrial District
Address: 5000 E Marginal Way S
Seattle, WA 98134
Phone: (206) 767-4777

#243
Henry's Tavern
Category: American, Seafood, Sports Bar
Average Price: Modest
Area: Sodo
Address: 1518 1st Ave S
Seattle, WA 98134
Phone: (206) 624-0501

#244
El Borracho
Category: Bar, Mexican, Vegan
Average Price: Modest
Area: Ballard
Address: 5465 Leary Ave NW
Seattle, WA 98107
Phone: (206) 582-1974

#245
Mission
Category: Latin American, Lounge, Mexican
Average Price: Modest
Area: Admiral
Address: 2325 California Ave SW
Seattle, WA 98127
Phone: (206) 937-8220

#246
Kate's Pub
Category: Pub, American
Average Price: Inexpensive
Area: Wallingford
Address: 309 NE 45th St
Seattle, WA 98127
Phone: (206) 547-6832

#247
Reservoir Tavern
Category: Dive Bar
Average Price: Inexpensive
Area: Mapleleaf
Address: 8509 Roosevelt Way NE
Seattle, WA 98115
Phone: (206) 528-2107

#248
Victory Lounge
Category: Sports Bar, Lounge
Average Price: Inexpensive
Area: South Lake Union
Address: 433 Eastlake Ave E
Seattle, WA 98109
Phone: (206) 382-4467

#249
Bad Jimmy's Brewing Co.
Category: Bar, Brewerie
Average Price: Inexpensive
Area: Fremont
Address: 4358 B Leary Way Nw
Seattle, WA 98107
Phone: (206) 789-1548

#250
Eastlake Bar & Grill
Category: Bar, Breakfast & Brunch, American
Average Price: Modest
Area: Eastlake
Address: 2947 Eastlake Ave E
Seattle, WA 98102
Phone: (206) 957-7777

#251
Prost! Tavern
Category: German, Pub
Average Price: Modest
Area: Phinney Ridge
Address: 7311 Greenwood Ave N
Seattle, WA 98103
Phone: (206) 706-5430

#252
Mcgilvra's
Category: Irish, Irish Pub
Average Price: Modest
Area: Madison Park
Address: 4234 E Madison St
Seattle, WA 98112
Phone: (206) 325-0834

#253
The Innkeeper
Category: Pub, Latin American, Caribbean
Average Price: Modest
Area: Belltown
Address: 2510 1st Ave
Seattle, WA 98121
Phone: (206) 441-7817

#254
The Matador
Category: Mexican, Bar, Tex-Mex
Average Price: Modest
Area: Ballard
Address: 2221 NW Market St
Seattle, WA 98107
Phone: (206) 297-2855

#255
Brave Horse Tavern
Category: American, Pub
Average Price: Modest
Area: South Lake Union
Address: 310 Terry Ave N
Seattle, WA 98109
Phone: (206) 971-0717

#256
Amorcito Lounge
Category: Bar
Average Price: Modest
Area: Beacon Hill
Address: 2410 Beacon Ave South
Seattle, WA 98144
Phone: (206) 323-1157

#257
Abay Ethiopian Cuisine
Category: Ethiopian, Bar, Vegetarian
Average Price: Modest
Area: Capitol Hill
Address: 2359 10th Ave E
Seattle, WA 98102
Phone: (206) 257-4778

#258
Teddy's Tavern
Category: Pub
Average Price: Inexpensive
Area: Roosevelt
Address: 1012 NE 65th St
Seattle, WA 98115
Phone: (206) 522-4950

#259
The W Hotel Bar
Category: Lounge, Restaurant
Average Price: Expensive
Area: Downtown
Address: 1112 4th Ave
Seattle, WA 98101
Phone: (206) 264-6000

#260
The Old Pequliar
Category: Pub, Irish
Average Price: Inexpensive
Area: Ballard
Address: 1722 NW Market St
Seattle, WA 98107
Phone: (206) 782-8886

#261
Metropole American Kitchen & Bar
Category: Bar, American
Average Price: Modest
Area: Downtown
Address: 820 Pike St
Seattle, WA 98101
Phone: (206) 832-5555

#262
Urbane
Category: Lounge, American
Average Price: Modest
Area: Downtown
Address: 1635 8th Ave
Seattle, WA 98101
Phone: (206) 676-4600

#263
Tug Inn
Category: Dive Bar, Karaoke
Average Price: Inexpensive
Area: High Point
Address: 2216 SW Orchard St
Seattle, WA 98106
Phone: (206) 768-8852

#264
TRACE
Category: American, Bar, Sushi Bar
Average Price: Modest
Area: Downtown
Address: 1112 4th Ave
Seattle, WA 98101
Phone: (206) 264-6060

#265
The House Sports Pub
Category: Sports Bar
Average Price: Modest
Area: Greenwood
Address: 8551 Greenwood Ave N
Seattle, WA 98103
Phone: (206) 403-1464

#266
Phinney Market Pub & Eatery
Category: Pub, Gastropub, Wine Bar
Average Price: Modest
Area: Phinney Ridge
Address: 5918 Phinney Ave N
Seattle, WA 98103
Phone: (206) 210-0105

#267
The Attic Alehouse & Eatery
Category: Pub, American
Average Price: Modest
Area: Madison Park
Address: 4226 E Madison St
Seattle, WA 98112
Phone: (206) 323-3131

#268
Pike Brewing Company
Category: Pub, Brewerie, American
Average Price: Modest
Area: Downtown
Address: 1415 1st Ave
Seattle, WA 98122
Phone: (206) 622-6044

#269
The Cask
Category: Wine Bar, Pub, Lounge
Average Price: Modest
Area: Admiral
Address: 2350 California Ave SW
Seattle, WA 98116
Phone: (206) 932-0977

#270
Feierabend
Category: German, Pub
Average Price: Modest
Area: South Lake Union
Address: 422 Yale Ave N
Seattle, WA 98109
Phone: (206) 340-2528

#271
The Night Owl Lounge
Category: Bar
Average Price: Expensive
Area: South Lake Union
Address: 13 Coins Restaurant
Seattle, WA 98101
Phone: (206) 682-2513

#272
Jelly Bar
Category: Lounge, Vietnamese
Average Price: Modest
Area: Downtown
Address: 1901 2nd Ave
Seattle, WA 98101
Phone: (206) 443-6266

#273
The Sloop Tavern
Category: Pub, Dive Bar, American
Average Price: Inexpensive
Area: Sunset Hill
Address: 2830 NW Market St
Seattle, WA 98107
Phone: (206) 782-3330

#274
Capitol Cider
Category: Pub, Cocktail Bar, Gluten-Free
Average Price: Modest
Area: Capitol Hill
Address: 818 E Pike St
Seattle, WA 98122
Phone: (206) 397-3564

#275
2bar Spirits
Category: Bar, Distilleries
Average Price: Modest
Area: Industrial District
Address: 2960 4th Ave S
Seattle, WA 98134
Phone: (206) 402-4340

#276
The Comedy Underground
Category: Comedy Club, Performing Arts
Average Price: Modest
Area: Pioneer Square
Address: 109 S Washington St
Seattle, WA 98104
Phone: (206) 628-0303

#277
Six Arms
Category: Pub, Brewerie, American
Average Price: Modest
Area: Capitol Hill
Address: 300 E Pike St.
Seattle, WA 98122
Phone: (206) 223-1698

#278
Collins Pub
Category: Pub, American
Average Price: Modest
Area: Pioneer Square
Address: 526 2nd Ave
Seattle, WA 98104
Phone: (206) 623-1016

#279
Mac's Triangle Pub
Category: Karaoke, Pub, Sports Bar
Average Price: Inexpensive
Area: Westwood
Address: 9454 Delridge Way SW
Seattle, WA 98106
Phone: (206) 763-0714

#280
Dimitriou's Jazz Alley
Category: Jazz, Blues, Music Venues
Average Price: Expensive
Area: Denny Triangle
Address: 2033 6th Ave
Seattle, WA 98121
Phone: (206) 441-9729

#281
Seattle Hookah Lounge
Category: Hookah Bar
Average Price: Modest
Area: University District
Address: 4701 Roosevelt Way NE
Seattle, WA 98105
Phone: (206) 708-6081

#282
Twisted Pasty
Category: Bar, American, British
Average Price: Modest
Area: Belltown
Address: 2525 4th Ave
Seattle, WA 98121
Phone: (206) 402-3831

#283
418 Public House
Category: Pub, Mexican
Average Price: Inexpensive
Area: Ballard, Phinney Ridge
Address: 418 NW 65th St
Seattle, WA 98117
Phone: (206) 783-0418

#284
Murphy's Pub
Category: Irish, Irish Pub
Average Price: Modest
Area: Wallingford
Address: 1928 N 45th St
Seattle, WA 98103
Phone: (206) 634-2110

#285
Hudson Public House
Category: Pub, American
Average Price: Modest
Area: Wedgwood
Address: 8014 15th Ave NE
Seattle, WA 98115
Phone: (206) 524-5070

#286
Spinnaker Bay Brewing
Category: Brewerie, Bar
Average Price: Inexpensive
Area: Columbia City
Address: 5718 Rainier Ave S
Seattle, WA 98118
Phone: (206) 725-2337

#287
The Lookout
Category: Pub, American
Average Price: Modest
Area: Capitol Hill
Address: 757 Bellevue Ave E
Seattle, WA 98102
Phone: (206) 329-0454

#288
The Siren Tavern
Category: Bar
Average Price: Inexpensive
Area: Industrial District
Address: 3403 4th Ave S
Seattle, WA 98134
Phone: (206) 223-9167

#289
Mcmenamins Queen Anne
Category: Pub, Brewerie, American
Average Price: Modest
Area: Lower Queen Anne
Address: 200 Roy St.
Seattle, WA 98109
Phone: (206) 285-4722

#290
Elysian Tangletown
Category: Brewerie, Pub, American
Average Price: Modest
Area: Wallingford
Address: 2106 N. 55th St
Seattle, WA 98103
Phone: (206) 547-5929

#291
Olde 99 Pub
Category: Sports Bar, American
Average Price: Modest
Area: Phinney Ridge
Address: 7305 Aurora Ave N
Seattle, WA 98103
Phone: (206) 687-7047

#292
The Baltic Room
Category: Dance Club, Lounge
Average Price: Modest
Area: Capitol Hill
Address: 1207 Pine St
Seattle, WA 98101
Phone: (206) 625-4444

#293
Red Papaya Ale & Spirits
Category: Vietnamese, Tapas Bar
Average Price: Modest
Area: Lower Queen Anne
Address: 530 1st Ave N
Seattle, WA 98109
Phone: (206) 283-6614

#294
The Cozy Nut Tavern
Category: Cocktail Bar
Average Price: Modest
Area: Greenwood
Address: 123 N 85th St
Seattle, WA 98103
Phone: (206) 784-2240

#295
Slim's Last Chance
Category: Bar, American
Average Price: Modest
Area: Georgetown
Address: 5606 1st Ave S
Seattle, WA 98108
Phone: (206) 762-7900

#296
Bush Garden Restaurant
Category: Japanese, Sushi Bar, Bar, Karaoke
Average Price: Modest
Area: International District
Address: 614 Maynard Ave S
Seattle, WA 98104
Phone: (206) 682-6830

#297
Fiddler's Inn Pub & Restaurant
Category: Pub, American
Average Price: Modest
Area: Wedgwood
Address: 9219 35th Ave NE
Seattle, WA 98115
Phone: (206) 525-0752

#298
Watershed Pub And Kitchen
Category: Pub, Pizza, Sandwiches
Average Price: Modest
Area: Mapleleaf
Address: 10104 3rd Ave NE
Seattle, WA 98125
Phone: (206) 729-7433

#299
Ten On 9th
Category: Cocktail Bar, American
Average Price: Modest
Area: South Lake Union
Address: 227 9th Ave N
Seattle, WA 98109
Phone: (206) 792-7221

#300
The Spectator Sports Bar
Category: Sports Bar, Burgers
Average Price: Inexpensive
Area: Lower Queen Anne
Address: 529 Queen Anne Ave N
Seattle, WA 98109
Phone: (206) 599-4263

#301
Al's Tavern
Category: Dive Bar, American
Average Price: Inexpensive
Area: Wallingford
Address: 2303 N 45th St
Seattle, WA 98103
Phone: (206) 545-9959

#302
Serendipity Cafe And Lounge
Category: Bakery, Bar, American
Average Price: Modest
Area: Magnolia
Address: 3222 W Mcgraw St
Seattle, WA 98199
Phone: (206) 282-9866

#303
Barrio Mexican Kitchen & Bar
Category: Mexican, Bar
Average Price: Modest
Area: Capitol Hill
Address: 1420 12th Ave
Seattle, WA 98122
Phone: (206) 588-8105

#304
New York Pizza & Bar
Category: Pizza, Burgers, Sports Bar
Average Price: Modest
Area: Lower Queen Anne
Address: 500 Mercer St
Seattle, WA 98109
Phone: (206) 913-2565

#305
Norm's Eatery & Ale House
Category: American, Pub
Average Price: Modest
Area: Fremont
Address: 460 N 36th St
Seattle, WA 98103
Phone: (206) 547-1417

#306
In The Red Wine Bar
Category: Wine Bar, Coffee, Tea, Tapas
Average Price: Modest
Area: Phinney Ridge
Address: 6510 Phinney Ave N
Seattle, WA 98103
Phone: (206) 420-8992

#307
Ampersand Lounge
Category: Lounge, Pool Hall
Average Price: Modest
Area: Belltown
Address: 113 Bell St
Seattle, WA 98121
Phone: (206) 239-0830

#308
Boxcar Ale House
Category: Dive Bar, Karaoke, Sports Bar
Average Price: Inexpensive
Area: Magnolia
Address: 3407 Gilman Ave W
Seattle, WA 98199
Phone: (206) 286-6418

Seattle Travel Guide 2016 / Shops, Restaurants, Arts, Entertainment & Nightlife

#309
Outwest Bar
Category: Gay Bar
Average Price: Modest
Area: Seaview
Address: 5401 California Ave SW
Seattle, WA 98136
Phone: (206) 937-1540

#310
The Iron Bull
Category: Sports Bar, American
Average Price: Inexpensive
Area: Wallingford
Address: 2121 N 45th St
Seattle, WA 98103
Phone: (206) 453-3901

#311
Betty
Category: American, Specialty Food, Cocktail Bar
Average Price: Modest
Area: Queen Anne
Address: 1507 Queen Anne Ave N
Seattle, WA 98109
Phone: (206) 352-3773

#312
The Celtic Swell
Category: Irish, Pub
Average Price: Modest
Area: Alki
Address: 2722 Alki Ave SW
Seattle, WA 98116
Phone: (206) 932-7935

#313
Mama's Mexican Kitchen
Category: Mexican, Bar
Average Price: Modest
Area: Belltown
Address: 2234 2nd Ave
Seattle, WA 98121
Phone: (206) 728-6262

#314
Twigs Bistro And Martini Bar
Category: American, Cocktail Bar
Average Price: Modest
Area: Northgate
Address: 401 NE Northgate Way
Seattle, WA 98125
Phone: (206) 367-1376

#315
Big Time Brewing Company
Category: Pub, Pizza, Brewerie
Average Price: Inexpensive
Area: University District
Address: 4133 University Wy NE
Seattle, WA 98105
Phone: (206) 545-4509

#316
Wedgwood Ale House & Cafe
Category: Pub, American
Average Price: Modest
Area: Wedgwood
Address: 8515 35th Ave NE
Seattle, WA 98115
Phone: (206) 527-2676

#317
The Saint
Category: Mexican, Bar
Average Price: Modest
Area: Capitol Hill
Address: 1416 E Olive Way
Seattle, WA 98122
Phone: (206) 323-9922

#318
The Atlantic Crossing
Category: Pub, British, Sports Bar
Average Price: Modest
Area: Roosevelt
Address: 6508 Roosevelt Way NE
Seattle, WA 98115
Phone: (206) 729-6266

#319
The Shanty Tavern
Category: Pub
Average Price: Inexpensive
Area: Wedgwood
Address: 9002 Lake City Way NE
Seattle, WA 98115
Phone: (206) 526-9854

#320
Hula Hula
Category: Karaoke, Lounge
Average Price: Modest
Area: Lower Queen Anne
Address: 106 1st Ave N
Seattle, WA 98109
Phone: (206) 284-5003

#321
The Ould Triangle
Category: Pub, Irish
Average Price: Inexpensive
Area: Greenwood
Address: 9736 Greenwood Ave N
Seattle, WA 98103
Phone: (206) 706-7798

#322
Central Pizza
Category: Bar, Pizza
Average Price: Modest
Area: Leschi
Address: 2901 S Jackson St
Seattle, WA 98144
Phone: (206) 802-0000

#323
Quinn's
Category: American, Pub
Average Price: Modest
Area: First Hill, Capitol Hill
Address: 1001 E Pike St
Seattle, WA 98122
Phone: (206) 325-7711

#324
Changes In Wallingford
Category: Gay Bar, Pub
Average Price: Inexpensive
Area: Wallingford
Address: 2103 N 45th St
Seattle, WA 98103
Phone: (206) 545-8363

#325
8oz Burger & Co
Category: Burgers, Bar
Average Price: Modest
Area: First Hill
Address: 1401 Broadway
Seattle, WA 98122
Phone: (206) 466-5989

#326
The Lost Pelican
Category: Gastropub, Cocktail Bar
Average Price: Modest
Area: Belltown
Address: 2400 1st Ave
Seattle, WA 98121
Phone: (206) 441-5132

#327
Rehab
Category: Pub
Average Price: Exclusive
Area: Alki
Address: 2424 55th Ave SW
Seattle, WA 98116
Phone: (206) 555-1234

#328
Industry Lounge
Category: Dive Bar, Burgers
Average Price: Inexpensive
Area: Georgetown
Address: 6601 E Marginal Way S
Seattle, WA 98108
Phone: (206) 762-3453

#329
Elysian Bar
Category: Cocktail Bar, American
Average Price: Modest
Area: Downtown
Address: 1516 2nd Ave
Seattle, WA 98101
Phone: (206) 467-4458

#330
Copper Coin
Category: Bar, American
Average Price: Modest
Area: Admiral
Address: 2329 California Ave SW
Seattle, WA 98116
Phone: (206) 420-3608

#331
Sam's Tavern
Category: Bar, Burgers, Barbeque
Average Price: Modest
Area: Capitol Hill
Address: 1024 E Pike St
Seattle, WA 98122
Phone: (206) 397-3344

#332
The Bourbon Bar
Category: Lounge
Average Price: Modest
Area: Columbia City
Address: 4916 Rainier Ave S
Seattle, WA 98118
Phone: (206) 420-8285

#333
Pub At Piper's Creek
Category: Pub, American
Average Price: Modest
Area: Broadview
Address: 10527 Greenwood Ave N
Seattle, WA 98133
Phone: (206) 417-5734

#334
Percy's & Co.
Category: Gastropub, Cocktail Bar
Average Price: Modest
Area: Ballard
Address: 5233 Ballard Ave NW
Seattle, WA 98107
Phone: (206) 420-3750

#335
The Tin Lizzie Lounge
Category: Lounge
Average Price: Modest
Area: Lower Queen Anne
Address: 600 Queen Anne Ave N
Seattle, WA 98109
Phone: (206) 282-7407

#336
Tommy Gun
Category: Bar
Average Price: Modest
Area: Capitol Hill
Address: 1703 E Olive Way
Seattle, WA 98102
Phone: (206) 323-4866

#337
Therapy Lounge
Category: Lounge, Dance Club
Average Price: Modest
Area: Capitol Hill
Address: 1509 Broadway
Seattle, WA 98122
Phone: (808) 391-7333

#338
Ayutthaya Thai
Category: Thai, Bar
Average Price: Modest
Area: First Hill, Capitol Hill
Address: 727 E Pike St
Seattle, WA 98122
Phone: (206) 324-8833

#339
Madison Pub
Category: Pub, Gay Bar
Average Price: Inexpensive
Area: Central District, Capitol Hill
Address: 1315 E Madison St
Seattle, WA 98122
Phone: (206) 325-6537

#340
The Canterbury Ale House
Category: Pub, Burgers
Average Price: Inexpensive
Area: Capitol Hill
Address: 534 15th Ave E
Seattle, WA 98112
Phone: (206) 325-3110

#341
Still Liquor
Category: Lounge, Cocktail Bar
Average Price: Modest
Area: Capitol Hill
Address: 1524 Minor Ave
Seattle, WA 98101
Phone: (206) 467-4075

#342
Barrel Tavern
Category: Bar
Average Price: Inexpensive
Area: Shorewood
Address: 11051 1st Ave S
Seattle, WA 98168
Phone: (206) 246-5488

#343
Lamplighter Public House
Category: American, Pub
Average Price: Modest
Area: Crown Hill
Address: 820 NW 85th St
Seattle, WA 98117
Phone: (206) 782-9690

#344
The Lobby Bar
Category: Gay Bar
Average Price: Modest
Area: Capitol Hill
Address: 916 E Pike St
Seattle, WA 98122
Phone: (206) 328-6703

#345
The Cuff Complex
Category: Dance Club, Gay Bar
Average Price: Modest
Area: Capitol Hill
Address: 1533 13th Ave
Seattle, WA 98122
Phone: (206) 323-1525

#346
Ba Bar
Category: Vietnamese, Bar, Bakery
Average Price: Modest
Area: Central District
Address: 550 12th Ave
Seattle, WA 98122
Phone: (206) 328-2030

#347
Tarasco Mexican Restaurant
Category: Mexican, Bar, Karaoke
Average Price: Inexpensive
Area: Phinney Ridge
Address: 1452 NW 70th St
Seattle, WA 98117
Phone: (206) 782-1485

#348
Zayda Buddy's Pizza & Bar
Category: Pizza, Bar
Average Price: Modest
Area: Ballard
Address: 5405 Leary Ave NW
Seattle, WA 98107
Phone: (206) 783-7777

#349
Kickin' Boot Whiskey Kitchen
Category: Bar, Southern
Average Price: Modest
Area: Ballard
Address: 5309 22nd Ave NW
Seattle, WA 98107
Phone: (206) 783-2668

#350
The 2 Bit Saloon
Category: Dive Bar
Average Price: Inexpensive
Area: Ballard
Address: 4818 17th Ave NW
Seattle, WA 98107
Phone: (206) 708-6917

#351
Prost! West Seattle
Category: Pub, German
Average Price: Modest
Area: Admiral
Address: 3407 California Ave SW
Seattle, WA 98116
Phone: (206) 420-7174

#352
The Hurricane Café
Category: Diner, American, Pub
Average Price: Inexpensive
Area: Denny Triangle
Address: 2230 7th Ave
Seattle, WA 98121
Phone: (206) 682-5858

#353
May Restaurant And Lounge
Category: Thai, Lounge
Average Price: Modest
Area: Wallingford
Address: 1612 N 45th St
Seattle, WA 98103
Phone: (206) 675-0037

#354
Wildrose
Category: Gay Bar, Arts, Entertainment
Average Price: Inexpensive
Area: Capitol Hill
Address: 1021 E Pike St
Seattle, WA 98122
Phone: (206) 324-9210

#355
Kells Irish Restaurant & Pub
Category: Irish, Irish Pub
Average Price: Modest
Area: Downtown
Address: 1916 Post Alley
Seattle, WA 98101
Phone: (206) 728-1916

#356
The Dubliner
Category: Pub, Irish
Average Price: Inexpensive
Area: Fremont
Address: 3517 Fremont Ave N
Seattle, WA 98103
Phone: (206) 548-1508

#357
Aladdin Hookah Lounge
Category: Hookah Bar, Music Venues
Average Price: Modest
Area: South Lake Union
Address: 1314 Denny Way
Seattle, WA 98109
Phone: (206) 261-7592

#358
Kremwerk
Category: Dance Club, Music Venues, Cocktail Bar
Average Price: Modest
Area: Denny Triangle
Address: 1809 Minor Ave
Seattle, WA 98101
Phone: (206) 682-2935

#359
Loulay Kitchen & Bar
Category: French, Bar
Average Price: Expensive
Area: Downtown
Address: 600 Union St
Seattle, WA 98101
Phone: (206) 402-4588

#360
Merchant's Cafe And Saloon
Category: Bar, Café
Average Price: Modest
Area: Pioneer Square
Address: 109 Yesler Way
Seattle, WA 98104
Phone: (206) 467-5070

#361
Row House Cafe
Category: Breakfast & Brunch, Comfort Food, Cocktail Bar
Average Price: Modest
Area: South Lake Union
Address: 1170 Republican St
Seattle, WA 98109
Phone: (206) 682-7632

#362
Grog
Category: Cocktail Bar
Average Price: Modest
Area: Ballard
Address: 5410 Ballard Ave NW
Seattle, WA 98107
Phone: (206) 783-5410

#363
King's Hookah Lounge
Category: Hookah Bar, Music Venues
Average Price: Modest
Area: International District
Address: 814 S Lane St
Seattle, WA 98104
Phone: (206) 518-8320

#364
Bleachers Pub
Category: Pub, Sports Bar, American
Average Price: Inexpensive
Area: Greenwood, Phinney Ridge
Address: 8118 Greenwood Ave N
Seattle, WA 98103
Phone: (206) 783-9919

Seattle Travel Guide 2016 / Shops, Restaurants, Arts, Entertainment & Nightlife

#365
Loretta's Northwesterner
Category: Bar, American, Burgers
Average Price: Inexpensive
Area: South Park
Address: 8617 14th Ave S
Seattle, WA 98108
Phone: (206) 327-9649

#366
Spitfire
Category: Sports Bar, Burgers
Average Price: Modest
Area: Belltown
Address: 2219 4th Ave
Seattle, WA 98121
Phone: (206) 441-7966

#367
Belltown Billiards
Category: Pool Hall, Dance Club, Venues, Event Space
Average Price: Modest
Area: Belltown
Address: 90 Blanchard St
Seattle, WA 98121
Phone: (206) 420-3146

#368
Jabu's Pub
Category: Pub, Karaoke
Average Price: Inexpensive
Area: Lower Queen Anne
Address: 174 Roy St
Seattle, WA 98109
Phone: (206) 284-9093

#369
Greenlake Wines & Wine Bar
Category: Tapas, Wine Bar
Average Price: Modest
Area: Greenlake
Address: 1400 N 80th St
Seattle, WA 98103
Phone: (206) 524-6909

#370
Elliott Bay Brewery & Pub
Category: Pub, Brewerie, American
Average Price: Modest
Area: Fairmount Park, Junction
Address: 4720 California Ave SW
Seattle, WA 98116
Phone: (206) 932-8695

#371
The Old Sage
Category: American, Gastropub, Lounge
Average Price: Modest
Area: Capitol Hill
Address: 1410 12th Ave
Seattle, WA 98122
Phone: (206) 641-9469

#372
Corretto
Category: Italian, Coffee, Tea, Cocktail Bar
Average Price: Modest
Area: Capitol Hill
Address: 416 Broadway Ave E
Seattle, WA 98102
Phone: (206) 328-7817

#373
Spur Gastropub
Category: American, Lounge, Gastropub
Average Price: Expensive
Area: Belltown
Address: 113 Blanchard St
Seattle, WA 98121
Phone: (206) 728-6706

#374
Admiral Pub
Category: American, Pub
Average Price: Inexpensive
Area: Admiral
Address: 2306 California Ave SW
Seattle, WA 98116
Phone: (206) 933-9500

#375
Poggie Tavern
Category: Bar
Average Price: Inexpensive
Area: Fairmount Park, Junction
Address: 4717 California Ave SW
Seattle, WA 98116
Phone: (206) 937-2165

#376
Four B's
Category: Pub, Burgers, Pool Hall
Average Price: Inexpensive
Area: Fremont
Address: 4300 Leary Way
Seattle, WA 98107
Phone: (206) 782-9024

#377
The Yard Cafe
Category: Bar, Mexican
Average Price: Modest
Area: Greenwood, Phinney Ridge
Address: 8313 Greenwood Ave N
Seattle, WA 98103
Phone: (206) 588-1746

#378
Ozzie's
Category: Dive Bar, American, Karaoke
Average Price: Inexpensive
Area: Lower Queen Anne
Address: 105 W Mercer St
Seattle, WA 98119
Phone: (206) 284-4010

#379
Russell's
Category: Pub, Tapas
Average Price: Modest
Area: Fremont
Address: 4111 Stone Way N
Seattle, WA 98103
Phone: (206) 547-1653

#380
Da Spot Hookah Lounge
Category: Hookah Bar
Average Price: Modest
Area: Denny Triangle
Address: 1914 Minor Ave
Seattle, WA 98101
Phone: (206) 228-9655

#381
The Masonry
Category: Bar, Pizza, Italian
Average Price: Modest
Area: Lower Queen Anne
Address: 20 Roy St
Seattle, WA 98109
Phone: (206) 453-4375

#382
Cyclops Cafe & Lounge
Category: Lounge, Burgers
Average Price: Modest
Area: Belltown
Address: 2421 1st Ave
Seattle, WA 98121
Phone: (206) 441-1677

#383
The Fuse Box Moto
Category: Dive Bar
Average Price: Inexpensive
Area: Fremont
Address: 4911 Aurora Ave N
Seattle, WA 98103
Phone: (206) 701-9411

#384
Chungee's Drink 'N Eat
Category: Bar, Chinese
Average Price: Modest
Area: Capitol Hill
Address: 1830 12th Ave
Seattle, WA 98122
Phone: (206) 323-1673

#385
World Of Beer
Category: Sports Bar, Beer, Wine, Spirits, Music Venues, American
Average Price: Modest
Area: Capitol Hill
Address: 500 E Pine St
Seattle, WA 98122
Phone: (206) 323-9110

#386
ART Restaurant & Lounge
Category: American, Lounge
Average Price: Expensive
Area: Downtown
Address: 99 Union St
Seattle, WA 98101
Phone: (206) 749-7070

#387
Molly Maguire's Pub & Fine Eatery
Category: Pub, Irish
Average Price: Modest
Area: Ballard, Phinney Ridge
Address: 610 NW 65th St
Seattle, WA 98117
Phone: (206) 789-9643

#388
The Chieftain Irish Pub & Restaurant
Category: Irish, American, Pub
Average Price: Modest
Area: Central District
Address: 908 12th Ave
Seattle, WA 98122
Phone: (206) 324-4100

#389
Terra Plata
Category: American, Bar
Average Price: Expensive
Area: Capitol Hill
Address: 1501 Melrose Ave
Seattle, WA 98122
Phone: (206) 325-1501

#390
Alibi Room
Category: Pizza, American, Lounge
Average Price: Modest
Area: Greenwood
Address: 10406 Holman Rd N
Seattle, WA 98133
Phone: (206) 783-4880

#391
Ballard Grill & Ale House
Category: Dive Bar, American
Average Price: Inexpensive
Area: Fremont
Address: 4300 Leary Way NW
Seattle, WA 98107
Phone: (206) 782-9024

#392
Octo Sushi & Happy Octo Bar
Category: Sushi Bar, Japanese, Cocktail Bar
Average Price: Modest
Area: Capitol Hill
Address: 1621 12th Ave
Seattle, WA 98122
Phone: (206) 805-8998

#393
Thunderbird Tavern
Category: Dive Bar
Average Price: Inexpensive
Area: Loyal Heights
Address: 7515 15th Ave NW
Seattle, WA 98117
Phone: (206) 781-2473

#394
Columbia City Ale House
Category: Pub, American
Average Price: Modest
Area: Columbia City
Address: 4914 Rainier Ave S
Seattle, WA 98118
Phone: (206) 723-5123

#395
Damn The Weather
Category: Bar, American
Average Price: Modest
Area: Pioneer Square
Address: 116 1st Ave S
Seattle, WA 98104
Phone: (206) 946-1283

#396
Manhattan
Category: Bar, Steakhouse, American
Average Price: Modest
Area: Capitol Hill
Address: 1419 12th Ave
Seattle, WA 98122
Phone: (206) 325-6574

#397
Schilling Cider House
Category: Bar
Average Price: Modest
Area: Fremont
Address: 708 N 34th St
Seattle, WA 98103
Phone: (206) 420-7088

#398
Taylor Shellfish Oyster Bar
Category: Seafood, Seafood Market, Wine Bar, Live/Raw Food
Average Price: Modest
Area: Pioneer Square
Address: 410 Occidental Ave S
Seattle, WA 98104
Phone: (206) 501-4060

#399
Altstadt Bierhalle & Brathaus
Category: German, Pub
Average Price: Modest
Area: Pioneer Square
Address: 209 1st Ave S
Seattle, WA 98108
Phone: (206) 602-6442

#400
Duke's Chowder House
Category: Seafood, American, Bar
Average Price: Modest
Area: South Lake Union, Eastlake
Address: 901 Fairview Ave N
Seattle, WA 98109
Phone: (206) 382-9963

#401
The Night Owl
Category: Hookah Bar
Average Price: Modest
Area: University District
Address: 4745 University Way NE
Seattle, WA 98105
Phone: (206) 729-2373

#402
Olaf's
Category: American, Sports Bar
Average Price: Inexpensive
Area: Ballard
Address: 6301 24th Ave Nw
Seattle, WA 98107
Phone: (206) 297-6122

#403
Heads Or Tails
Category: Sports Bar
Average Price: Inexpensive
Area: Haller Lake
Address: 12534 Aurora Ave N
Seattle, WA 98133
Phone: (206) 440-3288

#404
Bar Sue
Category: Bar
Average Price: Inexpensive
Area: Central District
Address: 1407 14th Ave
Seattle, WA 98122
Phone: (206) 328-0888

#405
Joe's Bar And Grill
Category: Dive Bar, Sports Bar
Average Price: Inexpensive
Area: International District
Address: 500 S King St
Seattle, WA 98104
Phone: (206) 223-9266

#406
The Triple Door
Category: Asian Fusion, Music Venues
Average Price: Expensive
Area: Downtown
Address: 216 Union St
Seattle, WA 98101
Phone: (206) 838-4333

Seattle Travel Guide 2016 / Shops, Restaurants, Arts, Entertainment & Nightlife

#407
Ed's Kort Haus
Category: Dive Bar, Burgers, American
Average Price: Modest
Area: Phinney Ridge
Address: 6732 Greenwood Ave N
Seattle, WA 98103
Phone: (206) 782-3575

#408
RN74
Category: American, French, Wine Bar
Average Price: Expensive
Area: Downtown
Address: 1433 4th Ave
Seattle, WA 98101
Phone: (206) 456-7474

#409
Restaurant Zoë
Category: American, Bar
Average Price: Expensive
Area: Central District
Address: 1318 E Union St
Seattle, WA 98122
Phone: (206) 256-2060

#410
Sun Liquor Distillery
Category: Burgers, Cocktail Bar
Average Price: Modest
Area: Capitol Hill
Address: 514 E Pike St
Seattle, WA 98122
Phone: (206) 720-1600

#411
Macleod's Scottish Pub
Category: Pub, Scottish
Average Price: Modest
Area: Ballard
Address: 5200 Ballard Ave NW
Seattle, WA 98107
Phone: (206) 687-7115

#412
Mike's Chili Parlor
Category: Dive Bar, American
Average Price: Inexpensive
Area: Ballard
Address: 1447 NW Ballard Way
Seattle, WA 98107
Phone: (206) 782-2808

#413
Paddy Coyne's Irish Pub
Category: Irish, Irish Pub
Average Price: Modest
Area: Interbay
Address: 2801 Alaskan Way
Seattle, WA 98121
Phone: (206) 737-8891

#414
Wonder Coffee & Sports Bar
Category: Café, Sports Bar, Ethiopian
Average Price: Inexpensive
Area: Central District
Address: 1800 S Jackson St
Seattle, WA 98144
Phone: (206) 538-0044

#415
Ocho
Category: Tapas Bar, Lounge, Spanish
Average Price: Modest
Area: Ballard
Address: 2325 NW Market St
Seattle, WA 98107
Phone: (206) 784-0699

#416
Trago Cocina & Lounge
Category: Mexican, Lounge
Average Price: Modest
Area: South Lake Union, Westlake
Address: 701 Westlake Ave N
Seattle, WA 98109
Phone: (206) 623-2949

#417
The Park Public House
Category: Pub, American, Sports Bar
Average Price: Modest
Area: Phinney Ridge
Address: 6114 Phinney Ave N
Seattle, WA 98103
Phone: (206) 789-8187

#418
Shultzy's Sausage
Category: Hot Dogs, German, Pub
Average Price: Modest
Area: University District
Address: 4114 University Way NE
Seattle, WA 98105
Phone: (206) 548-9461

#419
EETBAR
Category: Cocktail Bar
Average Price: Modest
Area: Ballard
Address: 1556 NW 56th St
Seattle, WA 98107
Phone: (206) 783-0131

#420
Flowers Bar & Restaurant
Category: Bar, American
Average Price: Inexpensive
Area: University District
Address: 4247 University Way NE
Seattle, WA 98105
Phone: (206) 633-1903

Seattle Travel Guide 2016 / Shops, Restaurants, Arts, Entertainment & Nightlife

#421
Kathy's Pizza, Grill & Sports Bar
Category: Sports Bar, Pizza, Karaoke
Average Price: Modest
Area: Bitter Lake
Address: 930 N 130th St
Seattle, WA 98133
Phone: (206) 829-9251

#422
Cure
Category: Bar, American
Average Price: Modest
Area: Capitol Hill
Address: 1641 Nagle Pl
Seattle, WA 98122
Phone: (206) 568-5475

#423
The Double Header
Category: Bar
Average Price: Modest
Area: Pioneer Square
Address: 407 2nd Ave
Seattle, WA 98104
Phone: (206) 624-8439

#424
The Rock Wood Fired Kitchen
Category: Pizza, Italian, Cocktail Bar
Average Price: Modest
Area: Lower Queen Anne
Address: 300 Roy St
Seattle, WA 98109
Phone: (206) 254-4900

#425
Crepe Cafe & Wine Bar
Category: French, Crêperie, Wine Bar
Average Price: Modest
Area: Ravenna
Address: 2118 NE 65th St
Seattle, WA 98115
Phone: (206) 527-7147

#426
Sluggers Seattle
Category: Sports Bar, American
Average Price: Modest
Area: Sodo
Address: 538 1st Ave S
Seattle, WA 98104
Phone: (206) 654-8070

#427
The Fireside Room
Category: Lounge, Tea Room, Music Venues
Average Price: Modest
Area: First Hill
Address: 900 Madison St
Seattle, WA 98104
Phone: (206) 622-6400

#428
Sonya's Bar & Grill
Category: Restaurant, Pub
Average Price: Modest
Area: Downtown
Address: 1919 1st Ave
Seattle, WA 98101
Phone: (206) 441-7996

#429
Box House Saloon
Category: Bar
Average Price: Modest
Area: Pioneer Square
Address: 124 S Washington St
Seattle, WA 98104
Phone: (206) 748-9975

#430
El Corazón
Category: Music Venues, Dive Bar
Average Price: Modest
Area: South Lake Union
Address: 109 Eastlake Ave E
Seattle, WA 98109
Phone: (206) 262-0482

#431
Seattle Eagle Tavern
Category: Dive Bar, Gay Bar
Average Price: Modest
Area: Capitol Hill
Address: 314 E Pike St
Seattle, WA 98122
Phone: (206) 621-7591

#432
Fountain Wine Bar & Lounge
Category: Wine Bar, Lounge
Average Price: Modest
Area: Downtown
Address: 1400 6th Ave
Seattle, WA 98101
Phone: (206) 621-9000

#433
Belltown Pub
Category: American, Pub
Average Price: Modest
Area: Belltown
Address: 2322 1st Ave
Seattle, WA 98121
Phone: (206) 448-6210

#434
El Camino
Category: Mexican, Bar
Average Price: Modest
Area: Fremont
Address: 607 N 35th St
Seattle, WA 98103
Phone: (206) 632-7303

#435
Revolver Bar
Category: Bar, Cajun, Creole
Average Price: Modest
Area: Capitol Hill
Address: 1514 E Olive Way
Seattle, WA 98122
Phone: (206) 860-7000

#436
Ballard Smoke Shop
Category: American, Dive Bar, Breakfast & Brunch
Average Price: Inexpensive
Area: Ballard
Address: 5439 Ballard Ave NW
Seattle, WA 98107
Phone: (206) 784-6611

#437
FX Mcrory's Steak Chop & Oyster House
Category: Seafood, Steakhouse, Sports Bar
Average Price: Modest
Area: Pioneer Square
Address: 419 Occidental Ave S
Seattle, WA 98104
Phone: (206) 623-4800

#438
Big Mario's New York Style Pizza
Category: Pizza, Dive Bar
Average Price: Inexpensive
Area: Capitol Hill
Address: 1009 E Pike St
Seattle, WA 98122
Phone: (206) 922-3875

#439
Tuck Seattle
Category: Dance Club, Performing Arts, Gay Bar
Average Price: Inexpensive
Area: Central District, Capitol Hill
Address: 1325 E Madison St
Seattle, WA 98122
Phone: (206) 324-8005

#440
The Gerald
Category: American, Gastropub
Average Price: Modest
Area: Ballard
Address: 5210 Ballard Ave NW
Seattle, WA 98107
Phone: (206) 432-9280

#441
The Blarney Stone Pub
Category: Irish, Irish Pub
Average Price: Modest
Area: Downtown
Address: 1416 1st Ave
Seattle, WA 98101
Phone: (206) 448-8439

#442
Bamboo Bar & Grill
Category: American, Sandwiches, Bar
Average Price: Modest
Area: Alki
Address: 2806 Alki Ave SW
Seattle, WA 98116
Phone: (206) 937-3023

#443
Roxbury Lanes & Roxy's Casino
Category: Bowling, Casino, Bar
Average Price: Modest
Area: White Center
Address: 2823 SW Roxbury St
Seattle, WA 98126
Phone: (206) 935-7400

#444
Anchors Down
Category: Hot Dogs, Pub, Dive Bar
Average Price: Modest
Area: Ballard
Address: 2016 NW Market St
Seattle, WA 98107
Phone: (206) 789-1396

#445
The Lodge Sports Grille
Category: Sports Bar, Pub, American
Average Price: Modest
Area: Pioneer Square
Address: 166 S King St
Seattle, WA 98104
Phone: (206) 538-0000

#446
La Isla Cuisine
Category: Latin American, Lounge, Puerto Rican
Average Price: Modest
Area: Ballard
Address: 2320 NW Market St
Seattle, WA 98107
Phone: (206) 789-0516

#447
Lock & Keel Tavern
Category: Pub
Average Price: Inexpensive
Area: Ballard
Address: 5144 Ballard Ave NW
Seattle, WA 98107
Phone: (206) 781-8023

#448
Eva Restaurant & Wine Bar
Category: American, Wine Bar
Average Price: Modest
Area: Wallingford
Address: 2227 N 56th St
Seattle, WA 98103
Phone: (206) 633-3538

Seattle Travel Guide 2016 / Shops, Restaurants, Arts, Entertainment & Nightlife

#449
Luso Food And Wine
Category: Portuguese, Wine Bar
Average Price: Inexpensive
Area: White Center
Address: 9614 16th Ave SW
Seattle, WA 98106
Phone: (206) 694-3524

#450
Cafe 56
Category: Seafood, Fish & Chips, Bar
Average Price: Modest
Area: Waterfront
Address: 1201 Alaskan Way
Seattle, WA 98101
Phone: (206) 623-4340

#451
E. Smith Mercantile Back Bar
Category: Cocktail Bar
Average Price: Modest
Area: Pioneer Square
Address: 208 1st Ave S
Seattle, WA 98104
Phone: (206) 641-7250

#452
Stellar Pizza & Ale
Category: Pizza, Bar
Average Price: Modest
Area: Georgetown
Address: 5513 Airport Way S
Seattle, WA 98108
Phone: (206) 763-1660

#453
El Borracho
Category: Mexican, Vegan, Bar
Average Price: Modest
Area: Downtown
Address: 1521 1st Ave
Seattle, WA 98101
Phone: (206) 538-0440

#454
Torchy's Restaurant & Wine Bar
Category: Wine Bar, American
Average Price: Modest
Area: Downtown
Address: 1325 6th Ave
Seattle, WA 98101
Phone: (206) 464-4626

#455
Fusion Ultra Lounge
Category: American, Lounge
Average Price: Modest
Area: University District
Address: 722 NE 45th St
Seattle, WA 98105
Phone: (206) 774-9296

#456
Elemental Pizza
Category: Pizza, Bar, Italian
Average Price: Modest
Area: University District
Address: 2630 NE University Village St
Seattle, WA 98105
Phone: (206) 524-4930

#457
Liam's
Category: Wine Bar, American
Average Price: Modest
Area: University District
Address: 2685 NE 46th St
Seattle, WA 98105
Phone: (206) 527-6089

#458
Outlander Brewery & Pub
Category: Brewerie, Pub
Average Price: Inexpensive
Area: Fremont
Address: 225 N 36th St
Seattle, WA 98103
Phone: (206) 486-4088

#459
Hattie's Hat Restaurant
Category: American, Lounge, Breakfast & Brunch
Average Price: Inexpensive
Area: Ballard
Address: 5231 Ballard Ave NW
Seattle, WA 98107
Phone: (206) 784-0175

#460
Locöl Barley & Vine
Category: Wine Bar, American
Average Price: Modest
Area: Roxhill, Gatewood
Address: 7902 35th Ave SW
Seattle, WA 98126
Phone: (206) 708-7725

#461
Hendrix Electric Lounge
Category: Lounge
Average Price: Modest
Area: Columbia City
Address: 4916 Rainier Ave S
Seattle, WA 98118
Phone: (206) 723-0088

#462
Showbox Sodo
Category: Music Venues, Burgers, Pizza
Average Price: Modest
Area: Industrial District
Address: 1700 1st Ave S
Seattle, WA 90104
Phone: (206) 652-0444

#463
Bad Albert's Tap & Grill
Category: Pub, American
Average Price: Modest
Area: Ballard
Address: 5100 Ballard Ave NW
Seattle, WA 98107
Phone: (206) 789-2000

#464
Tractor Tavern
Category: Music Venues
Average Price: Inexpensive
Area: Ballard
Address: 5213 Ballard Ave NW
Seattle, WA 98107
Phone: (206) 789-3599

#465
JOEY Kitchen At University Village
Category: American, Lounge
Average Price: Modest
Area: University District
Address: 2603 NE 46th St
Seattle, WA 98105
Phone: (206) 527-6188

#466
Royal Bar & Patio
Category: Bar, American
Average Price: Modest
Area: University District
Address: 5211 University Way NE
Seattle, WA 98105
Phone: (206) 659-0244

#467
Comedysportz
Category: Comedy Club, Performing Arts
Average Price: Inexpensive
Area: Fremont
Address: 3509 Fremont Ave N
Seattle, WA 98103
Phone: (425) 954-5618

#468
World Sports Grille
Category: Sports Bar, American, Pool Hall
Average Price: Modest
Area: South Lake Union, Westlake
Address: 731 Westlake Ave N
Seattle, WA 98109
Phone: (206) 223-0300

#469
Linda's Tavern
Category: Bar, American, Breakfast & Brunch
Average Price: Inexpensive
Area: Capitol Hill
Address: 707 E Pine St
Seattle, WA 98122
Phone: (206) 325-1220

#470
The Little London Plane
Category: Venues, Event Space, Tapas, Wine Bar
Average Price: Modest
Area: Pioneer Square
Address: 322 Occidental Ave S
Seattle, WA 98104
Phone: (206) 624-1374

#471
Hale's Ales Brewery & Pub
Category: Pub, Brewerie, American
Average Price: Modest
Area: Fremont
Address: 4301 Leary Way NW
Seattle, WA 98107
Phone: (206) 706-1544

#472
Finn Maccools Irish Pub & Restaurant
Category: Irish, Karaoke, Irish Pub
Average Price: Inexpensive
Area: University District
Address: 4217 University Way NE
Seattle, WA 98105
Phone: (206) 675-0885

#473
Auto Battery
Category: Sports Bar, Hot Dogs
Average Price: Inexpensive
Area: First Hill
Address: 1009 E Union St
Seattle, WA 98122
Phone: (206) 322-2886

#474
Bar Ferd'nand
Category: Wine Bar, Sandwiches
Average Price: Modest
Area: Capitol Hill
Address: 1531 Melrose Ave
Seattle, WA 98122
Phone: (206) 623-5882

#475
Ponti Seafood Grill
Category: Seafood, Bar
Average Price: Expensive
Area: Queen Anne
Address: 3014 3rd Ave N
Seattle, WA 98109
Phone: (206) 284-3000

#476
BOKA Restaurant + Bar
Category: American, Bar
Average Price: Modest
Area: Downtown
Address: 1010 1st Ave
Seattle, WA 98104
Phone: (206) 357-9000

Seattle Travel Guide 2016 / Shops, Restaurants, Arts, Entertainment & Nightlife

#477
Redline WS
Category: Sports Bar, American, Coffee
Average Price: Modest
Area: Fairmount Park
Address: 3478 SW Avalon Way
Seattle, WA 98126
Phone: (206) 258-4605

#478
Bai Pai
Category: Thai, Lounge
Average Price: Modest
Area: Ravenna
Address: 2316 NE 65th St
Seattle, WA 98127
Phone: (206) 527-4800

#479
Billy Beach Sushi And Bar
Category: Sushi Bar, Japanese, Bar
Average Price: Modest
Area: Ballard
Address: 5463 Leary Ave NW
Seattle, WA 98107
Phone: (206) 257-4616

#480
Maison Tavern
Category: Lounge, Tapas, Cocktail Bar
Average Price: Modest
Area: Industrial District
Address: 2946 1st Ave S
Seattle, WA 98134
Phone: (206) 382-7866

#481
Cafe Mox
Category: Bar, Café, Sandwiches
Average Price: Modest
Area: Ballard
Address: 5105 Leary Ave NW
Seattle, WA 98107
Phone: (206) 436-0540

#482
Pacific Inn Pub
Category: Dive Bar, American
Average Price: Inexpensive
Area: Fremont
Address: 3501 Stone Way N
Seattle, WA 98103
Phone: (206) 547-2967

#483
Rookies Sports Bar And Grill
Category: American, Sports Bar
Average Price: Modest
Area: Columbia City
Address: 3820 S Ferdinand St
Seattle, WA 98118
Phone: (206) 722-0301

#484
Thurston's Bistro & Lounge
Category: American, Cocktail Bar, Tapas Bar
Average Price: Modest
Area: Greenlake
Address: 6421 Latona Ave NE
Seattle, WA 98115
Phone: (206) 402-3553

#485
The Vera Project
Category: Music Venues,
Average Price: Inexpensive
Area: Lower Queen Anne
Address: 305 Harrison St
Seattle, WA 98109
Phone: (206) 956-8372

#486
Jet City Improv
Category: Performing Arts, Comedy Club,
Venues, Event Space
Average Price: Inexpensive
Area: University District
Address: 5510 University Way NE
Seattle, WA 98105
Phone: (206) 352-8291

#487
Center For Sex Positive Culture
Category: Adult Entertainment
Average Price: Modest
Area: Interbay, Queen Anne
Address: 1602 15th Ave W
Seattle, WA 98119
Phone: (206) 270-9746

#488
IL Bistro
Category: Italian, Lounge
Average Price: Expensive
Area: Downtown
Address: 93 Pike St
Seattle, WA 98101
Phone: (206) 682-3049

#489
Nacho Borracho
Category: Tex-Mex, Cocktail Bar, Mexican
Average Price: Modest
Area: Capitol Hill
Address: 209 Broadway E
Seattle, WA 98102
Phone: (206) 466-2434

#490
Re-Bar
Category: Dance Club
Average Price: Inexpensive
Area: Denny Triangle
Address: 1114 Howell St
Seattle, WA 98101
Phone: (206) 233-9873

#491
Clever Dunne's Irish House
Category: Irish, Irish Pub
Average Price: Inexpensive
Area: Capitol Hill
Address: 1501 E Olive Way
Seattle, WA 98122
Phone: (206) 709-8079

#492
Barboza
Category: Music Venues, Event Space
Average Price: Inexpensive
Area: First Hill, Capitol Hill
Address: 925 E Pike St
Seattle, WA 98122
Phone: (206) 709-9442

#493
Toronado Seattle
Category: Bar, American
Average Price: Modest
Area: Roosevelt
Address: 1205 NE 65th St
Seattle, WA 98115
Phone: (206) 525-0654

#494
Elephant & Castle
Category: British, Pub
Average Price: Modest
Area: Downtown
Address: 1415 Fifth Ave
Seattle, WA 98101
Phone: (206) 624-9977

#495
Marv's Broiler
Category: Dive Bar, American
Average Price: Inexpensive
Area: White Center
Address: 9808 16th Ave SW
Seattle, WA 98106
Phone: (206) 763-1412

#496
Nickerson Street Saloon
Category: Sports Bar, American
Average Price: Modest
Area: Queen Anne
Address: 318 Nickerson St
Seattle, WA 98109
Phone: (206) 284-8819

#497
Tak & Toni's Dome Stadium Tavern
Category: Dive Bar
Average Price: Inexpensive
Area: Pioneer Square
Address: 214 4th Ave S
Seattle, WA 98104
Phone: (206) 682-7612

#498
Buckley's In Belltown
Category: Pub, American
Average Price: Modest
Area: Belltown
Address: 2331 2nd Ave
Seattle, WA 98121
Phone: (206) 588-8879

#499
Retro Restaurant & Lounge
Category: American, Lounge
Average Price: Inexpensive
Area: Belltown
Address: 216 Stewart St
Seattle, WA 98101
Phone: (206) 441-7374

#500
Sully's Snowgoose Saloon
Category: Pub, Irish
Average Price: Inexpensive
Area: Phinney Ridge
Address: 6119 Phinney Ave N
Seattle, WA 98103
Phone: (206) 782-9231

Made in the USA
Lexington, KY
17 April 2016